Dmitry A. Tolstoy, Andrew D. White

Romanism in Russia

an historical study

Dmitry A. Tolstoy, Andrew D. White

Romanism in Russia
an historical study

ISBN/EAN: 9783337299668

Printed in Europe, USA, Canada, Australia, Japan

Cover: Foto ©Andreas Hilbeck / pixelio.de

More available books at **www.hansebooks.com**

ROMANISM IN RUSSIA:

AN HISTORICAL STUDY.

BY

THE COUNT DMITRY TOLSTOY,

MINISTER OF PUBLIC INSTRUCTION.

TRANSLATED BY

MRS. M'KIBBIN.

WITH PREFACE BY

THE RIGHT REV. ROBERT EDEN, D.D.,

Bishop of Moray, Ross, and Caithness, Primus.

VOL. I.

LONDON:

J. T. HAYES, LYALL PLACE, EATON SQUARE; AND
4, HENRIETTA STREET, COVENT GARDEN.

1874.

PREFACE.

NÓTHING could be more opportune than the appearance of these interesting volumes at this moment. The union of the Royal and Imperial Families of England and Russia, by the marriage of the Duke of Edinburgh, son of the Queen of England, with the only daughter of the Emperor of Russia, has shown, together with that of the Prince of Wales with a Princess of Denmark, that our Royal alliances are no longer restricted to the Protestant families of Germany. But this marriage is not only a union of Royal and Imperial families; it is also (and this invests it with an intense interest) the union of a son of the Church of England with a daughter of the Eastern Church. This fact cannot fail to awaken in the minds of all Englishmen, a desire to know something more than they do at present of that Church, of which the youthful Duchess of Edinburgh is a devout and faithful member. To that knowledge the present volumes will largely contribute.

The prevailing notion in the minds of most Englishmen has been, that the Russian Church, which is the most powerful branch of the great Eastern Church, is, in doctrine and discipline, much the same as the Church of Rome, although, I fear, it must be admitted that at present they know very little about it. When English travellers, who have witnessed on the Continent the Rites and Ceremonies of the Roman Church, have passed into Russia, and have witnessed there, for the first time, the striking Ritual of the Eastern Church, so different from the undemonstrative Ritual of their own, in their ignorance of the characteristics of all Eastern worship, they have jumped to the conclusion, that Churches which exhibit such gorgeous Ritual in the celebration of Divine Worship, and whose members reverently and devoutly cross themselves, cannot be very different from each other ; and they have thus raised an unfair prejudice against the Russian Church, a prejudice which has stood in the way of that approach towards Intercommunion between the Anglican and Eastern Churches which is so earnestly desired by many members of both Communions. Any information, therefore, which can serve to weaken or break down that prejudice, will contribute towards drawing these two Churches into closer communion. So long as it exists, and that the differences between the two Churches are supposed to be insuperable, so long will our approach towards each other be barred. "If," as the saintly and large-hearted Philaret, the late eminent Metropolitan of Moscow, said to me in the year 1866, " If the people of England think that the Russian Church is like the Roman, I am not surprised that they should entertain a very strong feeling against it." Yet so little did that great Prelate think that the revival of Intercommunion between the two Churches was impossible, that he expressed to me, in a very solemn manner, his deliberate opinion, that " the Bishops and learned men of the two Churches might be able to reconcile the differences." In the new and near relations into which we have now been brought, is it too much to hope that an attempt may be made to bring together, for such an object, " the Bishops and learned men of both Churches ?" The subject

is one well worthy of consideration, in the prospect
ere long of another " Lambeth Conference."
It must, however, be clearly understood, that
the revival of Intercommunion with the Eastern
Church does not of necessity imply *Union* with
that Church. We all know what Union with
Rome means. It simply means absorption. Rome
rejects Intercommunion with any Church which
will not accept all its dogmas, and recognise, not
only the Supremacy, but now also the Infallibility,
of the Pope. The fatal adoption of this latter
heresy by the Church of Rome, has rendered the
re-union of the rest of Christendom with that
Church an impossibility. The Intercommunion
which we desire to see revived amongst the Orthodox Churches of Christendom, is such Intercommunion as that which existed between the
members of independent Churches in the early
days of Christianity; when differences, which were
not of Faith, were not allowed to break unity;
when Polycarp could communicate with Anicetus;
when the Christian subjects of one Bishop passing
into the Diocese of another Bishop, and carrying
with them letters certifying that they were in full

communion with their own Bishop, were received as brethren, and were readily admitted to the Holy Eucharist. We are quite free to admit that, in the present divided state of Christendom, the revival of such Intercommunion must be the result of a mutual understanding between the Bishops of the different Churches, after such a Conference as that suggested by the venerable Philaret. And if, with the aim of accomplishing, in God's good time, the object of our common Redeemer's last prayer, that we "all may be one," the many points on which we agree are suffered in such a Conference, to have their due weight, as against the comparatively few on which we differ, such a mutual understanding may, with God's blessing, be arrived at.

That the eminent and distinguished Statesman who has given to us this Historical Sketch of "Romanism in Russia," should have sanctioned its translation into English, is an evidence of his desire that Englishmen should understand the relation in which the Russian Church has, from its earliest days, stood towards that of Rome, and in which it stands at the present time. Rome, be

it remembered, had no part in the conversion of
Russia to Christianity. That was the work of the
Eastern Church, and hence the Eastern character of
the Liturgy, Rites, and Ceremonies of the Russian
Church, retained to the present day with a tenacity
beyond all praise, in spite of the endeavours of the
Roman Curia, continued through many centuries,
to bring that Church under the Papal sway, and
to compel her to surrender those very Rites and
Ceremonies which she had received by tradition
from her Mother Church. The whole history of
that Church is indeed a noble protest against the
claims of Roman supremacy, which cannot fail to
attract the sympathies of English Churchmen.

Just cause, indeed, had the Russian Church to
complain of Rome's incessant efforts to proselytize
her members, and thus create a schism amongst
her children. It is then to be hoped that, in the
closer relations into which we shall now be drawn
with that Church, she will never sanction any
such attempts in England, or awaken the suspicion
that she holds as a principle that there is no
salvation out of the Eastern Church. It must not
be forgotten that important differences do exist be-

tween us ; differences, however, which may, we trust, be reconciled by "the Bishops and learned men of both Churches." And if it be found that we do indeed hold the " One Faith and One Baptism," let us hope and pray that we may, ere long, be united in one common Eucharist, and thus present to the World an objective unity which has not been witnessed for a thousand years.

R. E.

February, 1874.

CONTENTS.

VOL I.

CHAPTER I.

ATTEMPTS OF THE COURTS OF ROME TO CONVERT RUSSIA
TO ROMAN CATHOLICISM, FROM THE TENTH CENTURY
TILL THE CLOSE OF THE SIXTEENTH . . . 1

CHAPTER II.

THE CZAR JOHN IV. (THE TERRIBLE) AND THE JESUIT
POSSEVIN 33

CHAPTER III.

RÔLE OF CATHOLICISM IN THE TROUBLES OF RUSSIA AT
THE BEGINNING OF THE SEVENTEENTH CENTURY.—
EMBASSY OF THE CZAR ALEXIS TO ROME . . 84

CHAPTER IV.

ROMANISM IN RUSSIA FROM THE REIGN OF THE CZARS
PETER AND JOHN UNTIL THE ANNEXATION OF THE
WESTERN PROVINCES 122

CHAPTER V.

SKETCH OF THE HISTORY OF CATHOLICISM IN LITHUANIA
UNDER THE POLISH DOMINATION . . . 184

CHAPTER VI.

PAGE

Aperçu History of the Dioceses in Lithuania   .   244

CHAPTER VII.

State of the Latin Church in Russia during the
Reign of the Empress. Catherine II. .   .   . 327

ROMANISM IN RUSSIA.

CHAPTER I.

ATTEMPTS OF THE COURT OF ROME TO CONVERT
RUSSIA TO ROMAN CATHOLICISM, FROM THE
TENTH CENTURY TILL THE CLOSE OF THE
SIXTEENTH.

Contrast between the Roman and Greek Clergy.—Useless
efforts of the Popes to convert Russia to the Roman Church
from the tenth till the fifteenth century.—Intrigues of the
Popes against the Russian Princes.—Aversion of the Russians
to Roman Catholicism.—Writings of the Greek Clergy in
Russia against Romanism from the tenth till the twelfth
century.—Roman Catholicism at Novogorod and at Pskoff.—
Roman Catholicism at Kieff.—Latin Church at Novogorod in
the fifteenth century.—At this epoch Rome continues her
attempts at conversion.—Council of Florence.—Marriage of
John III. with Sophia Paleologue, arranged by the Pope with
the intention of converting the Russian Prince to Romanism.—
Relations of the Grand Dukes of Russia with Rome during
the sixteenth century.—Mission of the Dominican Schomberg,
1518.—Mission of Zacharie, Bishop of Gardieu, 1519.—Double
voyage of Paul Centurion, merchant, in Russia.—Mission of
John Francis, Bishop of Scaren, 1526.—Invitation to Russia
to take part in the Council of Trent.—Count Heberstein and
Stemberg sent to Russia with this aim, 1550.—Instruction

given to the Venetian, Giraldo, 1561.—Tenacity of Rome.—
Cardinal Maronius and the Russian envoys at the Diet of
Ratisbon.—Instructions given to Clenchen, agent of the Court
of Rome in Russia, 1576.—Conviction of Cobenzi, agent of
the Emperor (Roman), as to the facility of converting the
Russians to Romanism.—Error of Cobenzi.—Attachment of
the Russians to their faith and their aversion to Roman
Catholicism.—Testimony of Heberstein and of Herdenstein.

In uniting herself to the Greek Church which was
the cradle of the Faith, Russia became not only
Christian, but received from her principles and
institutions different to those which reigned in the
West, and which, under many circumstances,
determined her position with regard to othèr
European powers. It .was not so much the
dogmas of the hierarchical order, the spirit and
the tendencies of the Greek clergy, which separated Eastern Orthodoxy from Western Romanism;
Asceticism, the strict observance of Church prescriptions; reserve in all that concerned the
religious affairs of other Churches and the complete
absence of violent propagandism; such were the
characteristics of the Greek clergy.

The Roman priesthood, on the contrary, subtle,
active, and proud, after having recognised their
Patriarch as the visible representative of the
Saviour Himself, endeavoured without ceasing to
confirm his spiritual power at home, and to
propagate it abroad.

The clergy at all periods, and particularly at the foundation of the empires, exercising a great influence upon the people, the character of the Orthodox priesthood contributed to give the history of Russia a peculiar physiognomy, the traits of which differ essentially from those of the histories of Western nations. In the latter, the ecclesiastical corps was perpetually at war with the temporal power—with a nobility privileged and powerful—in nearly every page of whose chronicles we find kings, princes, and people excommunicated by the Pope or the bishops. The Roman priest propagated his faith by the sword; violence he raised to a social institution through the Inquisition; he made the *Compelle Intrare*, falsely interpreted, the principle and the base of his zeal. *In the history of Russia the contrary is to be found.* The clergy united their influence to that of the government; they sympathised with all classes of society, and more than once saved their country. During the space of ten centuries, the Patriarch Nikon was the only one who placed himself in opposition to the Czar, and—a significant fact—the antagonism of the two powers was not the subjection of the one to the profit of the other. The prince interfered as little. in spiritual matters as the clergy in political affairs. The two authorities marched side

by side in their respective spheres, and were only
rivals for the good of their country.

If Orthodoxy spread itself slowly, it was that
the clergy, strangers to violent propagandism,
applied themselves particularly to the care of the
faithful, and had the good sense never to dream
of the unstable conquests upon which the Roman
Church prided herself with so little reason. The
zeal of the priesthood was to be enlightened and
prudent, and their sole aim the glorification and
perfection of their own Church. Such was the
zeal of the Orthodox clergy.

With tendencies thus opposed, the two priesthoods met at the period when the history of
Russia commences.

Our first Christian King, Vladimir, had not yet
entered the Greek Church when the Pope proposed
to him to be baptized, and to introduce Romanism
into Russia. To the envoys of this mission
Vladimir replied, " Return home ! Our fathers
never would accept it."* Later, Vladimir, being
already a Christian, having joined the Church,
determined to convert his people and disseminate
Christianity throughout his dominions, the Court
of Rome in 988 made proposals to him to recognise

* "Russian Annals." Edition of the Commission Archéolo-
gique. Page 36.

her supremacy, and sent delegates to present him relics by way of a bribe. These attempts were equally ineffectual. When Russia had already become Christian and her Church actually in communion with that of Constantinople, Rome continued her, efforts, and the Russian chronicles report in the years 991 and 1000 the arrivals of new envoys.

The ancient history of our country repeatedly mentions the missions and epistles of the Popes towards the same end. At all those epochs when the country was in danger, when she was a prey to calamities, the Popes were always there to propose their good offices, and to promise the assistance of other powers, under the express condition that she should embrace Roman Catholicism. In 1075, the celebrated Pope Gregory VII. took advantage of the request addressed to him by the son of the Grand Duke Isaislaff; he begged the King of Poland to re-establish Isaislaff upon the throne, on condition that after being convinced of the power of the Pope, he should submit to Rome. In 1164-66, Pope Alexander III., despatched a Bishop to Russia, under pretence of learning that which for a very long time Rome well knew, the difference which existed between the Greek and Roman Churches. But the Metropolitan John, after having demonstrated in very modest terms that the Roman doctrine had no foundation, adroitly counselled the Pope to address himself to the Patriarch of Constantinople for more precise information, as this bishop was the principal pastor of the Eastern Church. "It is better for your Holiness," he wrote to Alexander, "to ask the Patriarch of Constantinople, your spiritual brother; you must display all your zeal to dispel false doctrine, in order that we may be united and have the same rites."*

In 1169, new ambassadors arrived again; but the greatest efforts of the Court of Rome to disseminate her doctrines, took place in the first half of the thirteenth century. The political circumstances of the time and the progress of Roman Catholicism in other countries, seemed to presage certain success. In 1204, Constantinople having been taken by the Crusaders, a Latin Patriarch replaced the Patriarch Greek. In 1201, the Order of the Porte Glaives was founded in Livonia, not far from the Russian frontier; and in the commencement of the same century, the Tartars began to ravage the country. Roman Catholicism triumphed, and Russia stood on the brink of ruin.

* "Monuments of the Russian Literature of the twelfth century." Page 209-211.

The Popes profited by circumstances so advantageous for them. The same year of the taking of Constantinople, a legate of Rome presented himself to Roman, Prince of Galiez, invited him to embrace Romanism, and promised him many temporal advantages. This embassy met with little success. Drawing his sword from its scabbard, Roman demanded of the legate, "Is the sword of Peter, which is in the possession of the Pope, like this? If so, he can take towns for himself, and give them to others; but his conduct will be contrary to the word of God, for the Saviour forbade Peter to carry a sword. As for me, I have the weapon which God has given me, and while it is at my side, I have no occasion to purchase cities otherwise than by blood, after the example of my ancestors, who have enlarged the limits of Russia." Three years later, Cardinal Vitalis arrived in Russia on a mission to convert the clergy and the laity to Romanism. This attempt was equally ineffectual. In 1227, Honorius III. addressed an invitation to all the Russian princes, and in 1231, Gregory IX. took the same step with regard to the Grand Duke George Wsrewolodowiez. Their epistles remained unanswered.

The attempt to convert the Grand Duke

Alexander Nevsky completely failed. In 1248, Pope Innocent IV. sent two cardinals with a letter to this prince, in which he intimated that in submitting to Rome his power should not be diminished but considerably augmented. "We know the true doctrine," replied the Prince to this Pope, "and decline to accept yours. We shall not even recognise it." In 1255 the same Pope sent the crown royal to Daniel, Prince of Galiez, on condition that he should accept it from the Court of Rome, his envoys promising assistance on the part of the Pope. The better to dispose the Prince to embrace Romanism, Innocent blamed the bishops of the West for interfering in the Greek Church, and promised to convoke a council to reunite the two churches. Daniel, hoping to receive succour against the Tartars through his intervention, decided to accept it from his hand, but soon finding himself deceived in his expectations he broke off all negotiations, and the exhortations of Alexander IV. had no effect on this Prince. History again mentions that in the year 1387 the Papacy once more directed envoys to turn their steps towards Moscow.*

---

* " Historica Russiæ Monumenta." Book i. p. 84.

Convinced by the experience of several centuries of the uselessness of trying to convert the Russians to Romanism, the Popes began to excite other princes against them; sometimes forbidding the Catholic monarchs of Christendom to make alliances with them; sometimes exciting these against them. In 1231, Pope Gregory IX. forbade the Bishop of Sémigal to conclude an armistice with the Russians, without the consent of the Legate. The following year he wrote to the Archbishop of Gnesno that the Polish Princes should not in their wars take the Russians, whom he called *Catolicæa fidei inimicos*, as allies.[*] Pope Alexander IV. authorised the Grand Duke of Lithuania to make war on Russia, and unite her provinces to his possessions; but this authorisation had no result, as peace was concluded between Mindogwie and Daniel, Prince of Galiez, the same year.

At last the same Pontiff had recourse to another expedient to propagate Romanism; he sent the Dominicans into Central Russia.

What was it that induced this aversion of the Russians to Popery?

In a biographical manuscript of the Grand Duke

---

[*] "Historica Russiæ Monumenta." Book i., p. 33.

Alexander Nevsky, preserved in the library of the Ecclesiastical Academy in St. Petersburg, we find amongst other information "La Confession de Saint Alexander Nevsky," containing a very succinct enumeration of the differences between the Greek and Roman churches. Does this confession actually appertain to the Grand Duke? Is it not a secondhand dissertation? No matter. It has its importance in an historical point of view, as we see by it how the contemporaries of this prince regarded Roman Catholicism. In examining the manuscript we find that no attention is paid to the political side of the question, that is, to the Supremacy of the Pope, while there is an elaborate mention made of the doctrines of that church; but it was the rites or exterior side of the divine office which repulsed the Russians. For example, the Azymes are called "stupid" in the manuscript. This production is an exact expression of an epoch when Theology, still in its infancy, attached more importance to the form than to the spirit—when the Liturgy appeared of more consequence than the dogmas. After a brief exposé of the orthodox doctrine, the manuscript finishes thus : "Behold our faith ! Those who do not profess it, or profess otherwise, be cursed ! And thus we curse you, miserable Latins." The envoys of the Pope on hearing these words went confusedly away.

One cannot doubt that the higher order of the clergy, and the princes their disciples, knew perfectly well the differences which existed between the two Churches. Accepting this fact, we shall therefore limit ourselves to a citation of some of the ecclesiastical works of that period which are still extant: the writings of Leon, Metropolitan of Kieff, who lived at the close of the tenth century, and which treats of the Azymes;* the letter of Theodosius to the Grand Duke Isaislaff upon the Latin and Varague religions; the controversies of George, Metropolitan of Kieff, 1065-79, with the Latins; the letter of the Metropolitan, John II. 1080-88, to Pope Clement III.; and three epistles against the Latins, attributed to the Metropolitan, Nicephorus, addressed, one to the Grand Duke Vladimir Monomach, one to a Prince whose name is not mentioned, and the third to the Prince of Mourome, Jaroslaw Swiatoslawiez, 1096-1129.

Desiring to understand the causes of the separation of the churches of the East and West, Monomach addressed himself to the Metropolitan, and the response to this question was the subject

---

* "Annuaires de la Société d'Histoire et d'Antiquités de Mosoow." Tom. v. 2, p. 1-18.

of the letter of Nicephorus, in which we find the
twenty principal points of separation enumerated,
with their explanations. In conclusion, the Metropolitan expresses himself thus : " And read this,
my prince, not once or twice, but many times,
thou, thyself, and thy sons. It behoves princes,
the elect of God, called to profess the·true faith,
to know thoroughly the words·of Christ, and the
fundamental basis of religion, that they may
defend it, preserve it in all its purity, and spread
it by every means in their power, amongst the
subjects whom God has confided to their care." *

In the eleventh century, the Grand Duke
Isaislaff Jaroslowiez sent the same question to
Theodosius, Prior of the Convent of Peczersk.
The treatise upon the Latin Church, which was
written in reply to this question, and to which we
have alluded elsewhere, contains not merely an
exposition of the exterior differences, which most
forcibly struck contemporaries, but also an explanation of the points of ecclesiastical discipline
which separated the two churches, and accused the
Roman clergy of grasping and worldly tendencies,
such as absolutions purely exterior; their custom
of going to battle sword in hand; proselytism,

---

* " Monuments de la Littérature Russe du douzième siècle."
Page 163.

extreme and violent, unflinching and inveterate, which never tolerated the exercise of another religion; and the celibacy of the clergy, so extremely repugnant to the Greeks. A contemporary better describes the ideas of the epoch :—

"They do not ask God but the Priests to pardon their sins, they do not take legitimate wives, but live in concubinage, which state does not hinder them performing the holy offices of religion, for in this state of concubinage they see no crime; their bishops openly keep mistresses; they go to war, and wear rings on their fingers. Great are the persecutions which they (the Latins) oblige Christians of other denominations, who live amongst them, to endure." Theodosius deduced from this that the Latin, or as it was then called in Russia, the Varèque religion, was pernicious, and its laws impure. He counselled the prince to be upon his guard, and exhorted the Orthodox not to be caught by the tricks of the Propaganda. "Therefore," he adds, "fly the religion of the Latins; hold not with their customs; imitate not their genuflexions, and do not listen to their sermons, for their doctrines are all false." In consequence of this view of the Roman Church, we find the Russians forbidden to contract marriages with Roman Catholics, and to have as little intercourse with them as possible. "It is forbidden," he again says, "to take wives from amongst them, or give thy daughters to them in marriage, to become their sponsors, to fraternise with them, to embrace them, or eat with them in the same vessel. To those of them who ask alms, give, for the love of God, but in their own dish; and if they have none, use thine own, but after they have eaten, wash it and purify it by prayer; for he who shall hold himself aloof from them, and guard his faith pure, shall be admitted to the right hand of God, and enter into his eternal rest. But those who pass over to them, shall be found on the left hand of God, in the midst of eternal tears, for there is no eternal life for those who live in the Latin religion."

These instructions, as well as those which follow, prove that the Russians of the eleventh century had frequent relations with Roman Catholics, and that the spirit of Latin propagandism was already perfectly known to them. The Russian clergy tried to preserve their flocks, as much by their advice as by the temporal power of the State, which was constantly allied with and sustained the Church. But, if on the one hand, the Russian clergy defied the Roman Propaganda, on the other they preached pity and demanded protection for the Roman

Catholic. They protected their own estate, and desired not that of another. "One should not praise their religion," continues the prior, "for he who praises their doctrine, indirectly blames his own; he who eulogises a religion different to the Orthodox faith has two beliefs, and therefore approaches heresy. And thou, my son, guard well thy actions, be not seduced by their dogmas, fly from them, cease not to value thy creed, and fortify thyself with good actions. Be charitable, not only to thy co-religionists, but to strangers. If one be naked, clothe him; if hungry and in distress, pity him. If amongst them there be heretics, even Latins, have the same mercy on them, save them from misery, and the recompense of God shall not fail thee. God himself nourishes and supports the world, the Pagan as well as the Christian. My son, if thou assist at or take part in a controversy between an orthodox and a heretic who would seduce the orthodox from the true faith, fly to the assistance of thy brother in the faith, sustain him, like a good pastor, save thy flock from the roaring lion; for if thou art silent thou wilt drive him from Christ and give him up to Satan. If such a one say to thee that God has given this religion, reply "Believest thou, miscreant, that God has two religions? Dost thou not know, to understand the dogmas of their faith, cursed and perverted by a false belief, that it is written, the Saviour hath said, "There is only one God, one baptism, and one faith."*

The other works referred to of the Russian clergy upon the Latin Church contain nearly the same ideas. It is unnecessary to make a more detailed mention of them.

According to several authentic documents, one cannot doubt that from the twelfth century there were Roman Catholics in several places in Russia, and not only Catholics but even priests of this Church, as well as chapels, particularly at Novogorod. It is from this period we date the commencement of the real Latin Propaganda in this country.

In the chronicle of Laurent, 1154, mention is made of an invasion of the Polowzi on Pereiaslaff and its environs, when several villages and a Roman Catholic chapel were burnt.

In the chronicle of Nikon, 1174, we find the Grand Duke of Kieff, Jaroslaw Isaislawier, imposing a tribute on the inhabitants of that city, and amongst others "the Latins" who resided there. At Ladoga there was a Roman church

---

* Manuscript belonging to Monsieur Pogodin, to be found in the Public Library of St. Petersburg.

called Nicolas. At Novogorod some Russians even commenced to baptize their children according to the rites of the Roman Catholic religion, for which they were subjected to public penitence for six weeks—"as people who had, so to speak, two religions." On the other hand, there were according to all probability also cases of conversion to the Greek faith; for we find at this epoch detailed instructions as to the manner in which Roman Catholics should be received into the Orthodox Church.

In general Novogorod and Pskoff as free and commercial towns, in constant communication with the Hanse, the neighbourhoods of Lithuania, of Livonia, and of Sweden were, more than all the other cities of Russia, exposed to Roman proselytism. Thus in the time of John Calita the Swedes tried to convert the Novogorodians; similar attempts on the part of Lithuania and Poland were repeated on several occasions. It seemed that the Propaganda might count upon eventual success in commercial cities, where for the most part the theological knowledge of the local clergy was not extensively developed, according to the testimony of the chronicle. But the case was altogether different at Kieff, where for a very long period the Russians had had relation with foreigners, and the clergy were much more civilised. "We hear," said one of the chroniclers, "that actually in Kieff there are theologians and learned men who write replies to different heresies and base them on the Holy Scriptures. Every one there learns and even tries to argue on and to defend orthodoxy against the attacks of strangers of other religions, and the Russians of the South learn from infancy to understand well the dogmas of their faith. With us, on the contrary, religious education is completely neglected; there are even priests who do not know how to recite the symbols of their faith, and dread even to speak of a religion which it puzzles them to explain. Do such men deserve even the name of Christian pastors? It is necessary to be Christian not only in name but in fact; for it is written "Show me thy faith by thy works." To confirm the people in the doctrines of the Greek Church, the bishops of other dioceses frequently visited and sojourned in these cities. Thus, in 1382, Nile, Patriarch of Constantinople sent Denys, Bishop of Sousdal to Pskoff and Novogorod, and he taught the people with the permission of the bishop of the place, in order that God might fortify them, writes the chronicler, against the seductions of late years, that their faith should not be tainted by heresy.

In the fifteenth century we find a Roman Catholic Church actually in Novogorod, about which a curious tradition is preserved. In 1416, with the consent of the Possadniks of Novogorod, several foreign merchants built a church in the Slave Street for the use of their factory, but not content with the celebration of the divine office for themselves, they conceived the project of making it an instrument of the Latin Propagand ; and without informing the bishop, they agreed with a painter (Russian) to paint the southern side of the exterior with the images of the Saviour and SS. Peter and Paul, and thus attract the population of the locality by its resemblance to the exterior ornaments of the Greek Church. " They caused these images to be executed by a Russian painter," adds the chronicle, "as all orthodox Christians have a horror of what is made by the hands of the Latins." " When the images were finished," says tradition, "there arose a terrible tempest, followed by thunder and lightning ; hail and rain struck the painting and effaced it completely ; shortly after a calm set in. The designs of the Latins were abortive, and orthodox Christians glorified God for this great miracle.

The Latin Propagand in the Russian possessions had naturally its source in Rome. Two letters of the year 1418 exist, by which Pope Martin V., named the King of Poland, Vladislas Jagellon, as well as the Grand Duke of Lithuania, his vicars general in the countries of Russia, exhorting them to exert all their efforts towards the re-union of the Eastern Church to Rome, and to bestow particular attention upon Novogorod and Pskoff.

These attempts of the Propagand were not particular or local. The scheme of the general conversion of Russia to Roman Catholicism had already been conceived for a long time ; and the Court of Rome, always faithful to its system, never ceased to send ambassadors into the country.

The council of Florence, if without any other result,* had in appearance forced the Court of Rome to postpone to a more opportune period the execution of her designs, without altogether abandoning her favourite view of seeing Russia converted to Romanism. With this aim, Pope Paul II. negotiated, in 1472, the marriage of Sophia, niece of the last Emperor Constantine Paleologue, with the Grand Duke John III. Wassitiewich. When Greece became a conquest to

---

* Histoire du Concile de Florence, by M. Gorsky, based upon the testimony of Syropoulo.

the Turks, the Princess Sophia left it with her
father and went to Rome, where she was educated
in the principles of the Council of Florence. The
Court of Rome founded on her its hopes of drawing
the Grand Duke to Romanism. This point gained,
the Pope did ‚not doubt of the possibility of
converting the Russian people subject to the will
of their sovereign. He was so much the more
disposed to believe in the possibility of this result,
as the alliance of a Russian prince with the
Imperial Greek house would give greater eclat to
autocracy. A legate of the name of Antoine
accompanied the princess to Russia. Once more,
however, Rome saw all her schemes and combinations frustrated. Sophia became a fervent orthodox in Moscow.

In the sixteenth century, the relations of the
sovereigns with Rome were frequent enough.

Rome was the more induced to seek an alliance
with Russia, and contract lasting bonds with the
Czars, from her constant fear of an invasion of the
Turks in Western Europe. At this epoch, the
Popes comprehended perfectly that such an alliance
would not be durable, unless based on a re-union of
the East and West,—religion then directing and
giving an impulse to politics. With this
view we find the frequent embassies of the

legates and agents of Rome, which followed
each other so rapidly in the course of the
sixteenth century.

In 1518, Pope Leo X., intending to proclaim
to the Council of Lateran a crusade against the
Sultan Selim, sent the Dominican, Nicolas Schomberg (afterwards Archbishop of Capua and a
Cardinal), on a mission to persuade the Grand
Duke Basil to accept the decision of the
Council of Florence, and to fight the Turks, conjointly with the other European sovereigns. He
enjoined him to promise the Grand Duke, as a
recompense, the crown royal, and to give the
Metropolitan the title of Patriarch. "All that
thou shalt promise the Czar for the adoption
of the Roman Catholic religion," he wrote, in
his instructions to the Dominican, " shall be
infallibly and positively confirmed by us without
the least change. Be persuaded that the performance shall justify the veracity of thy promises.
This embassy carried out according to the Pope's
intentions by the Grand Master of the German
order of Albrecht, had nevertheless no success. The
Grand Duke ordered his envoy Zamyski to inform
the Grand Master, " Our sovereign desires amity
and good relations with the Pope ; but as he has
always been firmly attached to the Greek religion,

inherited from his fathers, he intends, by the grace
of God, to hold to his faith."*

Notwithstanding this check, Leo X. the following
year, 1519, sent a new delegate, Zacharie, bishop
of Gardieu, who was then at Wilna for the
canonisation of St. Casimir, to make the same
propositions to the Grand Duke. This mission
had as little success as its predecessors.

In 1524, Paul Centurion, a Genoese merchant,
arrived in Russia, furnished with letters of recommendation by Leo X. His intention was to
explore a passage to India for commercial purposes
in spices, and he was enjoined to endeavour to
induce the Court of Russia to adopt the idea of the
re-union of the two churches. This same Genoese
was despatched a second time to Russia by Pope
Clement VII., to induce the Grand Duke to
acknowledge the supremacy of Rome, with the
habitual bribe of the Crown royal. According to
the testimony of Paul Jovius, Centurion persuaded
the Grand Duke to send Guerassimoff, or as he
was called by strangers, Erasme, as ambassador to
Rome—a man of already advanced age, who had
been educated in Livonia, and who held the
position of resident (Minister) to the Kings of

* Correspondance des Papes avec les Souverains de Russie.
16me siècle. P. 94-100.

Sweden and Denmark, Grand Master of the Prussian Order, and of the Emperor Maximilian. This embassy, to which Centurion united himself, arrived in Rome in 1526, with letters from the Grand Duke. In these epistles he expressed his disposition towards the Court of Rome, and his readiness to ally himself to the other Christian sovereigns against the infidels, but made no allusion to religion. This mission was therefore only one of simple politeness, and, notwithstanding the exquisite affability of the Pope and the attentions paid the Russian Envoy, had no other result.* They had prepared for the Russian envoy an apartment in the best part of the Palace of St. Peter; and Francis Cherato, Bishop of Aprutino received commands to accompany him through the city of Rome, and point out the antiquities.†

In 1526, the same Pope, Clement VII., at the time of the departure of Guerassimoff from Rome, sent with him Jean François, Bishop of Scarene, as his ambassador to Russia. The principal aim of this ambassador was to induce the Grand Duke to conclude an armistice with Sigismond, King of

---

* Correspondence of the Popes, &c., p. 15-16.

† Fragmento concernenti la legazione de Demetro Erasmo mandato a papa Clemente VII. de Basilo gran duca di Moscovia.

Poland; the bishop succeeded; and an armistice was concluded at Mojaisk for six years, and the same year the Grand Duke sent as ambassadors to Rome Troussoff and Ladyguin.* Details of this mission fail, but it is quite certain that it did not succeed.

From this epoch to the middle of the sixteenth century there was no relation between Rome and Russia. During this interval the Reformation had spread rapidly, not only in Western Europe but in Poland. Luther and Calvin had become more dangerous to Rome than the Sultans themselves. The interior organisation of the Roman Church was in peril, and war with the Reformation had become the principal pre-occupation of the Court of Rome, which believed itself destroying all opposition by convoking the famous Council of Trent. At the time of the first convocation of this Council, 1545-47, they thought not of Russia. But when the newly-elected Pope Julius III. again assembled this Council in 1550, after an interruption of three years, he despatched an embassy to Moscow composed of Count Herberstein and a certain Stemberg, who had already made a journey to Russia. These envoys were to

---

* Correspondence of the Popes, &c., p. 25.

persuade the Grand Duke to adhere to the reunion
of the churches, and they were strictly enjoined to
insist on his sending an ambassador to Rome.
Historical Russian *Monumenta* and the official
acts have not preserved any further details of this
mission, but we know that it was altogether
fruitless for the Pope, for the Czar Jean Was-
siliewich sent nobody there. In the month of May,
1552, the proceedings of the Council of Trent
were again interrupted without having terminated
the grave affairs for which it had been called ; and
this time it was adjourned for a lengthened period ;
for ten years later the successor of Julius III.,
Pope Pius IV., convoked it anew in January, 1562.
This pontiff sent another ambassador to John with
an invitation to the clergy to take part in the council.
But we do not find in the Russian archives any
details of this mission ; we do not even positively
know who were designated by the Pope to go
to Russia. We only know that at the commencement of the year 1561 in the month of April, the
Pope had designated as his envoy, Zacharie, Bishop
of Farene; and that, in the September of the same
year, he charged the Venetian, Jean Giraldo, to go
to Moscow with the same propositions. It is
probable that this bishop for some reasons unknown
did not go to Moscow, and that he was replaced by

the Venetian. Giraldo was charged to say that the Pope was gravely afflicted at the progress of the Lutheran heresy in Germany and other countries, and prayed the Czar to send Russian ministers to discuss the re-union of the two Churches. He desired also that some Russian youths, well educated and endowed with capacity, should be sent to Rome to finish their studies, learn the Latin language and the rites of the Roman Church, so as to be able in time to become the instructors of their fellow-countrymen. This idea, as we shall see hereafter, was never abandoned by the Court of Rome, and was put in execution, not with regard to Russians, it is true, but to the united Greeks. All the efforts made by the Popes to attract Russia to the Council of Trent were fruitless; the Council of Florence was too well known and too well remembered by the Russian clergy, and they comprehended perfectly well what sort of re-union the Papacy would establish between the Churches at the Council of Trent.

Let us, nevertheless, render justice to the prodigious tenacity of the Court of Rome, which would take no rebuff during several centuries, notwithstanding the continual checks experienced in her system of propagandism. Any other government after so many fruitless efforts, would have abandoned all projects against so distant a country, possessing customs and laws different to those of the West, of which the religion, the national existence, and the interior political organization had an exceptional character. Rome had more perseverance! She continued the same insinuating manœuvres, the same subterfuges, and the same seductions in nearly the same forms; hoping always for success, and consoling herself for all these checks in thinking that the Papacy lost nothing in reality.

Cardinal Maronius,* at the Council of Ratisbon, met the Russian envoys, and desiring to form relations with the Muscovite Government on the subject of religious affairs, requested them to take charge of letters for the Czar John, and for a certain Klenchen, then named agent in Russia. The plenipotentiaries replied that they were expressly forbidden to receive anything in the shape of letters, if not from the Emperor. The missives of Maronius did not, therefore reach their destination. Klenchen, doctor of theology, was sent to Russia in 1576, with detailed instructions composed by Cardinal Maronius by order of Pope Gregory XIII. These instructions are extremely curious. They discover the inten-

---

* Bishop of Modena, President of the Council of Trent, died 1560.

tions of the Court of Rome, and the means to be employed for success. Klenchen was ordered not only to induce the Czar to contract an alliance against the Turks, but what was particularly of more importance to Rome, to obtain the re-union of the two Churches; and to effect this, he was enjoined to represent to the Czar, with the greatest artifice and the most exquisite address, all the advantages of such a re-union; to explain to him that the Pope had exalted several sovereigns to the dignity of royalty, and that he should also attain the same by complying with the requisitions of Rome. He should remind the Czar that the Patriarch of Constantinople, chief of the Church in Russia, was a subject of the Sultan, and that consequently it was much more convenient and useful for Russia to submit to Rome. Cardinal Maronius being convinced that the Czar would eagerly consent to these propositions,* ordered Klenchen to carry the answer to the Pope himself, and, supporting himself by anterior examples, persuade the Russian government to send an embassy to Rome, as that would be very agreeable to the Pope and the cardinals,

---

* Maronii Cardinalis ad magnum Moscoviæ ducem et ad Rodulphum Clenchen epistolæ. "Non dubitamus magnum ducem pro sua prudentia sponte id facturum quod cupimus." *Vide* La Correspondance des Papes avec les Souverains de Russie.

writes Maronius, and serve as the first link in a
union so much to be desired. As far as one can
judge by the historical *Monumenta* of contemporaries, the mission of Klenchen remained only a
project, probably in consequence of the death of
the Emperor, which happened the 12th October,
1576.

The views of the Court of Rome with respect to
the conversion of Russia to Roman Catholicism
were participated in by other Catholic sovereigns,
as we find by a correspondence between Cobenzi,
the agent of the Roman Emperor, in 1576, and a
Latin bishop.   Proselytism appeared easy to
Cobenzi, as the Russians were very religious and
attached to their faith.   According to him, it
sufficed only to persuade them to put aside the
differences existing between the Roman Catholic
and Greek doctrines, and in passing over thus to
Romanism, they would preserve the same religious
spirit, the same zeal for the Church.   It would not
be difficult, he thought, to bring about this conversion, as the Czar desired a political alliance as
much with the Pope as with the Roman Emperor
and other European sovereigns.   He could assure
him that the Russian people had no aversion to
Rome ; on the contrary, many of them desired to
see the city with its sacred places, which reminded

them of martyrs for whom they had even more
veneration than the Latins themselves—particularly
for the Holy Virgin of Loretta, who was more
known to the Russians than to many French and
Germans. Cobenzi further believed in the possibility of this re-union, as the Russians much
disliked the Lutherans. When he expressed a
wish to see the image of St. Nicolas, the permission
had been accorded, because he belonged to the
Latin religion and not to the Lutheran. " Although the Russians do not recognise purgatory,"
he wrote, "nevertheless they pray for the dead in
such a manner that the only difference between
them and Roman Catholics lies only in the
words."

Cobenzi rejoiced not a little at the possibility of
such a brilliant future for Roman Catholicism.
The acquisition of Russia would not only cover all
the losses of Rome in France and Germany, in
consequence of the Reformation, but the compensation would be to her advantage. One single
consideration frightened him; it was that the
Russians, only recognising the seven Œcumenical
Councils, and rejecting all others, could not
venerate the Pope as universal Head of the
Church.

Such ideas about the Greek doctrine and those

who professed it, prove perhaps not so much his ignorance of the state of Russia as an exaggerated zeal for his own faith, and led Cobenzi to believe easy that which even for a more determined spirit offered insurmountable difficulties. Strangers who visited Rome before and after the correspondence quoted, testify to the attachment of the Russians to their own Church, and their aversion to the Latins. Herberstein relates that the Russians recognised as heretics and schismatics all those who did not strictly adhere to the seven Œcumenical Councils, and that they mistrusted them more than Mahometans, seeing in them only traitors to the universal and primitive Church. After him Heidenstein reports the same thing. "The Russians fly from the Latins as from a pest," he says, "and will have nothing in common with them."

We find the opinions of the Russians of the sixteenth century still more plainly expressed in the acts of the Czar John IV. (the Terrible), and in his discussions with the legate of the Pope, Possevin.

(33)

CHAPTER II.

THE CZAR JOHN IV. (THE TERRIBLE) AND THE
JESUIT POSSEVIN.

The war with Bathory, and his successes.—John, seeing
nothing else possible, determines to apply to the Pope to arrange
terms with Poland.—Advantageous position of the Polish
King.—The Pope receives John's overtures, and sends an
envoy to conduct negotiations.—Wary conduct of John, and
his private views as to the designs of Rome.—Possevin.—Interview with the councillors of the Czar.—Possevin negotiates
peace with Bathory, and returns for his reward.—Possevin
taken up by John on the return of the envoy.—Their interview.—John menaces the envoy with his heavy stick.—
His kindness to Possevin afterwards.—Ill success of the
envoy's mission to convert John.—Repeated attempts to do
so.—His views as to the probability of converting the
Russians at some future time.

WHEN Bathory, King of Poland, after seizing
Polotsk and Soukol, advanced towards the ancient
provinces of Russia, the Swedes on the north, the
Turks and Nogays on the south, threatened the
frontiers of the Grand Duchy of Moscow. John
IV., seeing the impossibility of defending his
newly-acquired provinces with success, decided to
try the mediation of Rome. Having neither allies

VOL I.   D

nor forces sufficient to arrest the progress of an enemy as active as Bathory, John believed that he might count upon the influence of the Pope to terminate the war. But his adversary being a Roman Catholic, and governing a people professing the same faith, had received the Pope's blessing to make war on Russia, and even been promised the support of other Catholic sovereigns. The intervention of Rome, therefore, in the pacification of the two countries was of the highest importance; his very inaction would be useful in the difficult position in which John was placed. On the 25th August, 1580, Istoma Schevriguin was consequently despatched to Rome to negotiate. Theodore Poplin accompanied him.

John foresaw that in return for any succour Rome might accord, she would exact, not territorial or material concessions, but concessions in matters of faith, and these might be of such a nature, that considering the attachment of the people to their faith, he could not, and would not, grant them. Positive evidence exists as to the Czar's knowledge of the views and tendencies of Rome—that he comprehended that in case she consented to aid him, her aim and ambition would be his own conversion and that of his people to Romanism. He would therefore leave Rome to her future experience on this subject, and make no engagement. This policy is evident throughout the instructions given to Schevriguin in the letter written by John himself with the greatest prudence to the Pontiff, and in the order given to the Pris-taw who should accompany the Pope's envoy from Smolensk to Staritska. This order expressly forbade the discussion of religion with the envoy, the Pristaw replying that he knew not how to read, and not even to mention religion. In his letter to the Pope and in his documentary instructions to Schevriguin, the Czar does not make the most distant allusion to this subject, and commanded his ambassador not to hold any conference on questions not specially mentioned in his instructions. If asked, had he any private communication to make, he should answer "only about the letter." Schevriguin fulfilled conscientiously the commands of the Czar; he adroitly eluded all approach to religious subjects, preserving the government on the one hand from all reproach on the part of those Russians who might disavow promises incompatible with the doctrines of the Greek church, and on the other side from all recrimination on the part of Rome for promises not fulfilled.

In the very circumstantial account which Schevriguin has given of this embassy, we cannot

discover a single negotiation on the all important
question. Possevin himself, the Pope's envoy,
does not make allusion to any engagements, and he
would scarcely have failed in remembering such, as
religion was the principal object of his mission to
Moscow. On his arrival in the capital, Possevin
handed in a memorandum of the affairs with which
he was charged, not omitting the grand point. On
this latter, however, John declined discussion, and
it was only on this point that Rome was induced to
take an active part in the affairs of the two
countries. John, by way of conciliation, had proposed an alliance of the Christian sovereigns of
Europe against the Turks; the proposal was not
contrary to his own faith, and it compromised him
in nothing with regard to Rome. But at heart he
could hardly entertain such an idea, as the position
of his own country was serious enough, and
exclusively claimed all his energy; but he would
manœuvre with Rome to attain certain ends, so
that the very term "alliance" should open up a
vast field for the hopes of propagandists of
that Court. In a political alliance, Rome
would naturally see a preliminary step towards a
religious union. Besides, he had still another bait,
another reward for any services he might receive
—the concession of a free route to Venetian

merchants and others through Russia to Persia.
Rome had for a long time desired this concession,
as Catholic missionaries usually accompanied the
merchants. Fully comprehending the consequences
of such a concession, John had refused it at the
time of the Pope's first overture to reconcile
him with Bathory; but he afterwards intimated
to Schevriguin that if similar proposals were
brought - forward, he should advise the sending
by the Holy Father of a special ambassador to
Russia, to arrange this business, or take upon
himself the commission when he should be returning home. By such means, John hoped for the
Pope's succour in assisting him to preserve the
integrity of his empire. The Russian ambassador
was received in Rome with great pomp. The most
magnificent equipages were placed at his disposal,
and he was taken to see all the marvels of the
ancient capital of the world, especially to see all
that might impress him with the excellence and
the splendour of the Roman Church, and the
expediency of the concentration of all Christian
confessions in her. He was introduced into a new
church built to receive the relics of Saints John
Chrysostom and Gregory. They invited him to
inspect a college where the Greeks studied Latin
theology—intended to facilitate the union of the

two churches—and, in fact, to see everything which
demonstrated the power and the omnipotence of
the Roman Church and the Roman Pontiff. He
remained in the Holy City more than a month, in
which interval nothing was spared that could strike
the senses or exalt the magnificence of the successor of St. Peter. But the Russian was not so
easily trapped. It was neither the riches of the
churches, nor the pomp of the Latin services, but
the uselessness of many of them, that impressed
his mind; and the very means which the Court of
Rome counted on to allure and dazzle his senses,
consequently to secure his influence in the
momentous affairs in hand, produced only the
contrary effect.

The overtures of John were received with much
suavity. More than once Rome had endeavoured
to extend her power to Russia, but this was the
first time that the sovereign of that empire had
seemed to anticipate her wishes, so at least she
flattered herself. At the close of May, 1581, the
Jesuit Possevin was selected to proceed to Moscow,
to negotiate a peace between John and Bathory,
and to sow the seeds of Romanism in Russia.
Antoine Possevin was born at Mantua, 1534, and
died 1611, at Ferrara. His ability and success in
the conversion of heretics was well known ; amongst

others attributed to him is that of John, King of
Sweden, who, in 1577, was said to have secretly
embraced Catholicism. The aim of his mission,
and the means to be practised towards its attain-
ment, are amply detailed in his instructions.
Bathory was first to be induced to conclude a truce
with Russia, but the affair was to be so arranged
that John should perfectly comprehend that he
owed it to Rome ; afterwards he was to be
influenced to form an alliance with the Pope, the
Emperor, and the other Christian sovereigns of
Europe, against the Turks. Having inspired John
with animosity against the infidels, this political
part of the programme should terminate, and they
should pass smoothly over to the other and, to
Rome, more important bearing of the question ;
Possevin proving to the Czar that an alliance could
hardly be durable or solid without union of Spirit,
and that this union could not · exist unless he
adhered to the Catholic Church and recognised the
Pope as its Head and as Christ's Vicar upon
earth ; adding, that from the earliest Christian
epochs he had been acknowledged to as such by all
Christian monarchs, Rome being considerated the
most exalted of all Christian ecclesiastical Sees.
His arguments should be based on the Council of
Florence, a copy of the acts of which in the Greek

language was forwarded for his use; and he should prove that this Council had unanimously recognised the Bishop of Rome as Head of the Church. The decisions of this council could not be expugned, the most enlightened theologians of the time taking part in it; and the Greek Emperor himself had, in the name of all the East, recognised its competency, its authority, and its indisputably wise resolutions. The Papal sovereignty had been discussed to its foundation, and with the assistance and intervention of the Holy Spirit, this Council came to a decision which confirmed fully and for ever the Pope's supremacy. The rôle of the Jesuit, however, was principally to play upon the passions of John, exciting his self-love, his vanity, his political and religious fanaticism, and twisting each and every weakness he might discover into a string to pull him in the desired direction. Assuredly the part allotted to Possevin in this great scheme was one not unworthy the well-known ability of the Jesuit. John's pride was to be attacked by a representation of the dependency of the Patriarch of Constantinople upon the Turkish Sultan, and his own shameful position as the dependent on the vassal of the Infidel—a position unworthy his exalted rank, his wisdom, and his power. How much better to acknowledge the

Pope as chief of the Church, whom all other Christian monarchs submitted to, and who was in truth the Vicar of Christ!

Supposing that the principal obstacle to such schemes might be found in the Russian clergy, who, partly through their hostile disposition towards the Latin Church and partly through their desire to preserve their own influence, would spare no pains to retain their sovereign in the faith of his fathers, the Pope charged the Jesuit to exert himself to conciliate and attract them. He was also specially commanded to procure permission for the construction of one or more Churches in Moscow, without which, he should add, foreigners could hardly come to open up a commerce with the country.

With these instructions, Possevin arrived in Russia. John's idea ran diametrically opposite. He knew that the chief object of this embassy was his own conversion to Catholicism, but he knew equally well that such hopes were vain. He resolved that he would not, and indeed could not, promise anything concerning spiritual affairs, but convinced of the orthodoxy of the Church to which he belonged, he would fight Rome with her own weapons, and actually endeavour to convert the Legate, sent to convert him, to his own belief.

Possevin and Schevriguin left Rome, and travelled
together as far as Prague, from whence the latter
departed for Denmark, while the Jesuit went to
Wilna, from which city he must pass through
Smolensk, on his way to Moscow. Accordingly
John wrote a letter on the 27th July to Sylvestre,
Bishop of Smolensk and Briansk, in which he
commanded him to permit Possevin on his arrival
to visit all the churches and convents, and personally to see beforehand that everything was in the
greatest order. If the Legate wished to see the
Church of the Holy Virgin, the Bishop should, at
that very time, himself officiate there with a full
chapter, and with the utmost pomp. But although
graciously receiving a stranger, the bishop should
not put himself on the same level, and the Czar particularly enjoined that Sylvestre should entice the
Legate to kiss his hand, but not to give him
apostolic benediction, as to other Christians, nor
even, though permitting him to enter the churches,
to let him approach the altar. This order of the
Czar was, without doubt, altogether unnecessary,
as it does not appear that the Jesuit tried to
see any of the churches, although we know by his
own words that he was presented to the Bishop of
Smolensk. Nevertheless the letter of John completely expresses the ideas and intentions of this

sovereign with regard to the reception of the Legate of the Pope. -

Having learned the state of affairs at Wilna, and augmented his suite by several Polish Jesuits, furnished with guides and a safe conduct by Bathory, Possevin on the 18th of August arrived at Staritza, where the Czar then was, accompanied by a numerous retinue. He was received with all the honours usually paid to the plenipotentiaries of powerful sovereigns, this distinguished reception being due no doubt to the politic consideration that John saw in the Pope the only possible mediator between himself and Bathory, the Emperor of Germany having declined to have anything to do with it. Two days afterwards, Possevin, presenting himself to the Czar, handed him the Pope's letter, in which, while accepting the proposition to arm against the Turks, Gregory XIII. explained that the sole base of an alliance between Christian sovereigns was love founded on the doctrines of Christ, of whom he himself was the earthly representative—that the Council of Florence, one hundred and fifty years before, as well as all the bishops of the Greek empire, and the Emperor Paléologue himself, had concurred in the supremacy of the Pope, but that those Greeks who had not recognised the authority of the Holy

See had been punished by all sorts of calamities, and had fallen under the yoke of the Infidel; that to act in concert with his Christian allies, against the Turks, and to consolidate his empire, he should be reconciled to Rome. Gregory also sent him a copy of the proceedings of the Council of Florence, requesting him to peruse it attentively, and to order the clergy to do so likewise, assuring him of its unquestionable value as good and true. In conclusion, he expressed his earnest desire to see John embrace Catholicism, promising him after that the fulfilment of everything likely to augment his earthly glory, and the happiness of his kingdom. Nor did the Holy Father forget the members of the Czar's family: he wrote to the two sons of John and to his wife, thinking that such compliments might assist the difficult task of the Legate. On his first interview with the Privy Council, the Jesuit from the outset advocated the re-union of the churches, stating, while recapitulating the contents of the Pope's letter, that the first four Œcumenical Councils had recognised the supreme authority of Rome, and the dogmas of the Latin theology, but that the Greek bishops had intentionally misinterpreted the decisions of these councils. As a proof of the opinions of the early Fathers concerning Catholicism, he referred to the fact that the relics of St. Chrysostom and St. Gregory lay in the Church of St. Peter at Rome—those of Saints Athanasius and Nicolas at Venice—while, moreover, the autograph works of the Fathers attested the verity of the Latin Church, a corroboration of which was to be found in the fact that, the heathen converted during the primitive days of Christianity adhered to this faith. The Greek Church he said being based upon the decisions of the Fathers, and these holy men recognising, as he pretended, the creed of the Roman Church, there was really no difference between the two beliefs ; farther, that the Council of Trent, which he urged should be regarded as legal authority, had completely expressed and confirmed the dogmas of the two Churches. In conclusion, he offered to copy out the works of the Greek Fathers for the Czar, or in case he should have to go to Bathory, that the two Jesuits who were with him should do it, and that while remaining for this purpose they could teach Latin, and at the same time learn Russian. He spoke of the colleges at Rome established for young clergy-men, wherein there were to be found pupils from all quarters of Europe, even from Greece, suggesting that some young Russians should be despatched, and that the Pope would educate them at his own expense. In acknowledging the Latin Church, John would acquire incomparably more glory than by the conquest of Tartar provinces—his authority over his own subjects would be consolidated, and all other Christian sovereigns would respect and look up to him; and that through the intercession of the Head of the Catholic Church, God would confer on him every terrestrial blessing, with power to annihilate the enemies of his empire.

The counsellors charged by the Czar to conduct this negotiation did not reply to the arguments of the Legate, but conversed generally about the affairs of Livonia, just then a source of inquietude to the government.

But the Jesuit was not so easily repulsed. On the 1st September he remitted a memorial, in which, while reviewing the subject of religion, he tranquillised the Czar by demonstrating that the union of the two Churches did not demand, as a necessity, changes in the Greek ceremonies and rites. He again reiterated that Rome was indispensable to his alliance with the rest of Christendom, and attributed the silence opposed by the government to his first propositions, to the fault of the translators who had not comprehended his ideas, hoping that the present memorandum would be attended to, as he should have to communicate with his own chief. Besides this he intimated a wish that the Czar in replying to the Pope's letter should style his Holiness " The Vicar of Christ," as it was customary among other sovereigns to do, and as the first four Œcumenical Councils and the writings of the holy Greek fathers warranted; this Possevin affirmed at least, though he knew without doubt that what he stated was untrue.

This memorial remained unanswered, and from this time the Jesuit despaired of success. He wrote to Rome, that not only did the Czar decline to listen to his propositions, but that he had even forbidden the translation of the despatch which he had presented on this subject. But on the 10th September he received a short and evasive reply to the effect that the Czar would himself converse with him personally on his return from the mission to Bathory. As to the alliance with the other sovereigns against the Turks, he scarcely succeeded better. " What alliance with Christian sovereigns is possible at this moment," said John, " We arm against the Infidel, and Bathory marches against us ! "

Thus Possevin was placed in such a position that not only could he not hope for success in his negotiations on the question of religion, but he could not even begin before having concluded a peace between John and Bathory. The conversion of Russia to Romanism, the alliance of John against the Turks—in a word, the chief object of his mission, plans so dear to Rome, all depended on the ability with which he should quickly conclude a convention between Russia and Poland. From this point only could he in reality commence operations, and it was exactly from this date that John intended his relations with Rome to close.

The Jesuit next turned his attention to the concession of a free route through Russia, for mercantile speculations and intercourse with Persia, a concession much desired by Rome for purposes especially her own. Not the Venetians only availed themselves of the commercial road to the East—missionaries invariably directed their footsteps towards the same quarter, and Possevin calculated that this route would neither be so dangerous nor so expensive, while it would certainly be much more advantageous for commercial purposes. He, therefore, in negotiating this point, said that on his arrival in Venice he should labour to convince the authorities of these advantages, and decide his Holiness at Rome to influence them to transact their commercial undertakings

by way of Russia. John, as we know, foresaw
the designs of the Jesuit, but would temporise
with him up to a certain point.

When the Legate left to go to Bathory, the
Czar had promised this route to the Venetians and
the ambassadors whom the Pope might send to the
Schah of Persia, as well as to any missionaries who
should accompany them ; but he distinctly gave
the priest to understand that his requests on this
head could not be realized until after the conclusion
of peace with Poland. Possevin himself comprehended this perfectly. "There is another route
towards India through Poland and Lithuania," he
said, with regard to the subject, "but it is
impossible to avail one's self of it from the continual hostility of the rulers of these countries,
who cannot live in peace and love with each
other." Hopes of ultimate success led the Legate
to follow the direction indicated by the Czar, and
he industriously applied himself to the task of
putting an end to the war. There is reason to
believe that the epistle of John to Bathory was
couched in such terms as to excite the hopes
of Possevin as to the certainty of his success
afterwards, as it alludes to the close resemblance
of the doctrines of the Eastern and Western
Churches. Without any further loss of time the

Jesuit quitted Staritza on the 14th of the same month, en route to Bathory.

The Jesuits Etienne Drenotzky, and Michael Morien, remained in Moscow as his representatives, and received elaborate regulations for their conduct in political and religious circumstances during his absence. They were enjoined to keep a journal of everything they saw and heard; to watch everything; to avoid all religious discussions, and to compromise themselves in nothing. They were particularly commanded to avoid all interviews with the Metropolitan, to postpone the distribution of works specially prepared by Possevin on theological subjects, until his return; not to make processions, as they were likely to excite the ridicule of the Lutherans, or even produce an émeute amongst the Russian population that might lead to their own expulsion. If questioned as to their faith or the rules of their Church, they should adroitly pose questions themselves, instead of directly replying, so as to embarrass their opponents; but if driven hard, and no answer suitable to or consistent with the views of their order was ready, they should postpone it till the following day. As a general rule they were to speak more of moral principles than dogmatical questions, and especially to evade the topic of the Greek Saints, pretending their ignorance on this head.

Suspecting from what he already knew of the Czar, that he might tamper with these two Jesuits while he was with Bathory, Possevin took precautions against such an eventuality, and commanded them neither to kiss the hand of, or accept the benediction of the Metropolitan either in the Churches or in private houses, confining themselves, if presented to him, to a formal salutation. Thus the rôle of the Jesuits, left in the capital as his representatives, was determined on with remarkable art, and was carried out under the guise of a prudent reserve, while waiting the time when their chief, returning from his mission, should base his propositions upon its result.

At this epoch, the King of Poland, on his victorious way towards Novogorod and Moscow, besieged Pskoff, and as he was well provisioned, he continued the siege, notwithstanding the energetic defence of the Russians. Bariatensky had been vanquished by Prince Radzivill, who had seized Porhoff and reached the banks of the Volga, and placed himself under the walls of Mojaisk. Livonia was occupied by the Swedes; Narva had been taken, and the envoy of the Turkish Sultan was actually in the camp of Bathory to propose him succours. John's position was almost desperate ; for not only had he to struggle against outward enemies, but to contend with the revolts of the Boyards, always hostile to his authority, who, profiting by the misfortunes of the war, had entered into a conspiracy against him, in which his eldest son, the heir to the throne, was concerned ; and it was under such disadvantages, that Possevin forced the proud conqueror, who had already refused even proposals for an armistice, to sign a treaty for ten years between Russia and Poland. The active part which the Jesuit took in this affair is testified to by the treaty itself which is counter-signed by him, and by the repeated attestations and acknowledgments which on many occasions he received from John afterwards.

This mission successfully brought to a close, Possevin hastened to return and claim the reward of his services. His arrival at Moscow dates 14th February, 1582. John had now a difficult card to play, in that having profited by the services of the Legate, he could hardly evade the compensation without clashing with Rome, and perhaps exciting anew the war just terminated. He at once took up his position however, and waited the march of events.

On the 16th, Possevin renewed the propositions
he had formerly made to the Council, in a memorandum to the Czar himself—viz., the armament
of John against the Turks—the union of the
churches, liberty for Latin priests to reside in
Russia, and the expulsion of the Lutherans from
Moscow, to whose inspiration Possevin attributed
the conduct of John with regard to the Pope ; and
last but not least the despatch of students to Rome
to study languages and theology. Such was the
memorial presented by the Legate, which closed
with a request that the Czar should first read
an Exposé upon religion, which he also presented
at the same time, and accord him an audience to
discuss matters personally. He guaranteed that
the Russian students educated in Rome should be
brought up in the Greek religion, and afterwards
sent back to their native land; that the Lutheran
clergymen residing in Moscow should be replaced
by other and worthier German ecclesiastics, *but
Catholics;* the final wind up being an energetic
attempt to procure a written undertaking that the
Venetians and other Roman Catholic residents
should in Russia enjoy the full exercise of their faith.

On the 21st of February, it was officially announced to Possevin by the Boyard Nizita
Romanowitch, in presence of the Court, that as

an acknowledgment of his active and successful
services in bringing about the peace with Bathory,
the Czar consented to enter into an alliance against
the Turks as soon as the other Christian sovereigns
had concluded the terms of such an alliance
between them; the Venetian and German traders
might have their clergymen, "but they should not
spread their doctrine amongst the Russians, or
erect churches; that every one should remain
in his own faith." "In our empire," added the
Czar, "there are many sects whom we cannot deprive of liberty; but as to churches, until
the present day none have been built in the
country." There existed no reason why the
Lutherans should be expelled; and as to the
students for the public schools of Rome, it was
evasively stated that it would be next to impossible
to find in so short a time suitable young men, but
that when found they should be despatched. The
greatest difficulty of all now remained to be dealt
with,—the discussion on the subject of the church,
to which the Czar had pledged himself, once the
treaty of peace was concluded with Bathory. But
if he would not consent to it at an epoch when his
empire was torn and devastated—when his only
hope of rescue lay in the Legate of Rome, he was
certainly less inclined to concede it after the

restoration of peace, when he had scarcely longer need of the services of Possevin or Possevin's master. The priest was consequently politely informed that as the Czar had not his Privy Council near him, it would be particularly inconvenient to discuss religion. " These discussions," the Czar intimated, " could hardly have any result, as every one is attached to his own opinion ; defending it might lead to useless disputes, which would only mutually irritate and annoy ; who knows if they might not even interrupt the good understanding just established between Russia and the Court of Rome ! "

When the determination of John was made known to the Legate, the latter, comprehending the position in which he was placed, perceived that his only hope lay in the skill with which he might manœuvre direct communications with the Czar. He accordingly expressed a wish that he might be permitted to have the communications, which the sovereign would personally make him, in writing, that he would reply to them ; but that in requesting an interview, he did not pretend to solicit a private audience, but to be received before the Boyards, as he knew that the Czar would no more be without them, then the head without its members. He affirmed that he did not come to dispute or argue, though at the same time he must remark that he could not conceive how anything disagreeable could result from a mere conversation; he meant only to prove the dogmatical analogy between the Greek and Latin Churches, and demonstrate that if some contradictions were found amongst them, it was owing to inequal translation by the Greek theologists; that the Council of Florence had virtually united the Churches, and that it would be well to carry out this union without delay. If the Czar would not receive him, he then begged leave to present another Exposé of his ideas on religion the following day.

Seeing the incessant solicitations of the Jesuit, and considering that written discussions might be indefinitely prolonged and also lead to further solicitation and inconvenience, John resolved to put an end to the affair. He therefore commanded Possevin to present himself and verbally explain what communications he had to make. In receiving him personally the Czar intended keeping the path he had chalked out for himself before the peace, namely—to manœuvre Rome, and avoid the question of religion. He had no intention of entering into preliminary negotiations on this point, but to convince the Legate that explanations were impossible, and by this means end an embassy that was as fatiguing as useless.

Possevin was received before the Boyards and some of the appanaged princes; but the Stolniks, Pristaws, and gentlemen of the Court were dismissed. After the usual ceremonial, he thus addressed the Czar:

"Eminent Sovereign, Czar and Grand Duke, My Master, Pope Gregory XIII. accepts the proposals of alliance which thou hast sent to him, the Inheritor of the Sovereignty of the Apostle Peter, by thy ambassador Schevriguin, in all faith and love, seeing no difference between the Greek and Latin faiths, and desiring the establishment only of one single Church and one belief according to the words of Christ, 'Que ma brebis paisse.' It is his earnest desire that we go to your churches and confess to your priests, and you to ours; and to attain this end he offers that if there be not in your empire a translation of all the works of the Fathers of the Greek Church, they can be procured at Rome, together with the works of St. John Chrysostom, and other illustrious saints, as well the decisions of the first four Œcumenical Councils, and the last Council of Florence which confirmed the re-union of the Latin and Greek faiths. By acknowledging such a union your Majesty shall have the Pope's friendship, and that of the Emperor of Germany and other Christian

monarchs; thy empire shall extend far beyond the
limits of the dominion of thy ancestors through
their conjoint efforts, and thou shalt become
Emperor of the East." The Jesuit farther
promised that neither the Churches nor the rites of
the Greek religion should be touched, that all
should remain as before; reminding John of his
promise, relative to this re-union, and liberty of
conscience to Catholics residing in Russia.

John several times interrupted him, denying that
he had written to the Pope on the subject of
religion, as even he himself had no right to enter
into negotiations of this kind without the permission of the Metropolitan and Council. He
begged Possevin to desist from a discussion which
was as useless as disagreeable, and that might end
in an unsatisfactory result. "You wish to speak
on religion," said the Czar, "and certainly, as the
Pope deputed you for this purpose, you are right to
do so; but I cannot reply to you, not having
obtained the consent of the Metropolitan and
Council." With regard to the route to Persia,
and liberty for Latin priests to reside in the
country, the promise formerly given was confirmed,
provided that divine service was celebrated neither
in public nor in churches.

Possevin repeatedly insisted that a discussion on

the matter could result in nothing disagreeable.
" Thou art a great sovereign," said he, "how then
shall I, the humblest of thy servants, dare to
pronounce one offensive word ?　I shall only communicate what His Holiness charged me to
say."　　.

" It is difficult to discuss spiritual affairs,"
replied the Czar, " seeing that for a long time the
Eastern Church has been separated from the
Western, and that we received Christianity from
the apostle St. Andrew who introduced it into the
country under Vladimir ; the whole land embraced
it and preserved it pure and entire ; while the
Roman Church established at the same time—
recollect what thou thyself told us at Staritza—
contains at this moment seventy different sects.
I was born in the Orthodox Faith !　By God's
help I will die in it.　Through His mercy I have
attained my fiftieth year, and it would ill become
me to change my opinions or desire a more extended empire.　I fix my aspirations only on a
future life, and the whole universe would not
tempt me to violate my conscience.　The earth is
the Lord's !　He can give it to whom He will.
But for what concerns thy statement that the
Greek and Roman churches have been re-united,
I beg to say that our religion is not the *Greek*

religion, but the orthodox faith, which differs on many points from the Latin. But I decline to discuss this subject, as I may say something superfluous or disagreeable to you, which I do not wish to do, heartily desiring to preserve those amicable relations commenced between myself and Pope Gregory XIII. I therefore request you not to continue the subject."

Possevin again repeated that he could not imagine how it could be disagreeable to the prince, and affected not to see that he fatigued him. But John's impetuous character, which often carried him beyond the limits he allowed himself, led him to reply to the priest again. He was certainly well versed in the dogmas of his church, and when occasions permitted, he liked it to be seen, not only in his conversation but in his writings. His impetuosity on this occasion carried him beyond his diplomatic determination not to approach prelimi- naries with Rome,—" I will not " said he " discuss the dogmas of the Catholic faith, but I will put one question—I see that you shave ! Neither ecclesias- tics nor laymen are commanded to do this, and you, a priest of Rome, have no beard ! Have the good- ness to inform me from what text this custom is taken ?" The embarrassed Jesuit replied that it was quite true he had no beard.

John's passion now carried him onward and he continued :—

"Schevriguin tells me that they carry the Pope about on a throne, and kneeling kiss his feet, upon the sole of whose shoe the Crucifixion is embroidered. The Cross of Christ in our church signifies the victory over sin—we adore it—we venerate the wood according to the traditions of the holy Apostles and the Fathers. But we never place it below the waist, nor even put the images of the Virgin and Saviour there either, that the eyes of the soul may see Him who is our model! Our altars are so arranged that holy things are never on a level with the stomach. Your Pope acts not according to the statutes of the Apostles and Fathers, or of the seven Œcumenical Councils; the ceremonies have been invented solely by the pride of man."

The Legate answered that such honours were paid to the Pope as the representative of the sovereignty of St. Peter; and that all Christian monarchs acknowledged him as such, a proof of which was to be found in the concentration of all holiness and religion in Rome.

"Thou art justified in speaking thus of thy sovereign," said John, "thou art wise to do so, but thy arguments are not based on the command-

ments of God, nor yet on apostolic tradition.
Pride does not become bishops. ' Call no one
master, for there is only One Master,' says Christ,
' ye are all brethren; neither call any one Rabbi,
for there is One Doctor !' And the Lord said again
to his disciples, ' Make no provision for the journey,
neither take gold or silver, neither staff or shoes,
neither two coats.' Remember also the Epistle of
the Apostle Peter, in which it is said ' Keep the
flock of Christ committed to thee ! Watch over
it, not with violence, but gently; not for gain, but
for charity; not for the sake of dominion, but
rather as the model of the flock. It is therefore
not becoming in Pope Gregory to exalt himself
upon a throne, as our envoy has informed us, and
as thou thyself hast confessed. It becomes him
better to be humble and to imitate the Apostle
Peter in spirit, after the commandment of our
Lord."

" From the time of the first Œcumenical
Council," continued the Czar, " there were four
Patriarchs or universal Doctors of the Church—
those of Constantinople, Antioch, Alexandria, and
Jerusalem ; and these sent Metropolitans into different countries. The ecclesiastical government
of our empire consists of a Metropolitan, archbishops and bishops, whom we respect and consult

in spiritual affairs. We style the Metropolitan "Father," we bow before him and he gives us his benediction when we implore it; and though we go with all our court to meet him we do not recognise him as God. Pope Gregory should not seat himself on a throne, and call himself the equal of Peter, and even of Christ; he is not Jesus Christ, and his throne is not a cloud, nor are those who carry him angels. Let him follow the example of St. Sylvestre, Adrian, and other holy men of the Church who walked in the doctrines of Christ, and neither proudly exalted themselves on a throne nor carried the Cross on their shoe, that people might kiss their feet. We acknowledge the Apostle Peter and several other Roman bishops, good and true' teachers of God's flock, such as Clement, Adrian, Sylvestre, Leon, and Gregory; but it is impossible to consider any one as the successor of the Apostles, who occupies their See without following our Lord's injunctions."

The reply of Possevin intimated that the power confided by Christ to his representatives did not depend upon their virtuous or reprehensible lives. "I pray thee, Illustrious Czar, to tell me if thou art the successor and legitimate inheritor of Vladimir, who lived five hundred years before thee?" When John replied in the affirmative,

Possevin went on :—" Then, if any one mocks thy
power and disobeys thee because thy ancestors had
human weaknesses and frailties—that they were
even abandoned to vices—would'st thou regard
them as worthy of eulogy or of punishment ? Thou
art a great sovereign in thy empire ! Why shall
we not exalt thee—glorify thee—even throw ourselves at thy feet !" In pronouncing these words
he threw himself at the feet of the Czar.

" In truth," answered John, ".our subjects owe
us obedience and respect, as they respected
Vladimir Monomach and all other great princes.
But if thou thinkest by that to justify the honours
paid to the Pope, I beg to observe that prelates,
as pupils of the Apostles, are expected to set an
example of humility, and not exalt themselves
above all other sovereigns. To potentates belongs
the honour due to potentates ; to prelates the
honour due to them as the servants of Christ.
Those Popes who have obeyed the commandments
of Christ and walked according to the Apostles and
the commands of the seven Œcumenical Councils,
have been truly equal to the Apostles ; but a Pope
who acts contrary to the doctrines of Christ and
Holy Scripture—such a Pope is not a pastor, but
a wolf !"

" If the Pope be a wolf, I have nothing to say

after that," said Possevin. "Why then hast thou
sent to him to succour thee? Why hast thou,
like thy predecessors, styled him Pastor of the
Church?"

At these words the Czar became furious, left his
seat, and, approaching the priest, menaced him
with his iron-clasped stick: "Hast thou been
brought up amongst peasants that thou darest use
such language towards us?" he exclaimed.

The terrified Jesuit hastened to excuse himself,
and afterwards most modestly replied to John's
attacks on the Papacy.

Hurried on by passion the Czar had overstepped
the bounds both of policy and prudence, but a
moment after and he saw that he must endeavour to
soften the impression his involuntary excitement
might cause,—an impression that could well militate
against him and rouse Rome, perhaps Bathory.
"I told thee before," he said more gently to the
trembling priest, "that religious discussions could
hardly terminate without something disagreeable.
But I did not mean to call your Pope a wolf; I
meant only the Pope who did not follow Christ's
commandments and the traditions of the Apostles.
Let our conversation here terminate."

Before dismissing him the Czar graciously presented him his hand to kiss, and the same day the

great officers in waiting carried the priest some of the dishes from the royal table.

After this interview, the Legate of Rome might well have comprehended that the intentions and views of his master could not be realized quite as easily as hitherto supposed. Nevertheless he did not renounce his projects, but persisted in believing that in time he should succeed. On the 22nd February, he presented another petition on the subject of the youths who were to be sent to Italy to be educated, in which he declared that he only desired it as a proof of the Czar's friendship for the Pope, adding, that many might be found in the neighbourhood of Pskoff. "Here," he said, "an opportunity was afforded the Czar of serving God, and adding lustre to his name ; but if he refused, the Pope would scarcely regret it, as so many pupils arrived in Rome for instruction, that very often many of them were obliged to be sent home again."

This memorial received no reply. On the 23rd February, however, Possevin received an invitation to present himself at the palace the following day. The frightened Jesuit believing that the crown of martyrdom awaited him, took the Communion, administered it to his followers, and then tremblingly set out. But John had not summoned the priest to martyrize him. He regretted the words he had used at the audience, and though excited, was profoundly politic, remembering that after all he owed the peace with his neighbour to the influence of the Pope. He had now requested the attendance of the Legate to be reconciled to him. John received him with much *empressement*, and after a few preliminary sentences said :

"When you insisted on discussing religious subjects with me, my Boyards were commanded to tell you, and I afterwards said the same thing to you myself, that they would produce disagreements, every one defending his own opinion. If I advocate my own church, you are impatient ; and if you eulogise yours it is unpleasant to me. But you were obstinate, and insisted on explaining the superiority of the Latin religion ; consequently, I made some observations which offended you. Forget what I said about the Pope, and do not write it to Rome ; notwithstanding the differences of our rites I desire the friendship of Pope Gregory as well as the other Christian sovereigns of Europe. I do not forget thy services and thy zeal, and shall certainly certify to the Pope that the peace was brought about through thy mediation with Bathory."

The Legate having thanked the Czar, said some words about religion which provoked neither con-

tradiction nor reply. After this reception he had
no further private access to the Czar; but he
continued his efforts through writing, and composed a dissertation upon the differences existing
between the Oriental and Western Churches,
which he sent to the sovereign. This dissertation
proved, as he believed, the superiority of the
Latin. He composed also a sermon on the
Procession of the Holy Spirit from the Father and
from the Son, which he considered might impress
the Russians, as well as a refutation of a dissenting
work, translated from the English, which had been
presented by English merchants to the Czar, in
which an analogy was traced between the Pope
and Antichrist. In defending Rome and in enu-
merating all the merits of her Pontiffs, he never
lost sight of the fact that the intervention of
Gregory XIII. had concluded the treaty with
Poland, and in conclusion stated that the "effusion
of Christian blood which had lasted for twenty-two
years had been arrested, not by Antichrist, but by
the Vicar of Christ on earth."

The theological treatises of Possevin did not
much interest John, but this prince, having repulsed
the attacks on the Russian faith, and dispelled the
Jesuit's hopes of his conversion, returned to his
original design of drawing him over to his own belief.

On the 4th of March there was a levee at the palace, at which the Legate presented himself; the saloons were full of people; the very staircases were crowded; and the vast building contained at least five thousand people. In the midst of such a crowd, the Leg&te found himself before John. "Our Boyards inform us that thou desirest to visit our temples and assist in the divine offices of the Orthodox Church. Thou shalt now have an opportunity of seeing all, as we go to the Church of the Holy Virgin, and thou canst accompany us. There thou shalt see with what faith we adore and implore the Holy Trinity, the Holy Virgin and the saints. Thou shalt see with what respect we bow before the miraculous images, and view the Mother of God painted by the Evangelist Luke. Pay special attention, we pray thee, to the manner in which we respect the Metropolitan, our Father, who prays for us. But thou shalt judge for thyself that we do not adore him as God—we do not carry him on a throne or kiss his feet—that is pride, not a religious custom. Thou sayest that the Pope is the representative of St. Peter, but St. Peter did not go on horseback, he walked on foot, even barefoot." Possevin replied that he had never expressed a desire to see the services of the Greek religion, but that however he would go to the Church, and again reiterated his explanations of the honours rendered the Pope. "Thou thyself, Prince," said he, "showest great respect to the Metropolitan during divine service. When he washes his hands, thou wettest thine eyes with the water."

"How? Thou wilt ever play the doctor," exclaimed John. "Thou comest hither to teach us? Dost thou know what thou sayest? Hast thou never had a correct explanation of the Mass?" Possevin was silent. "Then," continued the Czar, "I will explain it to thee. Before his sufferings the Saviour washed his hands and wet the eyes of those who served him, with the water. The Metropolitan, after washing his hands at Mass, refreshes his eyes with the water also; and we and all the people do the same, as a souvenir of the Passion of Christ, but not in honour of the Metropolitan."

Possevin had not a word to say in reply.

The Czar, intending to influence the imagination of the priest, and wishing to induce him to recognise orthodoxy, gave a grand religious fête in the Cathedral of Ouspensk, where a pompous ceremonial was prepared. The Legate was invited, and Eustace Pouschkin, Theodore Pissenisky and the great officers of the household were commanded to conduct him, and wait the arrival of the Czar at the doors of the building, so that he might see how the sovereign would be received by the Metropolitan with the Cross in his hand, and surrounded by all his clergy; and how the Czar would enter the Church after the Cross, Possevin to follow and enter after him.

Having arrived at the cathedral, Possevin would immediately enter the Church without waiting for the Czar, but was prevented by the Pristaws. He thereupon declared that he would return home; but the same officers obliged him to remain. The Czar on being informed of what had passed, and seeing how very difficult it would be to constrain the priest to bow before a Russian altar, sent his secretary to tell him that he only wished his presence to let him observe how the Russian sovereign was received by the Metropolitan, "and that he might not make any inconvenient mistakes;" but that if he declined waiting he could return home, and on presenting himself to the Ministry he would receive an answer to his despatches. The priest profited by this permission, and fled from the curiosity of the crowd. No longer hoping for a favourable response to his solicitations, he went to the Ministry, where he was officially informed that Roman Catholic churches would not be permitted in Russia, but that people professing this faith who came to or resided in the country had full liberty to worship as they liked, only that they must not proselytise the Russians. Such was the determination of the Czar.

Thus finished this remarkable episode in the history of Russia, which perfectly demonstrated the union existing between the temporal and the spiritual power. This union was not determined by any positive law, but resulted from social, political, and religious combinations, from habits and customs which have contributed to influence the national spirit of the country, without which he entire history of Russia would be incomplete.

The Pope addressed himself not to the Russian clergy, but to the Czar, on the subject of religion; but this sovereign, the absolute autocrat of his subjects, did not acknowledge his own authority over the Church. He discussed with the Legate the truths of his faith,—proved the verity of his belief,—and defended his religion in presence of the exigencies of Rome, and the intrigues of the Jesuits. But he declared that he would decide nothing in spiritual affairs, nor was he even commissioned to consider them, either by the synod or the Metropolitan. Our history proves this double fact, that the Government and the Church have always been intimately united, but that one of the two powers was never the slave of the other. Modern writers on Russia have denied this fact, and pretended that the spiritual power was constantly subject to the temporal, but an assertion like this proves great ignorance of the real relations existing between them, as also of the history of the empire. We affirm that in no other country were the two powers so independent of each other as in ours, notwithstanding the ties which united them. This reciprocal independence was never more strong than in the theological discussions of John the Terrible with the Legate of Pope Gregory XIII.

The Czar confided a letter to the Legate for the Pope, in which he simply acknowledged the copy of the acts of the Council of Florence, and the priest returned to Rome accompanied by Molianinoff as the envoy of the government, but he was not charged with any mission on spiritual matters; on the contrary, he was stringently prohibited even naming the alliance proposed against the Turks. His instructions contained the replies he should make to any questions or inuendoes relative to religion. "We are not commissioned to treat on these matters." "We have no authority to speak on this question." But it was certainly

John's wish to preserve amicable relations with
Rome. Knowing that his expressions about the Pope
to the Legate were a little too strong, and that
the constraint exercised over him at the church
was not a circumstance tending to strengthen the
friendship of Rome, he desired Molianinoff, in case
it were objected that he had called the Pope a
wolf, to reply that he had not heard it. As to
the Legate's detention at the door of the church,
he should say that at that time he was not at
Moscow, that he only knew that the same honours
were accorded him as were rendered to the Ambassadors of the Emperor or of the Sultan of Turkey.

Thus John's determination not to concede to
the Pope on religious matters remained unchanged.
He acted thus during the difficult time when his .
country was devastated by Bathory, and his only
safety lay in the mediation of Rome ; and his
conduct was the same, when, thanks to that intervention, he obtained peace. He succeeded in
evading all explanations on religion, employing the
concurrence of Rome for the defence of his country
without sacrificing the dogmas of his faith, or
conceding the establishment of the Latin Church
to the detriment of the Orthodox belief.

Bathory perfectly understood his Russian neighbour. Notwithstanding the attempts of Gregory,

John held both to his policy and his opinions. The theological struggle which ensued with the Legate was quite useless to both. Rome tried to convert John to Catholicism, and John endeavoured to make the Legate officially recognise his Church. The two champions stranded on their contradictory work. Rome only obtained permission through Possevin for Latin priests to reside in the country, conditionally, a concession up to this period refused. Through this concession, John obtained peace with a redoubtable enemy; preserved his conquests, and established the tranquillity and integrity of Russia.

The result of this mission may be appreciated, not only by its well-known consequences, but by the intentions entertained by the Legate at the period of his departure for Rome, and the means which he believed possible to introduce Romanism into Russia.

The first step in this direction was the establishment of an academy and seminary at Rome for Russians. It was expected that the magnificence of the Court and the distribution of presents to the students would attract a number of pupils. Similar establishments should be opened at Wilna and Polotsk in Poland, in which the young Russian prisoners should be instructed. Afterwards these same young men should be sent to the seminaries of

Olmutz and Prague, where, in their own language, they could influence their fellow-countrymen, the proximity of the Czech tongue facilitating the work. The aim of these seminaries was to excite religious fanaticism in the scholars, and accustom them to the means which were considered the surest for conversions. On finishing the course, they should be despatched to Russia, or into countries non-Catholic, to inculcate and propagate Catholicism.

He considered it absolutely necessary that the principal works of the Propagand and other Catholic books should be translated into Russian, and widely disseminated through the different schools and seminaries, but this work should be secretly and carefully effected. " If," said Possevin, " the decisions, translations and tra- ditions of the Council of Florence had, as intended, been spread in the East; if schools for the Greeks had been established in which the truths of the Roman Church had been explained, Mark of Ephesus himself would not have been strong enough to destroy such an important work." He added that Popes Eugene II., Innocent III., Gregory X., Alexander VI., Leo X., and Clement VII., all had in view the accomplishment of this grand aim, not only by the convocation of a council or the sending of a letter or a Legate, but by all these combined. He advised that the conversion of Russia should commence by obliging the Kings of Poland to confer different privileges and prerogatives to those Russian bishops who should recognise the Council of Florence. This he considered the best means of attacking Orthodoxy to the profit of Latinism. Particular attention, he said, should be paid to Lithuania, which, notwithstanding its political separation, still preserved ties with Russia, as formerly the Russian bishops were instituted by the Metropolitan of Kieff, subject to the King of Poland. Kind letters should be despatched to the bishops of the Greek rite in Lithuania, and no means neglected that could attract them to Romanism. Thus Possevin prepared what has since been called *The Union.* Before its organisation he had exactly determined and drawn out a programme of its character and signification with regard to Russia.

Possevin returned to Rome more persuaded than ever of the importance of the acquisition of Russia, but at the same time he comprehended the difficulties of the work. During his sojourn in the country, he had turned his attention to the study of its peculiarities, its social, political, and religious distinctions; its people, its laws, its government, and thoroughly understood and calculated on the obstacles to his aim; consequently, he planned out a thorough system of Propagandism, adapted to meet those difficulties,. which he embodied in the form of a memorandum.

Russia converted to Romanism, the East lay open to the views of this ambitious and designing Jesuit, the road through her being not *only surer and more convenient, but less expensive. "This affair," he said, "would not be the work of a day, or of a single embassy, but of centuries; of a course of the subtlest logic,—of unwearing and indefatigable patience,—of courage and perseverance! Armed with these, the Propagand might begin in Lithuania, by the establishment of seminaries in conjunction with the Jesuits, whose miracles would produce an extraordinary effect on the simple and ignorant people; and an alliance at the same time of the Czar with the other Roman Catholic sovereigns of Europe; as a constant and uninterrupted communication between those monarchs, but particularly with the Pope himself and the sovereign of Russia, would be one of the most effectual means of breaking the barriers of prejudice which prevented the religion of Rome penetrating into the country. It would be necessary to have a Nuncio at Moscow, to whom detailed instructions might be

given, not only as to his own action, but with
respect to all documetns sent to the government,
and the manner in which they were to be expressed.
Even the dress of this functionary was prescribed,
as well as every act of his public life calculated.
The Jesuit did not neglect the minutest details
that could possibly assist the work. Care should
be taken to send this Nuncio only at a propitious
period. His suite should be composed of few
individuals, so as not to excite suspicion; and the
persons composing it should not lodge near the
Czar's palace, or even enter it, except in cases of
absolute necessity. The Nunciature itself should.
be splendid in everything, with the exception of the
Nuncio, whom Possevin advised should be simply
and modestly dressed, as the people were accustomed to see their bishops in the ordinary monastic
habit. Indeed, the dress selected should be as
nearly as possible like that of the Russian bishops,
both in texture and colour, the more easily to
attract the vulgar. He quoted the opinion formerly
expressed by Albert di Campi to Clement VII.,
that a Nunciature to Russia should not exceed
four persons. He then went on to say that, on
arriving in Poland, they could find suitable persons,
accustomed to the climate and to dangerous journeys, whom they could attach to the suite as

interpreters ; he advocated the engagement of two such individuals in case of the death of one, as it was dangerous to confide in any one sent by the ministry, who might, through ignorance, duplicity, or attachment to his own faith, translate inexactly and falsely the documents entrusted to him, or, as had happened to himself, communicate certain words and circumstances not intended for publicity. These translators should not be taken from amongst Russians or Poles, because of their reciprocal tendencies, but chosen from the Sclave race of Bohemia or Lithuania, who might be found at the college of Wilna or Polotsk, the latter being at that time about to be founded. Also a doctor, understanding Czech or Russian ought to accompany them, in order to visit the sick, acquire their affection and gratitude, and profit by their weakness to draw their sympathy towards his Church. The Nuncio appointed, should, if at all possible, be a person who was conversant with the Czech or Russian tongue ; one who had carefully studied the differences between the Greek and Latin churches, and who should have read the thirteen treatises which he named, written against the Greek faith. He should have with him all the accessories for Divine Service, himself officiating as frequently as he could, to engage the attention of the people.

He is expressly advised to profess the greatest
veneration for the Russian Church, and conform all
his actions, when opportunities occurred, to the
popular customs; fasting when the Russians
fasted, but not fasting on the Saturdays, as
in his own Church; pretending respect for the
holy images of the Greek Church, as Cardinal
Como had exhorted Possevin himself to do by
order of the Pope, at the time of the Legate's
sojourn in Russia. He also proposed the translation of several Latin theological books into
Russian, and indicated the means of distributing
them. (1) To circulate them gratis in the schools
to pupils of Russian origin, or to those who
might be at the College of the Jesuits at Wilna.
To make extracts from the work of Gennadius
containing questions and answers on the doctrines
of the Oriental Church, and to engage the professors to constrain their pupils to send them to
their parents and friends. (2) To assign money
for the publication of the last five Treatises upon the
sovereign authority of the Pope by the same author,
and to circulate copies amongst the pupils of the College of Wilna as well as at the Jesuitical College of
Jaroslav, near Livoff; to send them to Olmutz
and Prague, and to John Erbest then in Russia.
(3) To translate and print the Latin catechism

by Peter Camsius in Russian at the expense of the Jesuits, who would voluntarily furnish the means for this purpose. (4) To print two or three folios of the chapter upon schism by Sandar, "*De la Monarchie,*" and to distribute them to the Russian scholars at the different Jesuitical establishments, and through the Czar's secretary, Jassinsky to send them to the employés of the Chancellery of Poland at Moscow. (5) To publish separately those voluminous works accessible to few, such as the Treatise of Thomas upon the errors of the Greeks. (6) To publish extracts in Russian from the colossal, and at that period, rare works of the Jesuit Pierre Scarga, containing a polemic against the Eastern Church. (7) To print the Bull of Pope Eugene IV. in Russian. (8) To compose in Russian, an extract from the Lives of the Saints, written in Polish, also by Scarga; and having circulated copies gratis to the Orthodox priests, to induce them to read it in their churches. (9) To translate the works of Eckius against Luther, and publish it in Russian, so as to convince the reader of the superiority of the Latin belief over the Lutheran. After terminating this work, which could be done in some months, it was necessary to proceed to the revision of the Sclavonic Evangelist, the Psalms and the Prayers, as well as the Lives of the Saints, and to publish them, first excluding those paragraphs and parts not corresponding with the Roman Catholic religious books ; and (finally), to publish the Latin Catechism in Russian.

These projects and schemes for converting the Russians to Romanism only discover Possevin's great ignorance of the Russian people. His zeal was too enthusiastic, too ardent ; and his interviews with the Czar should have certainly given him a better idea of the firmness of the nation in its faith.

CHAPTER III.

RÔLE OF CATHOLICISM IN THE TROUBLES OF
RUSSIA AT THE BEGINNING OF THE SEVEN-
TEENTH CENTURY. — EMBASSY OF THE CZAR
ALEXIS TO ROME.

Differences between the Greek and Roman Churches.—
Project of a new mission of Possevin to Moscow.—Missions of
Camuley, 1594 and 1597.—Imminent danger of the Russian
Church at the commencement of the seventeenth century.—
Mission of Sapicha, 1601.—The false Demetrius embraces
Catholicism, but with little sincerity.—Discontent of the
Russians.—Project of the Polish Jesuits to introduce the
union by means of a second impostor.—Election of Vladislas
to the throne of Russia under the condition of the preservation .
of the Greek faith.—Design of Sigismond, King of Poland, to
do away with the throne of Russia and introduce Catholicism.
—Philip of Sweden proposed as a candidate for the throne
under condition that he embraced the Greek faith.—The
dislike of the Russians' to Romanism increased by political
events.—Testimony of Olearius.—The means of violently
introducing Romanism having been averted, the Polish
Clergy recommend Vladislas prudence and moderation,
1617.—Passage through Russia for Roman Catholics going to
the East.—Mission of Louis Hayes, 1627.—Mixed marriages.—
The erection of Catholic Churches forbidden.—Mission of
Major Ménésius to Rome, 1673.—Errors and exaggerations of
the Court of Rome as to the mission of Ménésius.

IN his interviews with Possevin, the Czar John
was on every point faithful to his time, and to the

interests of his Church ; but if in his short conversations he had found it impossible to expose all
his ideas in detail, he had at least expressed his
sentiments of the spirit and tendency of Romanism.
It may not here be superfluous to quote a document
of the sixteenth century, containing the abjuration
of a Catholic who entered the orthodox church, by
which one may judge the odour in which the
Russian Church held Latinism.   This document
exhibits the differences both exterior and interior
between the two creeds; for example, the Procession of the Holy Spirit from the Father and
from the Son, baptism by sprinkling, the azymes,
the manner of making the sign of the Cross, the
use of milk and eggs during fasts, the celebration
of service several times a day on the same altar,
the custom of being seated during divine service,
organs in the church, and the habit of shaving the
beard ; the marriage of two brothers with two
sisters, and the celibacy of the clergy, so particularly repugnant to the Russians as well as
their intervention in temporal affairs.   The
act of abjuration runs thus :—" I curse all Latin
bishops who go to war, who lead men into
battle, who kill others and are themselves killed;
who after having dipped their hands in the
blood of their fellow-man and co-religionist, cele-

brate the service of God upon the altar; who are
not content to be only humble priests." What is
to be chiefly remarked is, that in this century, as
in the preceding, less importance was attached to
the supremacy of the Pope than to the dogmas and
ceremonies, so different to those of the Oriental
Church. In the aforesaid abjuration, there is not
the least allusion to the political phase of the
question. The supremacy of the Pope was looked
upon in a purely political, not dogmatical light,
and was not even dismissed as irrelevant to the
subject. But John attached more importance to it
than the clergy, who were occupied in explanations
on the doctrines of their own faith. The above-
mentioned formula commenced with the following
words :—" I pass from the Roman Church into the
true Christian Orthodox Church, established by the
saints and confirmed by the Holy Fathers of the
Seven Œcumenical Councils. I enter this Church,
not from any necessity or misfortune, neither
through persecution nor fear on the one side, nor
from promises, riches, or temptations of any nature
whatever, on the other; but I enter it sincerely,
with all my heart and soul, for the love of Christ
only, desiring to participate in the living doctrine
of the true and pure faith." This formula is not
one of simple words only. The Russian clergy did

not attract converts to their creed by means of a propagand like that of the Roman priesthood; certainly they did not refuse those who came to them from conviction; but they busied themselves more in the care of their flocks, trying to preserve them intact from the errors of Apostacy.

Rome did not consider the embassy of Possevin as an entire failure, though it was really such. The relations which he had had with the authorities of the empire and with a part of the clergy, his researches in Russia, and his description of his journey, together with his experience acquired in Moscow, of the spirit and character of the people, induced her to avail herself once more of his ability and knowledge. After the death of John, Gregory XIII. resolved to send him again on a similar errand—the re-union of the two churches; and on this occasion, Possevin was not to forget to remind the Czar Theodore, that his father owed the peace concluded with Bathory, to Rome.* At the same time, to gain the Boyards to his cause, this Pope addressed to them a letter. But this mission was never carried out; and the letters which Possevin should have presented, were forwarded through Lithuania to Moscow by a Russian courier in 1585. Sixtus V., the successor of

* Historica Russiæ Monumenta, B. II., p. 8-10.

Gregory, conceived the same project of sending Possevin to Russia; and, in a letter to the Czar, mentions the affectionate terms in which, according to him, the Papacy stood in the estimation of his father and grandfather, adding, that John IV. had entire confidence in the late Pope, and never forgot the services of Possevin in the conclusion of the peace with Poland. This embassy, however, was not carried out.

The idea of expelling the Turks by means of an alliance of the Christian sovereigns of Europe, never abandoned Rome, but the execution of the project was, she considered, inseparable from the re-union of the Greek and Latin Churches. To attain this end, Camuley, Cardinal priest of Piro-lame, was, in 1594, despatched to Moscow. Clement VIII. relied on the success of this embassy, as Camuley knew the Russian language, and for several centuries before there had never been an envoy who spoke it.

In his instructions Camuley was to present an emerald cross and an agate chaplet in his own name to the Czar; on the cross there were Greek letters engraven, that it might be the more acceptable to the prince. Amongst other things the Pope desired him, that if he heard any allusion made to the titles and privileges which the

Muscovite Czars arrogated to themselves, or to their pretended descent, on the ground of a genealogy expressly composed for the purpose, from the Roman Emperors, he should explain that all titles and dignities were confirmed by the Pope, and quote the example of Poland, Bohemia, and other kingdoms both east and west, enlarging on the power and influence of the Holy See and of the security of those who depend on it. "Such discourses" said the Pope, "inspire respect for the Chief of the Church ; and one may demonstrate the difference between the Pope and the Patriarch of Constantinople, who depends on the will of the Turkish Sultan, the principal enemy of Christendom."

In the Russian archives one finds nothing relative to the arrival of Camuley in Moscow, or of his stay in that city; consequently nothing on the subject of any negotiations entered into by him; but his departure on the 25th April, 1595, is noted. His mission was unsuccessful; he did not even return to Rome to render an account of it, but despatched the letters of the Czar to the Holy Father by a courier, while he himself remained at Wilna to superintend the propagand against the Calvinists, or, as he himself expressed it, to confirm the Christian religion in the churches of Wilna.

On the translation of Bishop Prince Radzivill to the See of Cracow, the diocese of Wilna remained for ten years without an ecclesiastical head, and was administered by prelates who were several times changed during this period, amongst the number of whom was Alexander Camulet, who officiated there as legate from March, 1595, till May, 1597.

While at Wilna, Camuley was ordered to prepare himself for a second embassy to Moscow, where he arrived at the end of May, 1597. To flatter the Czar, he assured him that he had several times written to the Pope informing him of the omnipotence of the Sovereign of Russia, and that every one in Rome was astonished at his account of it; that he had requested the Pope, in any letters which he might write, to address the Czar by the titles which Pope Gregory the XIII. had refused. The Pope had consented to this, and now addressed him by the titles desired. He added, that if the Poles and the Lutherans had known it, they never would have permitted him a pass to Moscow; that the King of Poland and the Polish nobles had tried to prevent the Pope giving him his proper titles, but that he paid no attention to them, as they depended entirely on the will of the Holy Father, who conferred them on whom he liked. But these attentions and attempts ended in nothing. The second embassy of Camulet ended like the first, and had no result. Otherwise the Czar received it with politeness.

We have now arrived at an epoch, which was for Russia a day of trial and a season of proof. In the beginning of the seventeenth century, Rome came, sword in hand, into the heart of the empire, threatening to stifle religion and nationality. In this dreadful crisis, it was religion that saved the nation; it was the faith which preserved the national independence. The struggle was sharp and prolonged. On the one side, Sigismond, King of Poland, impelled by fanaticism, pursued a sanguinary proselytism; on the other, intestine dissensions diminished the national forces, and prevented the election of a sovereign to the throne who was freely elected by the people.

Sigismond, who was continually at war with Sweden, hoped to ally himself with Russia, and at the same time introduce the germs of Romanism in a peaceful manner amongst her population. In 1601, he sent Sapicha to Boris Gondonoff, to bring about a lasting peace between the two states. The conditions of this treaty stipulated that Poles residing in Rnssia, who had there acquired property, should have full permission to exercise their

religion, and to erect, if they wished, churches on
their own estates; that in Moscow and other
cities, churches, colleges, and schools, at the
expense of the government, should also be established; "as," said Sapicha's instructions, "they
are indispensable, as much for strangers as for the
service of the Czar, with regard to the envoys of
other governments and foreign merchants, of whom
there are many in the empire." But Sigismond
was deceived. Sapicha was informed that foreigners
were permitted the full enjoyment of their faith,
but that the building of Roman Catholic churches
in Russia would not be allowed.

Sigismond and Rome showed little tolerance at
a time when the interior disorders of the nation
offered an opportunity for attempting the rights of
the church. Under pretence of establishing public
order, they meddled in State affairs, and Sigismond,
the pupil of the Jesuits, uniting his efforts with
those of his masters at Rome, the wonder only is
that the Orthodox faith was not completely crushed.
Poland recognised the false Demetrius, on the
express condition that he should turn Roman
Catholic, and induce the Russians to follow his
example. This usurper, whose real name was
Otrepieff, purchased the assistance and recognition of Poland, by consenting to the wishes of

Sigismond, who was instigated by the Jesuits. These ambitious priests commenced the education and training of Otrepieff. . Gaspar Sawicky taught him Latin; and though he had embraced Romanism through the Franciscans and not through the Jesuits, these latter continually surrounded him, and it was only through them that Sigismond was influenced to support the impostor.

It is not difficult, in tracing the ulterior career of this man, to discover indubitable proofs that he only apostatised from the faith of his fathers through self interest, and that conviction had nothing to do with it. Indeed he was little prepared to enter a Church altogether new to him. He knew a little Latin, as indispensable to the comprehension of the Roman rites; but when by the help of Poland he ascended the throne of Russia, he signed in a feeble and badly-formed hand, "Inperator." We do not find in any of the official reports of foreigners then in the country that after his ascension to the throne he conformed to the Catholic rites; but he had, it is true, two Jesuits with him, Nicolas Czernicky and Andrew Lawicky,* employing them, however, more as diplomats than for Proselytism. At the close of the year 1605, he

* Grevenbruck, p. 14.

94 ROMANISM IN RUSSIA.

despatched Lawicky to Rome to concert measures against the Turks. Rome herself believed so little in the sincerity of his conversion, that she missed no opportunities of confirming and influencing him in his new faith, the Pope himself exhorting him to firmness. Rangoni, Bishop of Regio and Macciwosky, urged him at the same time to convert the Russian people, and solely for this purpose Count Alexander Rangoni, the nephew of the Nuncio at Cracow, was sent to Moscow. " If," wrote Pope Paul V. to Cardinal Macciwosky, " Demetrius only remains faithful to the Catholic religion, we may hope in time to draw the Russians within the pale of the Church, for these people, as we know, are very obedient to their sovereigns." " One can do with the Russians what one likes," said the same Pope to Demetrius, " therefore command them, and they will obey." His marriage with Mary Miniszec, the daughter of the Palatine of Sendomar, was the corner-stone of the structure on which Rome depended for the overthrow of Orthodoxy, the Pope exhorting Demetrius to support his spouse in the doctrines of Romanism, relying on Mary to influence him to act with firmness and prudence. " The Palatine of Sendomar," wrote Cardinal Borghese to Rangoni, " will direct this business."

But if we impartially examine the political acts of Demetrius, we shall find, as far as circumstances permitted, he declined the dishonourable rôle allotted to him. Placed as he was in complete dependence on the Court of Rome and on Poland, it is astonishing that he did not commit any direct attentât on the Russian faith, nor did he commence to meddle with the doctrines of the Russian Church as they hoped. Even in his frequent relations with Rome, he constantly evaded mentioning religion or alluding to the re-union of the two Churches. At the time of his departure for Russia several Catholic priests accompanied him, but only a limited number, strictly sufficient to serve the spiritual requirements of his wife, his father-in-law, and the Polish soldiery. Demetrius never seconded the Propagand; and although the Jesuits at Moscow intended to establish a Roman College secretly, in conjunction with the arrival of Latin priests intended to be brought from Rome, they nevertheless adjourned their project and contented themselves with access to the Czar, which was otherwise extremely difficult.

A Catholic chapel was built for Mary's use, but on the pressing entreaties of Demetrius, and notwithstanding the formal refusal of the Pope, this Princess was crowned and married according to the rites of the Eastern Church—she received the sacrament from the Patriarch, prayed in the churches, and fasted, not on Saturdays but on Tuesdays like the Greeks, so that it may reasonably be supposed that had Demetrius continued on the throne the Court of Rome might have found her hopes as vain as past centuries of useless efforts had been.

In seconding, though in a dubious and undecided manner, the views of Rome, Demetrius drew upon himself the indignation of the Russians attached to their faith; and what further added to the public dissatisfaction was, that having been accustomed to the relaxed manners of the Poles, he, unlike those Czars who followed the prescriptions of the Church, did not observe the fasts, and sometimes even on fête days neglected to go to Mass. Not that he had any penchant for Latinism, but because of the boundless carelessness and presumption of his character. He ate veal, at that time contrary to custom. But what more than all else exasperated the people, was the way in which the Poles mocked at everything considered as sacred, bringing their dogs into the churches. Moscow,—supposing that the new sovereign intended to extirpate oxthodoxy—the more so as a suspicious correspondence with Rome was discovered, in which Demetrius engaged to erect Latin churches in the capital, conformable to an oath taken before his accession,—rose in arms, and the excitement became greater when the Patriarch Job, who had been deposed by the impostor, praying before the image of the Virgin, cried:—"The Christian Church, which was unshaken, is invaded by heresy; and we sinners implore thee, oh Holy Virgin, to let thy Son Christ confirm and render it immoveable." He then, says the chronicle, wept bitterly for hours. The inhabitants of Moscow, seeing the anger of God following them, concerted measures for dethroning the impostor and thereby saving the faith, broke out into tumult, the Poles were massacred and Demetrius was killed. Intentionally the excited crowd did not murder the Catholic priests, but if some of them fell it was owing to their being mistaken for Poles.

A second impostor, commonly styled the Brigand Touchkin, was also supported by Polish influence, and was regarded by the Jesuits as a likely and flexible instrument of the Propagand. They formed a plot as to the introduction of the "Union," which then began to be propagated in Lithuania, into Russia. The plan conceived was that the union should be kept from the

Czar himself, whose popularity might suffer, but be extended to the different personages in his suite, the guards and courtiers being selected from amongst Catholics, so that ultimately he might find himself surrounded by only the partisans of this doctrine. The different administrative employments and offices should be conferred only on those favourably disposed to the change. Discussions with the Russians should be conducted with the greatest prudence, and on these occasions hints should be thrown out of the necessity for seminaries, colleges, and the establishment of a Roman Catholic church in the capital. The clergy might be attracted by the promise of temporal advantages, at the same time their management of the property of the church was deprecated; but all this should be conducted in such a manner that the result should be the introduction of the "Union," arising from the very requirements of the people and the priesthood together. The Czar himself should be isolated from these intrigues, and his suite should only contain a certain number of Latin ecclesiastics, Russians predominating. Secrecy was specially énjoined as to all correspondence with Rome; and the better to facilitate the re-union of the churches, two or three priests of the united Greek faith should be placed near the Czarine, the same Mary Minisiec, daughter of the Palatine of Sendomar, who, speaking the language of the country, could converse with the Russians. All elements hostile to Rome should be dispersed, consequently the expulsion of the Lutherans should be effected, as well as the Greek Monks who came from Constantinople, and even the capital might be transferred to a city nearer the Polish frontier, so that the religious as well as the political centre of the empire might be attainable at an easy distance from the seat of the Propagand, and in which it would be more convenient to establish a Jesuitical college—in one word, the "Union" was to be planted in Russia by the same means so successfully used in Lithuania. As to the youth of the country, especially the noblesse, they were to be sent for education to Wilna, or, what was still more preferable, to Rome itself, or to other Italian cities where there were neither Colonists nor Lutherans.

This vast scheme of operations turned out however a dead letter, as the brigand Touchkin never reigned in Moscow, and this extensive, extended, and plausible programme was never put in execution.

The situation of Russia was at this time deplorable. On the one hand, Touchkin with the Poles

and the Cossacks, on the other the Polish army,
under the command of Zolkiewsky, surrounded
Moscow, while Sigismond besieged Smolensk. All
the country was agitated. Basil Ivanovitcsh
Shousky, the elected Czar did not fulfil public
expectation, and in this extremity it was considered
expedient to invite Vladislas, the son of Sigismond,
to the throne, so as to ward off the continuation of
the war, and obtain peace with Poland. The
Boyards of Touchkin, that is to say, the party
who followed the late impostor, Dimitry, were
the first to broach this subject, and sent
an ambassade to Smolensk for this purpose.
The principal and prime mover in this embassy
was Sultykoff. In the negotiations which followed,
the Russian envoys thought not of demanding
political rights or the confirmation of the privileges
of the noblesse, but rather that the new sovereign
Vladislas should preserve intact the national
church, and he himself enter within its pale. The
preservation and augmentation of churches of the
Russian faith, and of convents for the ecclesiastics
of the Greek rite were demanded; and it is recorded
that when Sultykoff supplicated the preservation of
the national church, he wept. But these conditions were such that the Jesuit King could
hardly consent to ; he could not however refuse the

propositions, as a categorical refusal would interrupt the negotiations. He therefore preserved silence on some points ; some he eluded altogether ; and for the remainder he gave only vague promises, never intended to be fulfilled. By this treaty, concluded Feburary 4th, 1610, Sigismond was obliged to maintain the Russian Church in the empire, not to tolerate Romanism, and to respect the Russian clergy. There is nothing said of the obligation of Vladislas to enter the Greek Church, but it was arranged that his consecration by the Patriarch was to be postponed until the pacification of the country. Sigismond added as a condition that a Roman Catholic chapel should be built at Moscow for the Poles who should accompany his son.

This treaty, as concluded only with some of the Boyards belonging to the impostor, was of no importance. But the idea of the election of Vladislas to the throne had become pretty general in Moscow and among the noblesse. Jolkiewsky in the capital gained over the greatest number of adherents to this plan, every one of whom imposed it as the first and chief condition that the Prince should enter the Russian Church. Shousky having been deposed, official negotiations were opened up between the leaders on both sides with regard to the candidature of the young prince.

Knowing the fanaticism of Sigismond, Jolkiewsky entered into no engagements relating to religion. "Faith," said he, "is the gift of God; it is impossible to dispose of the conscience of any one." A decision was, however, as necessary for the Poles as for the Russians, as the Polish troops receiving no pay refused to serve any longer, and announced their intention of returning home. Jolkiewsky, without waiting the determination of Sigismond, concluded the treaty concerning the election of Vladislas, stipulating that the Greek religion should be preserved intact, that the Russians should not be subjected to proselytism on the part of the Latin clergy, that Romanism should not be tolerated, and that no other churches than those of the national creed should be built. This last clause would paralyse the intention of Sigismond to erect a Roman Catholic chapel in Moscow. The treaty was signed August 17th, 1610.

Whosoever knows the ancient history of Russia and the characteristics of the Russian people, cannot but be astonished to find a stranger called to the throne without a positive and guaranteed undertaking that he should embrace the Greek faith, a sovereign of any other creed being impossible. But on consideration we are persuaded that, if the adoption of the Orthodox faith was not stipulated for in documentary guarantee, and as an article in the treaty, an assurance had been given and received that he should conform to the wishes of his new subjects. In point of fact this Prince was only fifteen years old, and the violent fanaticism of his father had scarcely had time to influence his mind. Arriving in Moscow while still a mere youth, and surrounded by but few Poles, as expressly decided on in the treaty, he would naturally receive new impressions and imperceptibly imbibe an attachment to the established religion, a sympathy which at that period was the prevailing characteristic of Russian society. It might justly be supposed that far from the companionship of his father, and removed from the influence of the Jesuits, he would ultimately enter the pale of the Greek Church. Such were no doubt the hopes which induced the people to consent to the election of a foreign prince to the throne of their empire. Jolkiewsky himself did not fail to impress upon every one that the prince was young and consequently impressionable, that it would be easy to influence him by new objects, and that he could embrace the Orthodox faith when he should be at

home in Moscow. Thus the conversion of
Vladislas, expected and hoped for on account of
his youth, was the basis of his election to the
throne of Russia.

On the other hand, the conversion of Russia to
Romanism was the one fixed idea of Sigismond,
who, on account of the tender years of his son,
determined that he himself should resolve a question so intimately connected with Poland. A
numerous embassy, with Philaret Romanoff at the
head, met him at Smolensk, to receive the ratifica-
tion of the treaty concluded with Jolkiewsky; but
properly and sincerely speaking, its aim was to
understand the king's views with respect to the
conversion of Vladislas. The instructions given
these envoys desire them to discuss "la grande
affaire." They were provided with answers to
every imaginable objection Sigismond might make,
and were especially to endeavour to obtain the
sanction of his father that before the boy's arrival,
he should profess the Greek faith at Smolensk, in
presence of the Metropolitan Philaret, and of Serge,
Archbishop of Briansk and Smolensk. Without
conforming to this measure, they were desired to
say it would be impossible that the clergy and the
Patriarch could go to meet him, as it was customary for them to do when a new Czar came to the

throne. If Sigismond objected that Vladislas belonged to the Roman faith, but would maintain the Greek Church in Russia, they should reply that since Russia had become Christian, more than six centuries ago, there had not been a single sovereign on the throne professing another creed, and that to tolerate any such thing would only excite disturbances. If Sigismond were to say, That as Vladislas had already been baptized then how could he be baptized a second time, no Christian being christened twice? they should answer, That true baptism is only practical according to the rites of the Greek Church, and that absolutely a Russian Czar must belong to the Orthodox religion, just as in Poland a sovereign of any other than the Established confession is never elected; and they should remind him that when he was himself elected, he had embraced Romanism. Should they not succeed in persuading the King that Vladislas should enter the Greek Church at Smolensk, then any other city might be named instead, provided he embraced the faith before entering Moscow. But should the King insist that the ceremony take place only in the capital, they were to procure a written promise to this effect, in the form of a letter to the Patriarch and the Boyards of the country. No doubt seems to

have remained in the minds of the Russians that
the young Prince, once removed from the influence
of his father's fanaticism and the Jesuits, would of
himself enter the Orthodox church. An injunction
not to discuss religious matters with the Roman
priests closed the instructions to these delegates,
and they were personally requested to beg the
Polish lords not to dissuade the prince from
entering the Russian Church. Another important stipulation in the arrangements with
the King of Poland was, that as on attaining
his majority Vladislas should marry, he should
take a Russian wife, otherwise the people would
be alarmed about their religion, as in the time of
Mary Miniszec. If Sigismond showed dissatisfaction on this head, it might be modified into a
condition that when of age he could not contract
any alliance without consulting the Patriarch and
the country, which in effect amounted to the same
thing.

The confirmation of a very important law was
required also, viz., that as the Orthodox church
never permitted any one, under pain of death, to
change his religion, this regulation should be
strictly carried out, together with the confiscation
of the estates of the offender by the State. This
clause, if confirmed by Sigismond, would effectually

disable the Propagand, and on this point the envoys were commanded to insist.

Moreover, once on the throne of Moscow, the sovereign of Russia should have no communication with the Pope, nor under any circumstances receive his benediction. If it were urged that in past times there had been communication and correspondence with Rome on the part of the Czars, the answer was that political and not religious negotiations had been conducted between the two courts, and that Vladislas might have similar communications, but strictly limited to political affairs, touching neither the Russian faith nor permitting the Propagand to take root in his empire. A particular stress was laid on the fact that Roman Catholic Churches were interdicted in Moscow.

Besides these diplomatic steps, the Patriarch Hermogene wrote a private letter to Sigismond relative to the baptism, which he earnestly requested, of Vladislas. "Give us your son," he said, "whom the Almighty loves and has elected Czar, that he may enter the Greek Church, a church which the Prophets and the Holy Fathers have foretold should remain for ever, and which shines, until the present, like the sun."

With the exception of the marriage of his son, and his change of faith, Sigismond pretended to

consent in general terms to the proposals of the
deputies; but to prolong the affair, he evasively
replied that the treaty before him must be laid
before the Diet to be confirmed. During this time
he continued to besiege Smolensk. The King did
not desire the voluntary union of Poland and
Russia; he intended, by means of the sceptre of
his son, to conquer Russia, and oblige her to
submit to his power; but the Polish Jesuits comprehended perfectly at this time that Romanism
would never willingly be accepted by the people,
and that it was not Russia which should become
Catholic, but that Vladislas should become Greek.
But the subjugation of Russia to the power of
Sigismond might permit the introduction by violence
of Romanism into the country, as had already been
effected in Lithuania, which sufficiently explains
why, though his son was elected sovereign of the
Empire, he continued the siege of Smolensk.

Some of the envoys of this embassy, siding with
the Pole, did not exact Vladislas' change of religion,
though consenting to his election, but Philaret
insisted, saying, " If he consents to accept our
faith, he shall be our King."

Notwithstanding the warning of Hermogene, the
apostle of the orthodox faith, as he is styled in the
annals of the period, some Boyards consented to

the conditions of the King of Poland, and expressed their readiness to do so in a letter to him. This step excited the anger of Hermogene, who cried in the midst of the people :—" I cannot support the Latin Chaunt, and I see in it the profanation of the faith, and the desolation of the Church." He released the people from allegiance to Vladislas, and by his influence roused Russia. The Poles were compelled to fly, and the country escaped the fate of her subjugated co-religionist Lithuania. Thus in preserving and defending the faith against armed Romanism, Russia was saved. Phileret and Hermogene were the victims of this deliverance. Hermogene was dethroned by the Polish party, confined, and soon after strangled in the Convent of Fezondoff, and Phileret was for nine years detained a prisoner in Poland.*

At this time the Swedes were under the walls of Tikvin. The Princes Pojarsky and Minin at Moscow, concerted measures with the Novgorodians to elect the brother of Gustavus Adolphus † to the throne; but not suffering, say the annals, the least infringement of the holy orthodox faith, decided that his election should depend on his acceptation of the doctrines of the ortho-

---

* Annales of Nikon, B. 8. p. 141-161.
† Born at Reval, 1601, died 1622,

dox Greek faith. This project, as well as the
previous election of Vladislas, prove that it was
not impossible at that period for the Russian
people to accept a foreign prince, but that the
least attempt on the national faith was enough to
raise the population into a desperate and bloody
struggle with an enemy already in possession of
the capital.

Historical events like these illustrate sufficiently
the opinion of the Russians as to the Roman
Church. Its rites shocked and disgusted the
whole community. They were so entirely different
to the rites of the Russians that comparison only
strengthened the aversion both to ceremonials and
dogmas. As the clergy became more educated,
greater importance was attached to the dogmatical
differences, which were the substantial impediments
to a re-union of the churches of the West and
East. Moreover, the spirit of the Latin clergy,
who invariably meddled in temporal affairs, was
found to be incompatible with Russian ideas as
to the peculiar duties of the priesthood. The
perseveringly-carried-out efforts of Rome to persuade as to the indispensable necessity of the
union of the churches, had totally different consequences to those anticipated; her exertions only
stimulated the obstinacy of the people. In short

the religious persecutions by Sigismond which roused all Russia for the defence of the faith, and the terrible souvenirs of this bloody struggle rendered Catholicism not only impossible but odious throughout the land. Olearius, who thirty years afterwards visited our country, says that the Russians willingly permitted people of all nations and religions to reside amongst them, Lutherans, Reformers, Turks, Tartars, Persians, and Armenians, but that they would not suffer either Jews or Papists, whose very name displeased them.

This firmness of the Russians in their faith, forced the Poles to abandon all hopes of converting them, but the Polish clergy did not quite resign all hopes of ultimate success. After the death of his father, Vladislas undertook an expedition into the empire with the intention of carrying out the designs in which his father had been frustrated; and Gemoitsky, Archbishop of Gniezno, pronounced this speech before him at Warsaw:—"God honours those who try to spread the Catholic faith, who respect the priesthood, who serve the Church and gratefully accept her councils. The Almighty, through your royal highness, permits the light of His truth to penetrate the darkness of the road which leads to truth and peace; but in this

important affair to which your attentions are
directed, it is necessary to pursue it with
moderation, as the people are unenlightened and
must not be constrained by violence, but attracted,
little by little, by the pious example set by yourself,
and the priests who shall accompany you." But
Vladislas had not the fanaticism of his father;
besides, circumstances had changed; and the
Polish Propaganda, impotent against the national
faith at an epoch when Russia was in deep distress,
became impossible with the restoration of public
order, and a regular government established under
the Czars Alexis and Michael. By the year
1612, these attempts to introduce Romanism into
Russia through the assistance of Poland, entirely
ceased.

Some European Catholic sovereigns tried to
obtain from the government permission for Roman
priests to reside in the country, and to erect
churches; but their solicitations failed. In 1627,
Louis XIII. despatched Louis de Hayes to the
Czar Michael Feodorovilsh to negotiate a treaty
between Russia and France, and demanded the
establishment of a Catholic chapel in Moscow for
French subjects. A refusal was given; and later,
in a treaty concluded with the help of Olearius for
commercial purposes, it was stipulated that no

passage through Russia should be available to people of the Latin creed; but these restrictive measures were afterwards abrogated, as travellers were freely permitted the route to Persia and India without any inquiry as to religion. In 1674, the Dominicans Azarius and Antoine passed through Moscow, en route to the East, and brought with them letters from the Pope, from the Emperor of Germany, and other sovereigns to the Schah of Persia, to induce him to declare war against the Turks. The same year the Spaniard, Pierre Cuberius, and an Italian named Cavagniole, arrived in the capital, also on their way to Persia and India as missionaries, and requested the assistance of the Czar. In 1677, a route through Smolensk, Moscow, and Astracan was accorded to the envoy of Clement X., who had been to negotiate an alliance with Persia against the Ottomans, and who received, according to the etiquette of the period, a free pass, with guides and other necessaries.

In speaking of the aversion of the Russians to Romanism, Olearius says that though they never forced people to embrace their faith, they did not permit mixed marriages, but exacted that the two spouses should profess the Greek faith.*

---

* Les voyages du Sieur Olearius.

At the close of the seventeenth century, Roman Catholics residing in Russia, were not allowed to erect churches. Rome then comprehended that her efforts were ineffectual; and when, on some occasions, the ambassadors of foreign monarchs spoke in favour of the erection of one or more, for the convenience of the residents, they were answered very curtly, that at Rome there did not exist, until to-day, a single Russian Church.

Since the time of the false Demetrius, with one exception, there had not been any transaction with Rome, and this was a political, not a religious one. The constantly encroaching power of the Turks, and the invasion of Poland by them in 1672, the taking of Kameniez Podolsk, and the danger which menaced that part of Little Russia which had been annexed, induced the Czar Alexis to succour Poland. He not only sent troops to the Crimea to produce a diversion there, but even intended to rouse all Europe against them, and wrote to the different sovereigns, inviting them to join the alliance. Matweeff, the Minister of Foreign Affairs, informed the Czar that, conformably to his desire, he had prepared the letters to the Courts of Spain, France, England, Denmark, and Sweden, and requested to be informed if he should also address one to the Pope. " Since the time of the false Demetrius," said he, "we have had no relations with Rome, and if now a letter be despatched to the Pope, it will flatter him into an alliance to help Poland, in which he would be seconded by the other European sovereigns, who carefully obey him." The Czar therefore agreed to it, and Paul Menesius was the person deputed to convey it to the Eternal City. But this plan failed. Europe occupied with internal convulsions, had neither time nor inclination to league against Turkey, and the only two powers who consented to the scheme were the Elector of Brandenburg and the King of Sweden. In his letter to the Pope, the Czar only styled him "Preceptor of the Roman Church," and desired his envoy to salute him at the audience with a simple bow only; that if told to kiss his foot, he should not do so, but merely kiss his hand; that if the Pope did not rise in pronouncing the name of the Czar at the audience, he might say "that the German Emperor, from a sentiment of love and respect for the sovereign of Russia, rises and uncovers when he inquires about his health." Should the Pope desire one of his chamberlains to take the letter and present it to him, the envoy should refuse, and insist on presenting it with his own hands, "that the honour of their sovereign should be cared for."

I 2

During the journey to Rome Paul Menesius, Major of Infantry, who was the special ambassador on this occasion, was greatly perplexed as to how he should escape kissing the Pope's foot, if required to do so, and as he knew was the custom even among sovereigns who visited the Holy See. He communicated his uneasiness to Matweeff, who told him that Catholic monarchs kissed the Pope's foot, as they belonged to the same Church, but as for themselves they were strictly forbidden in their instructions to dó any such thing. Menesius arrived in Rome the 8th of August, 1673, and was received by Count Lesley, a Jesuit deputed to attend him. Lodgings were prepared for him at Montecavalo, not far from the palace. Before official reception, Cardinal Alfieri, the nephew of Clement X., whose influence over the Pope was unlimited, had long conferences with Menesius on the subject of the reception. He said that the Pope would not himself either receive from or give the letters for the Czar to Menesius, and that he would not rise on speaking of him, exacting at the same time that the ambassador should kiss the Pope's foot. "If," said he, "the Emperor of Germany or any other sovereign came to Rome, he would not be received unless he conformed to this custom." "I am expressly forbidden to do so," replied Menesius, "as my sovereign does not profess the Catholic faith. Before the separation of the two Churches, the Greeks did not kiss the Pope's foot ; and, moreover, if it be exacted from me, I must be permitted to quit Rome immediately." Valuing an alliance with the Russian Prince, and seeing the obstinacy of the ambassador, the point was waived, but Menesius was advised to kiss at least the cassock, which he refused to do. He was received in solemn and official audience on the 18th August, when the master of the ceremonies endeavoured by force to make him kneel, as likewise the secretary, but they both refused, and did not even once conform to this custom, excusing themselves, that, being the representatives of the Czar and the bearers of his letter, they could not possibly do. The Grand Chamberlain would have jerked the head of the latter, and called the attention of Alfieri to it ; but the Cardinal forbade violence, and the secretary only made a bow to the Pope. The epistle of the Pope in reply to the letter of the Czar, commenced thus :—" To our well-beloved son, the illustrious Alexis Michaelowitsch, Grand Duke of Russia." This title was considered as incomplete, and the Russians refused to receive it. A council of Cardinals was therefore convoked, and despatches were sent off and received from different

Courts. The upshot of all was that the Pope had
a confidential interview with Menesius, from which
nothing resulted, and on the 20th September the
ambassador left Rome without a letter, Cardinal
Alfieri informing him that the answer to the
Czar would be forwarded by an envoy extraordinary.

It is a remarkable fact that Menesius was himself a Roman Catholic, and a very fervent one. In
his will he charged General Patrick Gordon, a
disciple and friend of the Jesuits, to bring up his
son in the Catholic faith. If during his embassy
he obstinately refused to follow the ceremonial
customary at the Court of Rome, it was because he
perfectly comprehended his position as the representative of the Czar, the envoy of the Majesty of
Russia, and that not in his own quality of Catholic
must he uphold the dignity he represented.

Rome was offended at the title given by the
Czar, "Maestro della chiesa Romano," to the
Pope, complaining that it was unsuitable to
the dignity of the inheritor of the Prince of the
Apostles, and the Father of the Faithful. But she
would not lose the present opportunity of renewing
relations with the Russian empire. After the
departure of Menesius, the savants of Rome discussed, by order of the Pope, whether they should

give the sovereign of Russia the title of Czar, and this discussion produced several treatises. A decision was at length arrived at that the letters should be addressed to Alexis Michaelowitsch, Czar or King, as the Emperor of Germany and the King of Poland employed this style. This title employed by the Pope signified that he elevated him to the dignity royal. Much importance was erroneously attached to these learned dissertations. In the Eternal City this mission to the Holy Father was received and looked upon as a very uncommon event, as well as a very important one. "Until now," it was argued, " embassies from Russia were only replies to initiatives taken by Rome ; this time it is the powerful Czar himself, who, under very different circumstances to those of John IV., who required the Pope's assistance, sent a plenipotentiary to His Holiness." The conclusion come to was that some secret aim,—some underhand intention,—lay beneath an act of diplomatic courtesy. They believed that the Czar desired to introduce Roman-ism into his dominions ; and to profit by it a mission without any regard to expense should be sent to obtain at once, while the charm was working, certain privileges and concessions which had for so many centuries been sighed for in vain :

a church in Moscow,—Roman Catholic priests in
that city,—the organisation of the most pompous
ceremonies,—the establishment in short of all the
paraphernalia of Popery,—these ought to be obtained through, as they considered, the penchant of
the prince for Western manners and customs, and
his intention to spread civilisation, in conjunction
with a taste for the Greek and Latin languages,
throughout the land.   To flatter his taste for
educated men, several savants should be attached
to the church at Moscow; and these priests could
ultimately become the preceptors of the people, in
producing insidiously and gradually the union of
the two Churches.   Thus Rome schemed, under
pretence of education and civilisation, to arrive at
results both vast and difficult, results which accomplished, point by point, would bring about the
re-union of the Eastern and Western Churches, and
crown her long-continued and persevering efforts
by the conversion of a great empire to the doctrines.
of her Church.   But when and where have not the
Jesuits similarly schemed and dreamed and worked?
The keystone of this chimerical illusion was the
confirmation of vain titles by him who claimed the
right to confer them on temporal sovereigns as the
representative of S. Peter, a right founded not on
Scriptural authority, but based on and proceeding

from the pride of an arrogant power. But the Court of Rome, more prudent than some of her zealous advisers, paid little attention to these treatises, and sent no embassy to Russia. Experience had already sufficiently demonstrated, how unpractical, uncertain, and futile all her efforts had been !

CHAPTER IV.

ROMANISM IN RUSSIA FROM THE REIGN OF THE CZARS PETER AND JOHN UNTIL THE ANNEXATION OF THE WESTERN PROVINCES.

Entry of strangers of the Roman Catholic faith into the service of Russia.—Successive arrival of the Jesuits at Moscow in the suite of the Ministry of the Roman Emperor, 1684-7.— Purchase of a house for the Jesuits at Moscow, 1685.—Jesuitical Propaganda at Moscow.—Expulsion of the Jesuits from Moscow, 1688.—Protection of the Jesuits by Prince Basil Galitzen.—Passage from the Testament of the Patriarch Joachim, concerning the Latin Propaganda, 1690. — Steps taken by the Jesuits for their recall to Russia.—Intervention of Curzius, the envoy of the Roman Emperor, in favour of the Order, 1691.—General Patrick Gordon represents the Catholics in Russia at this epoch.—The Government refuse the Catholics permission to build a church at Moscow.—Notwithstanding this the Catholics build one at Moscow.—The Missionaries penetrate to Moscow.—The Jesuits re-introduced into the Empire.—Second expulsion of the Order from Russia, 1719.—Religious liberty under the reign of Peter the Great.— Mixed marriages.—The Capucins called to Russia, 1720.— Struggle between the Capucins and the Franciscans.—These Orders replaced by the Dominicans, 1724.—Relations with the Holy See.—Journey of Sebastian Knabe, Archbishop of Naxivane, 1684.—Girowsky, Minister of the Roman Emperor, continues the negotiation entered into by the Archbishop.— Dulois and Curzius defeated in the same negotiation, 1685.— Project of an ambassade to Rome, 1697.—Journey of Field

Marshal Shérématief to Rome, 1698.—Mission of Prince
Kourakin to Rome, 1707.—At the time of the Czar Peter the
Great at Paris, the Nuncio Bentivoglio tries to dispose him
towards Romanism, 1717.—Rome endeavours to procure a
Concordat with Russia, 1721.—Proposition of the Sorbonne to
re-unite the Churches of the East and of the West, 1717.—
Response of the Russian Bishops to this proposition, 1718.—
The Emperor Peter has little sympathy for Catholicism.—
Catholicism under the successors of Peter the Great.—Latin
Propaganda at Astracan among the Armenians.—Dissensions
between the clergy and the parishioners of the Church at
Petersburg.—Regulations of the Empress Catherine II. for
this Church, 1769.—The regulations of 1769 extended to the
Catholic Churches of the Colonies of Saratoff and the South
of Russia.—The number of Catholics very limited in the
Empire until the annexation of the Western Provinces.

THE intimate relations of Russia with Western
Europe, and the many strangers who had accepted
an invitation to enter the service of the Czar,
entirely changed the state of the Catholic Church
in the country. Nevertheless the number of
foreigners in comparison to the population, were so
limited, that the celebration of their church ceremonials and services, though enough for their
requirements, could scarcely argue the success for
the Propaganda. Formerly, as we know, the
Lutherans and other colonists enjoyed entire liberty
of conscience ; they had churches at Moscow, but
they did not proselytise. The Roman clergy, on
the contrary, tried not only to procure for their
co-religionists liberty of worship, but their ultimate

aim was the conversion of the whole country, and those foreigners belonging to their church residing in Russia, were the auxiliaries by whom they hoped to carry out their intentions.

In 1684, several disguised Jesuits came to Russia, in the suite of Girowsky, Ambassador of the German Emperor, and the couriers selected for the Russian service at Vienna were almost always nominated from this Order. Baron Keller, the Dutch Minister at Moscow, thus describes one of these messengers :—

" The courier of His Imperial Majesty, whom I mentioned in my letter of the 9th June, brings only complimentary letters on the occasion of the marriage of the eldest Czar. The courier is a Jesuit named Vota. He is dressed with as much elegance as if he were the first courier of Europe, and bears the title of Imperial Secretary. They say he is by birth a Frenchman."

At the time of his departure from Moscow, Girowsky left his confessor Schmidt behind him, to celebrate religious rites for the Catholic officers in the service of the government. In 1685, Albert Dubois and Curzius, courier of the Emperor of Germany, arrived in Moscow, and in 1687, Tichawsky followed them, furnished with letters of recommendation by his own government, so that very

soon there was a Jesuit colony established in the
capital. The Roman Propaganda, which formerly
arrived under Polish protection, now visited Russia,
through the patronage of the Emperor of Germany,
and it was at the expense of this sovereign, and
through the mediation of Curzius, that a house
was bought for the Jesuits, but was registered
only in the name of an Italian, of the name
of Guasconi. This man was a lay Jesuit, who,
under the guise of a merchant, was nothing
less than an agent of the Order. Without loss of
time they commenced to work by founding a school
for Russian children. They distributed Roman
Catholic books translated into the vernacular
tongue, together with images to second their views.
They interfered in temporal affairs, and acted as
the agents of other powers without even taking
the trouble to dissimulate their intentions. In
their absolute ignorance of the spirit of Russia
they comprehended not the attachment of the
people to their faith, and considered it an easy
work to introduce Romanism into Russia. One of
their designs was to occupy the Patriarchal chair.*
Their seductions and hypocrisy would hardly

---

* Extract of a letter from the Jesuit Jaconovitsch, to the
post-master Sangala, complaining that Moscow would not have
him for Patriarch.—See *Archives*.

however attract many adepts, as their actions were so extremely antagonistic to their words, and their lives gave the lie to their sermons.

In 1688, the Czars John and Peter, in accordance with the custom of their ancestors, made a pilgrimage to the Troitza Convent. The Patriarch Joachim, displeased already at the Rascolnik schism, seeing the new danger which threatened, told the princes that formerly the Jesuits were not permitted to establish themselves in Russia, and that there was a great difference between the Eastern and the Roman churches. "Rome has apostatised and separated from the apostolic faith, and since Jesuitism has taken root in Moscow, many of the true believers have been seduced." He therefore demanded their expulsion, particularly as no diplomatic difficulty could intervene. The Jesuits had domiciled themselves in Moscow of their own accord, notwithstanding that the government had at different periods refused, though they were backed by the powerful influence of the Emperor of Germany, to permit them to do so, except in one or two instances, where policy, demanding an alliance with a foreign power, had tolerated their presence for a limited time. As political circumstances had changed, he demanded and urged their expulsion, which was determined on. Care was taken to dismiss them graciously, and to furnish them with horses and provisions as far as the frontier of Lithuania, and the Court of Vienna was carefully informed that such provision was made for them on account of the Emperor's interest in the Order. They quitted the capital regretfully, sorry tô leave the work just commenced, undone, and before starting left no stone unturned to put off the misfortune. They asked to be allowed to remain long enough to sell the house they had bought, which stood in the German quarter. The delay of a few days was given, but they requested to remain till they could communicate with Vienna, and receive an answer; hoping, without doubt, to profit by the intercession of the Emperor on their behalf. But they were informed that this was useless, and that the Czars would themselves inform the Court of Vienna after their departure. This new check did not discourage them. They addressed themselves to Dovenant, the Polish ambassador, who not daring to interfere in their favour officially, the ukase for their expulsion being already published, endeavoured to arrange the affair through another channel. Oukrainzow, afterwards so celebrated under Peter the Great, was at that time Secretary of Foreign Affairs, and to him Dovenant turned for assistance, desiring that the Jesuits might be permitted to remain a little longer in the capitals, but Oukrainzow not only categorically refused, but expressed his astonishment that such a request should be made in favour of individuals not Poles, but in reality German subjects. They were therefore obliged to leave Russia.* The following year a Jesuit named Terpilowsky attemped to introduce himself into Moscow, but being discovered was expelled.†

For this unexpected blow, which upset all their schemes, the Order cared comparatively little, as they were protected by Prince Basil Galitzen the favourite of the Czarina Sophie. The German Emperor, knowing that the Catholics in Russia owed the Prince many obligations for liberties granted during the residence of the Jesuits in Moscow, thanked him, and the Order glorified his name, as they said, through all Europe. But this time the Patriarch was more powerful than the Prince. In his will, made in 1690, Joachim besought the Czar not to tolerate the Latin Propaganda, and not to allow the holy images of the Russian Church to be painted after the model of the Italian; to forbid the erection of Catholic

---

* " Recueil des lois."
† Posselt's " Day-book of General Patrick Gordon."

churches; and concluded by observing that in no other part of Europe were there Russian churches.

Nevertheless, the Jesuits did not lose all hope, as the intervention of the Court of Vienna, and those strangers serving in the army of the Czar, was their anchor for the future. Only one little cloud in the horizon disquieted them—that priests of another Order should be sent for; and they concerted measures against such a contingency, begging the Polish Minister to say that the Catholic community of Moscow did not desire priests of any other Order; and they requested General Patrick Gordon, who at that time represented the most influential part of the Catholic society in the capital, to state that they did not demand any from the government. They represented all the advantages their Order conferred on the country,—the education of youth,—economy to the State, as they required no subsidy;—and in short portrayed themselves as the most amiable and accomplished class in Europe. Gordon was exhorted to obtain their recall by every means possible, and in the meantime so to manœuvre that nothing was undertaken as to other ecclesiastics before receiving the reply of the Emperor from Vienna.

The hopes of the Jesuits as to the influence of the Emperor of Germany were not vain, for in

1691, Curzius, the envoy of this potentate, appeared in Moscow on a special mission in their behalf. He immediately announced himself to General Gordon, and the house of Guasconi became the centre of their re-unions.* After having assured the government of the unalterable friendship of the Emperor, the envoy said that his master was very sensible of the protection which had been accorded the Jesuits in Russia, and that he had sent him to testify his gratitude, and with his own hands to present the Czar a letter from the Emperor. At the same time, he must express his astonishment at their expulsion, and hoped that on further consideration they would be recalled ; he hoped that this request would be attended to, and not refused ; that as Christians of other denominations, Lutherans, Calvinists, etc., had full liberty of worship in the land, even so the Catholic community might be permitted to have clergymen to fulfil the offices of religion ; the Greek faith, he added, was not persecuted in Hungary and Servia, which countries formed part of the Imperial dominion.

Curzius was informed that the building of Roman chapels and the establishment of schools was forbidden, and that the Jesuits should abso-

---

* Posselt's Tagebuch des Gen. Patrick Gordon. Vol. ii., 444-494.

lutely not be recalled, as their conduct had not
conformed to the conditions on which their presence in the centre of a population professing the
Greek faith depended ; that these conditions had
been granted only out of the friendship of the Czar
for the Emperor, and were only for a limited time.
They had undertaken to live quietly and to celebrate the service of their church in their houses,
instead of which they had interfered in things
which did not concern them, had corresponded
with a foreign power, attracted Russian children to
their schools, and established a complete system of
Propagand. Other countries, it was said, complained of the conduct of these priests, and suffered
from their meddling propensities. Even in Venice
they were not tolerated.

Curzius defended them, assuring the Government that these reproaches were unmerited, and
that they were caluminated purely through the
intrigues of the Lutherans and Calvinists of Moscow ; that the Fathers were as much distinguished
for their scientific accomplishments as for their
Christian humanity ; that they had only one aim,
that of fulfilling the duties of the ministry to which
they had been called, and of which they were an
ornament, and that if they had unintentionally
infringed the conditions on which they were

allowed to reside in the capital, it would be easy to enact more stringent regulations, to prevent future irregularities. "In Venice and in England," said he, "there are also Jesuits, but they are changed every three years, and in the latter country they are disguised as laymen, so as not to excite popular tumults, and to facilitate their intercourse with Catholics." But Curzius perfectly comprehended that he could not insist on their recall, that there was little chance of it, and contented himself with diplomatising, stating that if they were again permitted to reside in Moscow, they might also, as in Venice, be changed every three years, and he proposed to draw up rules to be sanctioned by the government, as to their conduct and action while in Russia, and to guarantee the exact fulfilment of them. The house which had been purchased by the German Emperor should be registered as that of Guasconi. "Besides," added he, "what a scandal their expulsion will create throughout Europe. All sorts of calumnies will be circulated about them. The Lutherans and the Calvinists will spread it over Christendom, the entire Order will suffer, and nobody will defend these innocent martyrs. Therefore the Emperor of Germany wishes their recall to re-establish them in public opinion."

He was answered, that it was strange if the
Emperor was angry at their expulsion, for they
had not fulfilled their duty or the conditions on
which they had been allowed to reside in the
country ; that the reason of their expulsion was
that they had commenced to proselytise, and not
confined their action to their own parishioners ;
that it was .quite unnecessary in them to make
converts, as the Russians had been for centuries
Christians, and were sincerely attached to their
religion ; and that in chasing them there was
nothing offensive to the Emperor, who could, if he
really desired their establishment in foreign lands,
send them to countries where the people had no
knowledge of the true God, and lived in the darkness of idolatry, amongst whom they could preach
Romanism.   That as to the Lutherans and the
Calvinists, although their doctrine differed much
from that of the Russian creed, they lived very
peacefully in Moscow, occupying themselves solely
with their own affairs.   As to whether they had
calumniated the Jesuits or no, the government did
not trouble itself to inquire.   With regard to the
house of the Jesuits, occupied by Guasconi, this
man could do as he liked, but it was excessively
strange and inconvenient to use the name of the
Emperor in connection with it.   Throughout the

German Empire, it was added, there is no house to be found belonging to the Russian Czars.

These conferences closed by a notification that the government of the Czars, taking into consideration the wishes of the Catholics in their service, consented that one Roman priest, not a Jesuit, should reside in the capital, but that it was absolutely a *sine qua non* that he should be a monk of another order, that he should reside in a private house, and neither interfere in temporal affairs nor try to proselytise. If they sent a disguised Jesuit, he should be immediately chased beyond the frontiers, and no more Catholic priests should in future enter Russia.

Curzius then demanded permission for a curate to be appointed to this priest, and that, until they arrived from abroad, the Dominican attached to the embassy at Moscow should temporarily fulfil the duties of the Church, a request acceded to by the government.

Curzius, counting on a better result, drew up beforehand a memorandum of his demands to be signed, in case they were conceded by the Czars. This document, bearing date 1691, still exists, and in it the recall of the Jesuits is consented to, together with the permission to erect Catholic Churches, to allow public religious processions, and many privileges to be continued and confirmed by the existing government and their successors. Without doubt Curzius deserves credit for cleverness. He had endeavoured to have the house recognised as the property of the Emperor, to afford at any future time an excuse for meddling in the affairs of the Catholics of Russia, and the possibility of further concessions.

The permanent establishment of Catholicism in the country became more and more a necessity from the successive arrival of strangers, but at this epoch it was new to Russia. Our statesmen of the period perfectly comprehended the spirit of this doctrine, and admirably traced the line of demarcation between religion and proselytism, between spiritual requirements and the pretensions of the Roman clergy. In Russia, the Catholics had the right of liberty of conscience; nobody constrained them to change their religion; but, on the other hand, their clergy were absolutely forbidden to make converts.

Events justified the penetration of our politicians of that period. It was not religion, but the love of domination that led the Jesuits to undertake the Propagand in Russia. It would give them more political influence throughout Europe, a better position amongst strangers of the same creed,

serving the Czar ; it would open up the avenues of
social and public life, through which they could
guide, and rule, and reign, and strengthen the bul-
warks of Rome, at the same time that they could
more effectually support the Emperor of Germany.

Catholic interests in Russia were at this period
represented by General Patrick Gordon, whose
fervency and fanaticism are well known. Educated
in the Jesuitical school of Braunsberg, he was all
his life devoted to the Order, and during the long
term of his service he corresponded constantly with
them abroad, sending his three sons to be brought
up by them in France, Germany, and England. In
1684, at his instigation no doubt, he presented a
petition from his co-religionists in Moscow, which
was supported by Girowsky and Blumberg, the
envoys of Austria, who demanded in the name of
the Emperor, that a church might be erected in
the capital for those Catholics who faithfully and
devotedly served his august Majesty the Czar, and
for the use of the various trading companies
residing in the German quarter, who regularly paid
all taxes and imposts according to law, and who
have not a house of prayer or pastors for their
spiritual wants, while the Calvinists and Lutherans
have clergy and churches. The Czar replied that
he would confer with the Patriarch. Two years

elapsed without the desired authority, when the
government reiterated the permission already given
as to liberty of worship, but refused to allow the
erection of a chapel. The Emperor was obstinate,
reiterated his requests, and insisted always that
the church should not only be built, but be furnished with a bell, that the service should be
public, and that all this should be confirmed by
the Czar for himself and successors officially. "We
cannot even listen to such propositions," was
the reply ; "to permit a church at Moscow is an
impossibility." In 1686, the Boyard Boris Petrovitch
Shéremeteff, Ambassador at Vienna, expressed the
same determination on the part of his government.
The Emperor graciously offered to write to the
Czar, and to hand his letter to the envoy himself,
conditionally that the above request be conceded
and confirmed. Shéremeteff replied that Catholic
priests, with liberty to celebrate their religious
services at Moscow, were only tolerated through
the friendship of the sovereign of Russia for His
Majesty, neither induced by nor resulting from
any obligation or constraint ; that the intrigues of
the clergy had offended and irritated the people,
and that in future the government would be more
circumspect with regard to Catholic ecclesiastics.
It would be exceedingly difficult to accord to

secular priests that which had been denied to the
Jesuits when they were actually in the country,
and what had also been refused to His Majesty
himself, and so constantly demanded in his
embassies.

The Dominican, Bleer, followed the mission of
Curzius, in December, 1692, accompanied by the
missionaries Le Clerc and Eroch. Gordon directed
this mission. He surveyed their actions, and kept
Curzius informed regularly as to their activity and
their progress in the Russian language, and even
wrote to the Emperor of Germany, telling him
that the Romanists of Russia owed him their
establishment. He was, at this date, the principal
instrument of the Propagand in this country. But
the missionaries soon commenced to imitate the
Jesuits, only acting with greater prudence and
secresy. It is probable that they were only
disguised Jesuits. Five years later three more
arrived, with Guarlente, Ambassador of Austria.

Afterwards these priests decided to act on their
own authority, and to have a chapel by hook or by
crook. They therefore built a wooden one beside
the house of which Guasconi was the proprietor,
pretending that Gordon had commanded it, and
dug in the German quarter a cellar, for, as they
said, the interment of the General's family. It

was not quite finished when the suspicions of the
people were aroused, and the authorities informed.
The Minister for Foreign Affairs reported the case
to the Czar Peter, then at Azoff. Peter replied
that he had never authorised such a construction,
ordered it to be stopped, and desired that the
priest should be interrogated as to who had commanded it. Proceedings were commenced, and
the Jesuits, knowing the high favour in which
Gordon stood at Court, threw all the blame upon
him, Guasconi confessing that all the plans and
orders were issued only by the General. Guasconi
pretended to ignore as to whether Gordon had
authority or not, but the true state of the case
stood thus :—In 1694, the Czar went in a carriage
with Gordon to a marriage of some of the strangers
serving in the army, and passing through the street
where the Catholics had decided to build a church,
Gordon drew his attention to the subject, to which
the Czar did not reply. Gordon interpreted this
silence as an intimation that the authority to build
would not be withheld. The priests, who on
their own responsibility had commenced this work,
persuaded by the guarantee of such permission,
continued it. The authority required was later
conceded, for which concession the priests promised
a glorious victory over the Turks. The Minister
for Foreign Affairs made many inquiries on the

subject, and was informed by Gordon's son that after the prohibition to continue it, a petition had been sent to General Gordon, then with the Czar at Azoff, who had obtained it, but whether in writing or verbally, was not known. This was the first church erected in Moscow, of the Catholic faith, which received the name of SS. Peter and Paul. It exists at present, with its primitive architecture and without any considerable changes in its construction.* Bergholz, gentleman of the Chamber of the Princess Anne,† daughter of Peter the Great, visited it in 1722, and tells us that its interior was ornamented with pictures and other decorations, and possessed a very fine organ.

We have accurate dates as to the arrival of a Roman Catholic bishop in the year 1698. He arrived for the service of the engineers and military of the Catholic persuasion in the army of the Czar, who had been engaged by His Majesty during his first journey abroad. But we cannot exactly fix the date when the Capucins established themselves, as it is founded only on Roman Catholic records. There is no trace of them in any official documents; we only know that they were called much later to Moscow. It is true that there exists a document bearing the signature of Peter

---

* Arch. prin. des Moscow.
† Married to the Duke of Holstein.

and signed with the Great Seal, but it is entirely
apocryphal, as it is drawn up by some one who
knew not the language. This false document
permits, in honour of the alliance of the Czar and
Augustus II., of Poland, the erection of a church
and a convent in the capital of Moscow, as well as
public processions, and every one is enjoined to
pay respect to the Capucins.

The great aim of the Jesuits was to be officially
recognised. As secular priests, they had established
themselves constantly in the country, under pretence of missions to Persia and India. Many of
them had arrived from time to time in the suite of
the Ambassador of the Emperor of Germany as
confessors, and were furnished with letters of
protection by that sovereign. Thanks to the
ignorance of some of the Russian authorities and
the desire to preserve amicable relations with the
empire of Germany, they began a new era in
Russia. They received a subsidy of 800 thalers
per year from the Emperor. Their church at
Moscow was very handsome, and they preached in
Polish or German. In Petersburg, the new capital
of the Empire, they appeared as civilians, and in
Moscow as secular priests, but afterwards they
threw off the mask, opened schools and boldly
assembled Russian children for instruction. They

succeeded so far that they even persuaded the
Minister for Foreign Affairs to place students for
the diplomatic service in their establishments, to
learn, as they pretended, Latin and German.
Ladyjensky, converted at Moscow, entered the
Order and took successful steps to obtain and take
with him the estates he possessed in the country.
But it was chiefly amongst the higher classes of
society that they made the most converts. They
continued their connection with Vienna as before,
and acted as spies. The most enterprising of
them was Engel, sent by the Bishop of Inflandt to
Petersburg in 1715, with a letter of recommendation to the Chancellor of the Empire, Golowin. The
difficulties made by Austria as to the extradition
of the Czarewich Alexis, irritated and cooled the
Czar Peter, and afterwards produced a rupture.
Bleer, the ambassador, suspected of intrigues in
favour of Alexis, was compelled to quit the country,
but Peter did not expel him himself; he demanded
his recall by the Court of Vienna ; and when he did
at last receive the order of departure, he contrived
to remain several months longer at Petersburg.

The German Emperor, however, less polite,
abruptly dismissed Wesselowsky, and desired him
to quit Austria within a week. The Russian
General Consul was also expelled, though he

never mixed in politics, and confined himself quite to the transaction of commercial interests. To resent this affront, Peter, on the 17th April, 1719, ordered the expulsion of the Jesuits.

The Order had foreseen this for a considerable period, and had taken precautions for such an emergency. In 1719 they had received a secret warning as to how their correspondence with foreign countries should be carried on, and were to send their letters and documents through the Austrian embassy, so that when on the 25th of April the Jesuit. Engel was summoned before the Chancellor to have his papers examined, nothing of any importance was found. Rowmianzoff, who had conducted the affair of the Czarewich Alexis, was charged with their expulsion. A captain of the regiment of Bielozersk escorted them to the frontier, the government furnishing them with horses and furs and other necessities for the road. A declaration as to the causes of their dismission was despatched to the different foreign powers, and England concurred in the opinion that the determination of the Emperor Peter in this affair was perfectly justifiable.

Thus, in the course of thirty years, the Jesuits, who had twice introduced themselves into Russia, had been twice expelled. The first time the

Church, indignant at their barefaced proselytism, had roused herself to repel the threatened danger; it was not the civil power but the Patriarch who expelled them. The second time the voice of Russia made itself heard, and they were banished, not by the spiritual power, but by the Czar. It was not for their religious opinions, or because their church and its rites were repugnant to the feelings of the Russians, but as the protegés of the German Emperor, as the engines of a foreign power, and for political reasons. Here there is a striking contrast between Old and New Russia— between a government penetrated and actuated by the traditional religious spirit and a government founded on new European principles.

Under the reign of Peter the Great the Catholics of Russia enjoyed full liberty of worship in both the capitals and in the provinces. Taking advantage of the alliance of the Czar Peter with Augustus of Poland, the Roman Catholic clergy tried to obtain a written confirmation of their privileges through the good offices of the Jesuit confessor of the king; and in 1704, when Peter lay under the walls of Narva, in the war with Charles XII. Dzialynski, the Polish envoy exerted himself to obtain a charter in their favour, and this act was signed at Grodno the 12th of December, 1705, by which the Czar promised that neither now nor at any future time should they be forbidden the use of their religious rites in either the capitals or in the provinces ; and that they might erect a stone church, " which concession was granted solely out of regard for the Polish Diet." The first church, as we have seen, was built at Moscow ; afterwards others were constructed without preliminary authorisation at Petersburg and Astracan. This last city was selected as the centre of the Propagand for the east, and more especially for the Armenians. Under pretence of visiting Asia, Latin ecclesiastics had from time to time arrived there, and actually built a church for the merchants of different countries trading with the East, establishing in reality a depôt for proselytism, directed against the Armenian nation. In 1716 the Jesuit Milan wrote to Engel :—" The Capucins at Astracan have nothing to do if they are not employed amongst the Armenians." These priests lived very quietly in the city, dressed in the habits of their Order ; they were not only attached to the Church, but some resided in some of the families of the foreign merchants. A Franciscan of Turin lived in the house of the Contre Admiral Zmiewicz, and others at St. Petersburg were engaged as tutors to the children of noble families residing there.

The Holy Synod permitted mixed marriages, in the year 1721, conditionally that before the conclusion of the ceremony the strangers should give a written undertaking not to convert their spouses, and that the children of such marriages should be brought up Orthodox.

After the second expulsion of the Jesuits, the Capucins were called from France and Switzerland to replace them, but before this they had already been located at Astracan.* Patricius of Milan was their Superior, and was afterwards called to St. Petersburg to superintend the Order. The Pope, hearing of the expulsion of the Jesuits, sent the Franciscans to officiate instead, and named Le Père Doleggio, who was returning from Persia, as their chief. On his arrival at St. Petersburg, acting on his authority from the Pope, he set aside the Capucins; a proceeding which caused a ferment, and divided the Catholic community into two parts—the Catholics properly speaking, and the Papists. The first thought only of carrying out the services of religion; the second of aiding and abetting the designs of Rome. In Sept., 1720, Patricius appealed to the authority of the Czar against the Franciscans, presenting a

---

* Six arrived in 1720, and were attached to the church at St. Petersburg, and six were sent to Moscow.

petition in which he and his coadjutors complained that they were banished from the Church on pretence that they were not sufficiently learned. "It is true, august monarch," he wrote, "that humble and without scientific accomplishments I have consecrated my life to religion, convinced that for a monk it is not science but religion with which he should occupy his time in his cell."

The same day Pierre Tolstoy, a Privy Councillor, announced the Czar's pleasure to the Foreign Office, that Patricius and his brethren should remain connected with the Catholic Church as before, and that there should be no hindrance to them in their duties. A ukase of the 14th September confirmed this, but the day following Doleggio presented a memorial supporting the rights which he attributed to the Franciscans, with regard to the Church at St. Petersburg. No reply was given to this petition. The General of the Capucins wrote from Rome to thank the Czar for the protection accorded his brethren, but Patricius paid dearly for his triumph. A complaint was forwarded to Rome by the Franciscans on the subject, and the conclave, in a very harshly-worded letter, severely reprimanded him. In his fright he flew to the Foreign Office. But the protection of Rome, instead of helping the Franciscans, was injurious.

In 1721, two letters addressed by the Pope and the conclave to the Franciscans were seized, and examined by the Holy Synod, at the request of the Foreign Office. In these epistles they were informed that measures were being taken for the recall of the Capucins, and they were requested to propagate the Roman creed by every. means in Russia. The Synod, however, could not actively interfere, as the Patriarch had formerly done, in an affair with foreigners, but despatched a memorandum to the Czar, with the following remark :—

"It is necessary to regard the Franciscans at St. Petersburg as the spies of the Pope. As to the instructions of Rome, they are sometimes absolutely inhuman, supporting even attempts on the lives of sovereigns, as history sufficiently demonstrates by examples in which monks have executed such crimes."

At the request of the Synod, the Czar ordered proceedings to be instituted against the Franciscans, and that the Foreign Office should register a list of the Roman Catholics in the Empire, their localization, etc., as well as supply information as to the number of ecclesiastics annually arriving in Russia. The Franciscans, however, rested undisturbed and continued their intrigues against the Capucins, which resulted in their dismissal.

A ukase ordered the administration of the Church at St. Petersburg to remain for four years vested in the hands of the Franciscans, directed and superintended by their Superior, and the Capucins were consequently expelled from their duties in connection with the Church.

On its part, the government exacted that the Franciscans while permitted to officiate as they desired, should style themselves "Curators of Souls" or simply "Curates" and not missionaries, as they were elected to celebrate divine service for their parishioners, but not allowed to proselytise.

But the Franciscans did not long enjoy their triumphs, for the French ambassador, who belonged to the Gallican or Catholic party, defended the Capucins, and owing to his interest they were, on the 4th of May of the same year, reinstated as coadjutors for the religious services. This struggle between the Orders, so painful to their parishioners, was exceedingly embarrassing to the government ; both parties trying to obtain the protection of the Foreign Ministers, and meddling in affairs which did not concern them, continually beset the Ministries. To put an end to these disorders, both Capucins and Franciscans were, in November, 1724, ordered to quit Russia, and the Dominicans were appointed to replace them. The govern-

ment "imagined that the rules of this Order
forbade their meddling in temporal affairs;" but
the truth was the Dominicans were summoned
in compliment to Benedict XIII. who belonged
to their brotherhood, as the Czar having by
the treaty of Nusztadt become Protector of the
Greek Church in Poland, wished to soften religious
animosities by making himself agreeable to the
Pope, so that it was entirely owing to political
considerations that the Dominicans were called to
Russia and installed in St. Petersburg. Until their
arrival the Franciscans might officiate in the
Church, but conditionally that they lived peaceably
with each other—in case of contravention they
should be sent off.*

We must now glance for a moment at the
relations of the government with the Court of Rome;
remarking first that during the reign of the Czars
Peter and John Alexiewich, there were no direct
rapports with Rome, but negotiations only on the
subject of the titles which should be respectively
employed in addressing their respective sovereigns.
These negotiations were generally conducted
through the mediation of the envoys of the German
Emperor at the Russian Court.

In 1684, Sebastian Knabé, Archbishop of

---

* Arch. prin. de Moscow.

Naxivane, ambassador of Austria to Persia, stopped
on his way at Moscow, and informed the Foreign
Office that Pope Innocent XI., both verbally and by
writing, desired to renew relations with Russia,
which relations had been formerly broken off in
consequence of difficulties relative to titles; that
the Pope consented to give the Czar his full title,
and begged the Minister to give him a form of the
style, that it might be despatched to Rome.   The
government expressed their readiness to renew
relations with the Pope, but to this end a plenipotentiary should be sent by Rome.   The desired
formula was the same day handed to the Archbishop,
with the title of the Czars written *in extenso.*   As
to that of the Pope, the same style was employed
as that used by the Czar Alexis Michaelowich.
Having looked at them, the Archbishop returned
them to the Ministry, saying, that if the Czars did
not consent to give the Pope the title of "Very
Holy Lord and Father" he could not accept them.
As this was refused, he left for Persia.   After his
departure Girowsky, the Austrian Minister at
Moscow, renewed negotiations, and the Government
agreed to style the Pope "Very Pious and very
Illustrious Lord, Innocent XI., Pope and very
worthy Pastor of the Roman Church;" but as
nothing came of the affair, Girowsky quitted

Moscow, without obtaining any concession or any other result.

In 1685 Albert Dubois, attaché to the mission of Curzius, arrived from Vienna, with proposals from the Pope relative to an alliance against the Turks, and the re-establishment of relations with Rome. But before entering into negotiations, a discussion arose about titles. Although Dubois carried a letter from the Pope, it was Curzius who commenced preliminaries, the Emperor of Germany being the mediator between the two Courts. He said that, in compliance with the desire of the Emperor, the Pope had given the Czars their full titles, but that unless these sovereigns should accord the Holy Father his complete title also, they should withhold the epistle. The Foreign Office however was dissatisfied with the style adopted towards the Czars, and declared that the Russian government could only address His Holiness in the style delivered in the formula to Girowsky, declining to use that of the period of John Vassielewich which had not been employed since a patriarch had been established in the country. Curzius at length declared himself content, and professed his readiness to accord the Czar that which he demanded, after which he presented the Pope's letter. To his astonishment he found that this epistle did not correspond with a copy which had been previously handed him, and that in the original the titles were considerably abridged. In consequence of this incident, the reply to the Pope, which had been prepared, was not remitted, and Curzius was dismissed. Indirect rapport, however, between the two courts continued as before.

During the reign of Peter, an embassy was despatched to Innocent XII., for the purpose of renewing relations and forming an alliance against the Turks. Generals Lefort and Golowin composed this mission, to which Woznitzyn was attached, but not reaching Rome for some unforseen cause, they were obliged to return home.

As Field-Marshal Boris Shéremeteff was going to Italy to study the organisation of the armament of the Knights of Malta, the Emperor charged him with a letter to the Pope, his visit having otherwise no official character. Shéremeteff intended visiting Rome, attracted there by his veneration for the Apostles Peter and Paul, and the relics to be found in the Eternal City; but his chief inducement was in pursuance of a vow he had made during a war with the Turks, that he would visit the tombs of these holy saints. He arrived in Rome, March 21st, 1698, accompanied by his two brothers and a numerous suite, and was received

with much distinction. The religious devotion of
the Marshal, his profound veneration for the relics
to be seen in this Catholic capital, the treaty of
alliance which he had concluded with Poland against
the infidels, and the many victories he had gained
over the enemies of Christianity, all predisposed
Rome in his favour. Notwithstanding that the
Czar addressed the Pope as before, "Ouczitel de
l'Eglise de Rome," Innocent XII. with his own
hands received the letter, and the General was
permitted to carry his hat in his hand, and his
sword at his side, during the audience, nor was he
obliged to kiss the Pope's foot as was customary.
He was presented with gifts and images, and his
holiness received from him also some rich Russian
furs. After a residence of fifteen days he left for
Malta, but returned in a short time, and received
the Pope's reply to the Czar. The Jesuits of Rome
and Venice seeing the Boyard's devotion to the
relics of the saints, augured his easy conversion, and were lavish of flattery and compliments. They transformed the Academy into
a salle d'armes to please the warrior, their
pupils representing the combats of the heroes
of antiquity, executing the military exercises
on foot and on wooden horses. "It is mani-
festly the approach of Christ's Kingdom,"

wrote a Jesuit, " and this conversion will give
us at Moscow an apostle, but it must remain
a secret.   It is to be desired that a Father knew
the Sclave language in order that he might converse with him on religious subjects."   But the
Jesuits were deceived for their pains.

Again, the successes of Charles XII. of Sweden
in Russia, which led to the possibility of his
invading Poland and dethroning Augustus, the
ally of Peter, naturally induced the Czar to court
allies against the Swedish prince, and on this
occasion he thought of Rome.   At this time
Poland was divided into two parties—one for
Augustus, who was on the throne, the other for
Stanislas Lesczinsky, the creature of Charles.   The
former trying to reserve their political rights
remained faithful to Augustus, and even after his
abdication refused to acknowledge Stanislas, and
proceeded to a new election ; the latter, obedient
to the conqueror, acknowledged allegiance only to
Stanislas.   Peter, supporting the opposition of
the Poles to the *élève* of Sweden, naturally turned
his thoughts on Rome, as Charles XII., being a
Lutheran as well as Stanislas, would hardly be
agreeable to the Latin clergy.   In 1707 he sent
Prince Boris Kourakin to Clement XI. not exactly
as ambassador, but in a sort of incognito, with a

semi-official character.　Kourakin was charged
with a letter to the Pope and one to the Cardinal
Archbishop of State, Paulluci, and opened the
negotiation very cleverly.　He assured the Pope
and the Archbishop that in waging war on Charles
the Czar Peter defended not only his own interests
but those of Catholicism, as the King of Sweden
being a Lutheran and the Protector of the Lutheran
confession, was the natural and constant enemy of
the Roman Church, a sufficient proof of which was
to be found in the fact that during the last war a
great number of Roman Churches had been devastated, or transformed into Lutheran temples, and
that the doctrine of Luther if it took root in
Poland, might spread from thence as from a centre
of heresy.　Prince Kourakin then followed up his
subject by requesting the Pope to fulminate a Bull
in which, conjointly with Russia, he refused to
acknowledge Stanislas as king, and encouraged the
Poles to elect a new sovereign who might be
useful, not alone to Russia, but to the Roman
Church in Poland as well as to Rome herself.
" If," he said, " the Swedes should be permitted
to confirm Stanislas on the throne, contrary to the
will and consent of the Holy Father, it would lead
not only to a deconsolidation of the Papal power,
but serve as a precedent for the entire extinction of

the Papal authority and faith in Poland." By way
of disposing Rome to his views, Kourakin stated
that it was purely out of personal regard for His
Holiness that the Czar had accorded the Catholics
in his empire entire liberty of worship, with the
erection of churches at Moscow, and a free route to
the East for the Chinese and Persian missionaries.
Rome promised concurrence in the views of Peter,
but did not decide on openly annulling the election
of Stanislas.

The principal aim of Kourakin in this negotiation was the dethronement of Stanislas; and the
allusion which he threw out as to the religious
liberty of the Catholics in Russia, was a means
towards this end, and a bait to prepossess Rome the
more in favour of the project. But for Rome on
the contrary, these negotiations on the subject of
Poland were but secondary, serving as the basis for
the demands for new favours and concessions for
the Romanists of Russia. On his first interview
the Holy Father thanked the Czar for benefits
already conferred on his Church, begging Kourakin
to transmit his acknowledgments for the same to
Peter, but immediately afterwards requested the
confirmation of these concessions in writing by a
charter, something in the form of a concordat,
sealed with the Great Seal, etc. To which Kourakin

replied that such a charter could not be at present delivered, but that, conformably to a promise made by the Czar to Augustus II. of Poland, a written authority was often given for the erection of Roman Catholic churches in Russia. Desiring however to assure the co-operation of Rome towards the result aimed 'at by the Russian government, the Prince evasively added that such a charter should be conferred on the Catholics after the war with the Swedes, if throughout this period the Pope maintained his friendship with Russia. As there existed nothing controvertible in this, it was not opposed. At a later date they endeavoured to obtain a written confirmation of the above-named concessions—the free exercise of religious rites, the erection of churches, and a free route towards the East;—but Kourakin could promise no such a certificate, and the Pope was obliged to content himself with repeating the promises made to him by the envoy, in his letter to the Czar.

Kourakin remained seven months in Rome, received much kindness from the Pope, but scarcely preserved his own and his sovereign's dignity as Menesuis had done in 1673, for he condescended to bend his knee before him, and sometimes even kissed his foot.*

---

* Arch. de Moscow. See also Hist. Russ. Mon. Vol. ii., pp. 284, 285.

That political views almost always swayed Peter more than religious interests can scarcely be doubted; a fact which is proved by the statement of Kourakin at an audience when he told the Pope " that in Lithuania, where they destroy the Orthodox Churches, the Czar, according to existing treaties with Poland, having the right to prevent it by force, nevertheless does not do so, though the incorporation of Russians in the Union is not effected by conviction but by violence, yet, out of love for the Pope he leaves the Union complete liberty of action, and only begs the Holy See to recognise as King of Poland the sovereign whom the Poles themselves should elect." The Pope replied by thanking Peter for his kindness towards the Union. This episode is sufficiently illustrative of the tendency of Peter's government."

After Kourakin's departure, the Nuncio at Warsaw was directed to obtain through the influence of Augustus II. the confirmation by charter of those privileges so ardently desired. The Nuncio drew a glowing picture of this glorious epoch in the annals of the Empire and the Church; nevertheless the Czar did not accord it, but continued, as formerly, to protect his Roman Catholic subjects in full liberty of conscience.*

* Hist. Russ. Mon. Vol. ii., pp. 286-297.

In 1717, Peter being expected at Paris, prepara-
tions were made to receive him; and Bentivoglio,
Archbishop of Carthage, asked the Secretary of
State how he should comport himself during the
sojourn of the Prince, and demanded if he should
not seize this opportunity to obtain greater concessions for the Catholics in Russia, which hitherto
the Popes had in vain desired. In reply to this
Bentivoglio was commanded to ' procure them if
possible, and to endeavour to arrange at the same
time for the presence of a Nuncio at St. Petersburg,
the secretary sending him also a formula of the
ceremony to be observed in addressing the Czar.
Paulucci, the Cardinal Secretary, the same who
had formerly conducted negotiations, sent him
directions as to how he should manage Kourakin
and artfully lead any conversation he might have
with the Czar towards the subject of the Church,
and the necessity of a Nuncio at St. Petersburg,
pretending that as the stay of the prince at Paris
would be so short, he could afterwards explain and
arrange matters at greater length in the Russian
capital.   The Duke of Orleans promised his
assistance to this scheme ; and Bentivoglio put it in
train, adding in his interview with Kourakin that
Rome had great influence over Poland, and
the politics of other powers, accompanying his

dissertation by an accusation against the Gallican Church of promoting dissensions in the Church in France, because some of the bishops had refused obedience to the head of the Church. At Kourakin's request an audience was granted the archbishop, who in a very recherché discourse eulogised the eminent qualities and exploits of the Czar, and hoped he would continue his kindness to the Roman Catholics of his empire. The prince made a flattering reply, but to the despair of his hearer did not mention religion. Kourakin also evaded all allusion to it, and sent him to the Vice Chancellor, Shafiroff, who informed him that if the Pope thought proper he could despatch a plenipotentiary to Russia. The efforts of Bentevoglio were, therefore, fruitless, and finding himself disappointed, he changed his plans. The Czar, after quitting Paris, went to Amsterdam, and from thence to Spa, where Bentevoglio desired the Nuncio at Cologne, to try to see him. As Peter did not like receptions while on his journeys, the Nuncio did not dare enter the town without permission, and sent Count Cavalchino to Amsterdam to the Chancellor Count Golowin to procure it, and to ask if the Czar would receive him. In case of refusal, he begged Cavalchino to try if he himself could not manage to obtain an audience, at which he could explain the views of Rome, and influence the Czar to further concessions. Cavalchino did procure this audience for himself, and was received with much affability, but it had, for Rome, no satisfactory result, the permission being given only for a plenipotentiary to appear in St. Petersburg.* Thus the pursuit of the Czar from Amsterdam to Spa was quite useless.

The hopes of the Papacy now centered in the person who should proceed to St. Petersburg. From the accession of Peter her aim had been the establishment of a regular embassy there, which might politically assist the spread of Romanism in the empire, and so bring about the union of the two Churches; and notwithstanding successive checks, she, had never abandoned the idea, but adjourned it from time to time on learning that Peter was well disposed towards her. The flattering reception which he had accorded Cavalchino induced a renewal of the attempt, particularly as he declared that Peter was kindly disposed towards the Pope, and that Golowin and Shafiroff, the Vice-Chancellor, had a liking for Catholicism. A letter was immediately despatched

---

* Correspondence entre le Noirce de Cologne et le Chancelier. Hist. Russ. Mon.—Vol. ii., pp. 331 et 332.

to Rome, in which ample considerations were discussed as to the sending of some one to Russia, Cavalchino advising a person who knew Russian, mathematics, and architecture, who had a general knowledge of the arts and sciences, to be selected as the best means of attracting the favour and liberality of the sovereign of Russia; and as Peter patronised everything likely to contribute to the civilization and interest of his subjects, he might be easily gained over by the present of a statue or some new tableau. This programme, like many another undertaken before it, was never executed, and the dissensions to which we alluded in a former page having broken out, ended by a rupture, and the expulsion of the Jesuits from the Empire.

Peter's taste for the arts, which Cavalchino had not failed to remark, led him to search all Europe for *chefs-d'œuvre* to enrich his new capital. Twice he sent to Rome to purchase statuary. In 1718, Kologriwoff bought an antique statue of Venus from that city and confided it for repairs to a sculptor, Legros. Falconieri, governor of Rome, being apprised of this circumstance, forbade its delivery. The Chancellor, Count Golowin, charged the Russian Minister at Venice to demand its restitution; and a long correspondence with the Cardinals ensued,

M 2

which ended in the Venus being deposited with Count Ragousinsky for the buyer. Cardinal Ottoboni having been the most active agent in its restitution, the Czar wrote and thanked him, promising to attend to a request the Cardinal had made for the relics of St. Briget, which were in Sweden, to be sent to Rome. This statué of Venus was not only to purchase the bones of a saint greatly venerated by the Roman Church, but was to lead to more serious results. A species of Concordat, signed with the Great Seal, giving an undertaking for himself and his successors, was to be obtained from the Czar, which would secure those priveliges so ardently longed for by Rome to the Catholics of Russia, through which she could attain a political and religious footing in the Empire, which might eventually enable her to unite the Eastern and Western Churches. The most desired of these concessions was the erection of Roman Churches without any control whatever of the government. As the Jesuits had been expelled two years before, it was thought unnecessary to mention them in the note written by Ottoboni to his agent in St. Petersburg; the remark being, "that the Pope will send missionaries who may be agreeable to His Majesty—Capucins, Benedictines, or the Barefooted Carmelites, who never interfere in temporal affairs

and preach only the Gospel. Besides, they will
be prohibited, under pain of severe chastisement,
meddling in civil or political affairs." The programme of Ottoboni contained also the establishment of schools, colleges, and universities, where
the sciences *and even Latin theology* might be
taught. A free passage for missionaries to the
East was also desirable. We know that this
passage was never interdicted. The execution and
confirmation of all these demands almost amounted
to the establishment of ultramontanism in its fullest
extent,—there would be indeed a state within a
state—in return for which Rome promised the
following titles to the Russian sovereign :—" Sere-
nissimo, Potentissimo, ac Magno Domino Czari et
Magno Duci Petro Primo, universæ, Magnae,
Parvæ et Albæ Russiæ autocratori, nec non Mag-
norum Dominiorum Orientalium, Occidentalium et
Septentrionalium paterno, avitoque hærdi successori,
Domino et Dominatori," as well as some statues and
antiquities. It would really appear as if the
government meant to accept these propositions, as
the question of appointing a Cardinal Protector for
Russian interests—then the custom amongst foreign
potentates—was discussed, as we find by a note
from Peter Tolstoy to the Ministry explaining the
signification of the title " Cardinal Protector " of

France. Thus the antique statue of Venus, which at present embellishes the Hermitage of St. Petersburg, was nearly costing Russia a Concordat, which might have ended darkly for the country. By a happy chance Russia escaped it. The 8th March, 1721, Clement XI. died, and Ragousinsky comprehending the absurdity of the whole affair, wrote to the Czar that he had better defer the sending of this document until after the election of another Pope. The Czar followed this advice; and the newly-elected Pope, not following up the question, Rome lost an advantage she had struggled for centuries to obtain.

During his journey through Europe, the Czar, as we have just said, visited Paris, and on the 14th July, went to the Sorbonne. While in the library he examined several books written in the Sclave language, which had caught his quick eye, and the doctors of the college seized the opportunity to draw His Majesty into a conversation upon the possibility of a re-union of the Eastern and Western Churches. In the course of the conversation, the Czar coolly remarked the striking differences between them, quoting two which had forced themselves upon him, but adding that his attention was given more to war and politics than to religion, and that if they desired to discuss the subject with the Russian Bishops they could do so, and he should propose to the latter to reply to any questions addressed. The theologians of the College immediately set about preparing a note on the subject, hastily, they said, as the Czar was about to leave, in which they touched on the principal differences of the Russian and Latin theology, trying to evade the polemical style so habitual to Western disputants. They did not consider it necessary, they said, to discuss either the rules or the ecclesiastical discipline, as in many churches the services differed; nor yet even the sacrament of the Eucharist, for all Catholic countries followed their own customs, as far as they conformed with the dogmas of their Head; so that the Russians could preserve their own rites like the United Greeks, provided that in so doing they threw no discredit upon those of the Latin Church. Their reasoning upon the dogmas of their own or the Greek faith were exceedingly shallow; nor did they give any satisfactory explanation of the Procession of the Holy Spirit, which is one of the most important differences of the Churches. They only arrived at the conclusion that both should have the same symbols of faith, but that the Russians need not have the famous Filioque of the Roman theology. It only remained to examine the *ecclesiastico-politico* dogma of the Pope's supremacy, and on this point the Sorbonne showed itself even more conciliatory. According His Holiness the same authority as to other bishops, with pre-eminence over them as the successor of St. Peter, but denying his infallibility, they proceeded to blame the tendency of the Papacy to interfere in temporal affairs, and saw no reason why Russia, in accepting Catholic unity, should submit to ordinances composed at Rome, particularly as these were not generally followed by many other countries essentially Catholic. "Such," said the doctors, " are our ideas, and although the Ultramontanes differ from us, they nevertheless do not hinder our being sound Catholics."

Etienne Jaworsky and Theophane Procopowich drew up two replies to this document in 1718, the contents of both being similar; but that of the latter was preferred, probably because his style was more bombastic, and interspersed with allusions to the Popes as the chief cause of the separation of the Churches. The Russian bishops thanked the Sorbonne for its worthy efforts at reconciliation, declaring that this was also the hope of the Russian Church, which daily prayed for the unity of the East and West, but regretting that they could not acquiesce in the reasoning of the reverend doctors. The bishops, however, had no right to decide or even to examine the question, as other countries professed the Greek faith, and referred the learned professors to the four Eastern Patriarchs, or, what was still better, abandon it to the decision of the Most High. This letter was signed by four of the principal bishops of the Orthodox Church, and was despatched to the Sorbonne in 1720.

The Jesuits of Moscow, who knew the contents of the letter written by the doctors of the Sorbonne, were deeply mortified at such an *exposé* of the views of the Church of France; and they wondered that nineteen priests of the College should dare present such a note to the Czar, without the signature of a single bishop; but if these boldly took upon themselves, they said, to promulgate such views, they had their antagonists even in the Gallican Church. At St. Petersburg itself there could be found many adherents of this Church, as in 1719 a Franciscan clergyman actually resided there who had little sympathy for the Jesuits. If the re-union of the Eastern and Western Churches were ever an accomplished fact, it would be assuredly as much through the Gallican doctrine as through that of Ultramontanism, the grand obstacle of all being Rome. Gallicanism commended itself more than Ultramontanism to this prince, for Peter had even Protestant tendencies. The brochures published in Holland against Rome found a favourable reception at his hands, and were even translated into Russian. At the Fêtes at the Palace, it was not uncommon to give ridiculous representations of the conclave of Cardinals, Zotoff playing with *empressement* the part of the Pope.*

After the death of Peter, the difficulties with the Catholic priesthood lasted a long time. The Capucins and the Franciscans excited the suspicions of the government, and fomented dissensions amongst the Catholic community. Chrysologue, an Austrian Capucin, endeavoured to excite Peter, the grandson of the late Emperor and the son of Alexis, against Catherine I., but this priest was expelled to Reval, and after a time finally banished.

At the close of 1728, the Abbé Jubet arrived from Paris, as tutor to the children of the Princess Irene Dolgorouky, *née* Princess Galitzen. This lady was the wife of Prince Serge Petrovich Dolgorouky, and had been converted to Romanism in Holland in 1727, by her friend the Princess of Aremberg, and received into the church of Rome by the Archbishop of Utrecht. The Abbé Jubet was neither more nor

---

* Memoires Secrets de la Cour de Russie sous les regnes de Pierre le Grand et de Catherine I.

less than an agent of the Sorbonne, who, with Fouquet and others, were selected, after a two years' debate, to go to Russia furnished with full powers, and backed by satisfactory credentials, to open preliminaries with the Russian clergy as to the eventful union. He was protected by the Duke of Liria, the Spanish Ámbassador, who was extremely intimate with Dolgorouky, the darling of Peter II., through whose influence Jubet was named Almoner to the Spanish Embassy, with permission to reside at the house of the Princess. Jubet was indeed specially protected by the whole Dolgorouky family, at that time in power, the two brothers of the princess being members of the Privy Council. The country house of one of the Galitzens served for a place of assembly for those who favoured the union; but these re-unions, as unconstitutionally assembled, and unrecognised by any episcopal authority, were useless. The Abbé was expelled in 1732. At a period somewhat later, several Capucins arrived from Austria, and were attached to the church at Moscow; the Dominicans only administering the church at St. Petersburg.

But notwithstanding difficulties, the Roman Propagand slowly progressed, through the influence of Polish emigrants, who converted the Russians after settling in the country. These immigrations

were however, in 1730, prohibited by law; and
proselytism was by a special clause forbidden
under pain of severe penalty. At Astracan on the
Caspian, it had more success, as further removed
from the observation of the authorities, who, until
too late to arrest it, did not discover its progress. In the time of Peter the Great, Roman
missionaries had arrived there, pretending to go
to Persia, and having delayed their departure
from the city from one period to another, had
in the interim built a church without any official
warrant. It was only in 1721 that the Foreign
Office thought of asking the Governor of Astracan
what number of Catholics lived there; what priests
they had; if there was a church there; and what
his opinion was about the Capucins, if they
could be permitted to settle there, requesting any
information he could give. The celebrated Wo-
lynski, who was then the Governor, replied that
there were many foreigners, principally merchants
there, both Germans and Armenians, of whom
many professed the Catholic faith, and that
according to his opinion he saw no reason why
these priests should not reside there; that on the
contrary their presence would serve the interests of
civilization in the country, as they taught Latin
and other languages. But the Armenians, whom

the question more narrowly concerned, foresaw the danger which threatened their Church, and declined to pronounce any opinion.

These forebodings were soon after fulfilled ; but Rome, acting with great prudence, in an almost imperceptible manner drew the Armenians, without forcing them, to Catholicism.   She gradually introduced the rites of the Roman Church into the Armenian, preserving the ancient ceremonies—that is to say the exterior of the faith—while little by little sapping the basis of the primitive dogmas, to which the mass of the people, seeing the exterior still the same, and little suspecting such duplicity, were blind.   Rome in one word introduced the Union into the Armenian Church, as she had before done into the Greek, and thus formed that mixture which is still to be found in the Armenian services, and which exists until the present day.   From Astracan the missionaries of Rome spread themselves into Persia, where they tried to convert the population.   Mohammedans and Armenians were equally the object of their spiritual solicitude there, and they actually succeeded so well that they enjoyed the favour of some satraps falling back upon Southern Russia for an asylum in case of danger.   By the middle of the century they had established themselves openly, under the

name of the Roman Mission. But a cloud appeared in the horizon of their success. Bakounin,
the Russian consul at Guiliany, determined to call the
attention of the government to them; and in 1746
he reported the intrigues of the Jesuits in Persia,
their proselytism of the Armenian peasantry, and
remarked on their constant correspondence with the
Capucins of Astracan. He concluded his report
thus :—" If the dervishes of India and Persia are
not permitted to enter Russia, because of their
propensity for espionage, how much more dangerous
are the Latin priests on this very same score." A
certain Capucin who for seven years had proselytised
in Persia, left it to return to Italy, but stopping at
Astracan on his way, he coolly continued his labours.
The Ministry aroused, took measures to stop this
insidious and dangerous Propagand; the Capucin
was ordered to be expelled, and the Consul was commanded not to give passports or permit " *these
vagabond priests,*" as they were styled, to sail in
Russian vessels. The Capucin who was distinguished by fanaticism and bigotry, was warned to
evade in future conversions amongst the people, if
he desired to escape exemplary punishment, and
enjoined to be quite quiet, contenting himself like
his co-religionists with the free exercise of his faith
as tolerated by law. But these precautions came

too late. The Capucins continued to convert the
Armenians as before, baptizing in the Roman
Church all the children born of mixed marriages
between Catholics and Armenians. But the
Armenians themselves were excited, and loudly
accused the Propagandists menacing the Capucins
with expulsion, so that Rome had to interfere and
invoke the Russian government for protection for
these priests. The Armenian clergy roused themselves. Etienne, Archbishop of Astracan, complained
in 1755 against them, exposing their actions, and
presenting a list of persons whom they had proselytised. When it was known that this memorandum
had appeared at the Foreign Office, two Capucins
left for St. Petersburg to advocate their defence, and
by way of retaliation brought with them a certain
Armenian book containing a critique on the dogmas
of the Greek Church. Through such an *exposé* of the
ideas of the Armenian Church on the Russian creed,
they hoped to work up a scheme, not only to defeat
the petition presented against them, but to obtain
official authority for the conversion of Armenians
not Russian subjects, with an injunction to the
Archbishop not to complain again and to keep
his discontent to himself. But there existed at
this very same moment, in St. Petersburg, positive
proofs that the missionaries had also tried to

convert Russians as well as Armenians at Astracan.
They were commanded to reply to this charge; but
instead of doing so eluded it, demanding permission
to leave for Rome to concert with their superiors
as to their defence, but threatening the Vice
Chancellor, Count Woronzoff that in case the affair
were decided against them, they should appeal to
foreign sovereigns for protection. The Holy Synod
insisted on an inquiry; saying, that the culprits if
found guilty should be punished, but the Foreign
Office over-ruled it, and the case was quashed.
Naturally the Armenians were dissatisfied at this
result, as it threw discredit on them, and the
Ministry justified itself by the following *exposé* of
the reasons which actuated the government.

"With respect to the accused Capucin, it would
not be prudent to proceed with that severity against
him, which existing laws justify; as even were his
crime evident, the Emperor of Austria, who holds
the same faith, would defend him, and under
present circumstances it would not be politic
to have any coolness with that Court. It is therefore better to let the affair drop, and banish the
priest, seeing that if once convicted, it would be
exceedingly difficult to execute the sentence;" in
other words, tolerance was sacrificed to policy, as
genuine tolerance consists in preventing one Church

ᵣersecuting another. The Roman Catholic missionaries, intolerant and overbearing in their own Church, were this time, as the Jesuits had formerly been by Peter I., protected by reason of the foreign policy of the government; and since the reign of this Emperor, the system pursued by Russia with regard to strangers domiciled in the empire, did not consist in equalising their rights, but in making them serve as political instruments, protecting them when an alliance was desirable, and withdrawing this protection when a demonstration was intended. In the present case, policy did not require such a course, but on the contrary; it was not Russia which required an alliance with Austria, but Austria to whom it was essential. Frederic the Great was not dangerous for Russia, but for Austria; he did not make war on the Czar, but on the House of Hapsburg; and an act of justice on the Capucins of Austria, who had violated the conditions on which they were tolerated in the country, could hardly be dangerous for the government, Austria having more at heart the defence of her States against the Prussian troops, than of fanatical missionaries against Russian justice. Sound policy was, however, sacrificed to expediency, and the Capucins enjoyed even more protection than ever. The following year Count

Esterhazy, the governor of Astracan, was enjoined
" to show the Catholic priests every protection,
and to try to reconcile them with the Armenian
clergy." Thanks to this injunction, they redoubled
their energy and no longer veiled their proselytising
propensities, openly trying to convert the Russians
to Catholicism. The Archbishop of Astracan did
not cease to complain, remarking at the same time,
that there were really no born Catholics, for that
all had been converted. This inactivity of the
government produced such fruit for Rome, that in
the city, where, until the time of Peter I., there
was not a single Catholic by birth, in 1760 there
were eighty-seven families converted to Catholicism.
Fifty-three of these families depended on the
Russian government, and together formed a fourth
part of the population of the town.

As to the Dominicans at St. Petersburg, they did
not live in very cordial relations with their parish-
oners. Sent to Russia by Rome, they were
exceedingly circumscribed in their usefulness, as,
knowing only Italian, they were of little service
either to the Germans, French, or Poles. Their
superiors depended only on Rome, and in no case
respected the rights of the community, regarding
the estates of the Church, not as belonging to their
parishioners, but to Rome, to whom only they

owed allegiance. Although they personally made no sacrifices in favour of the Church, they yet collected and saved money, which they placed out at high interest for their own profit; and finally ended by returning to Italy without rendering any account of the Church funds, leaving only debts behind them for their parishioners. These last, oppressed by the clergy, demanded authority from Rome to select their own priests, to elect a superior and inspectors for the administration of the Church property; but for several years the conclave gave no reply, sending, however, their own superiors. The community at that time confided their interests to the Empress Catherine II., and begged her Majesty to establish a regular administration for the Church at St. Petersburg. In 1766, the Foreign Office was commanded to take steps that the Franciscans should come to Russia; and in 1769, the Empress published regulations for the Church at St. Petersburg, the principal of which were as follows :—

1. The Franciscans should officiate in the parish to the number of five or six, and not four as formerly, and these priests should from time to time celebrate divine service at Cronstadt, Revel, Yambourg, and Riga.

2. Eight inspectors or syndics should be selected by the parishioners; and these, as adjuncts to the

superior, who should also be chosen by the congre-
gregation, should regulate the pecuniary affairs of
the parish.

3. Attached to the church there should be a
school for the education of Roman Catholic children,
but of no other confession of faith.

4. The church, the school, and other buildings,
should, without exception, belong to the municipal
community.

5. The clergy were to abstain from all proselytism.

6. The superior direction of the affairs of the
Church, should, as well as the decision in all
litigious matters between the clergy and their
people, be referred to the Minister of Justice for
the affairs of Livonia, Esthonia, and Finland, conditionally that the Ministry did not interfere with
the dogmas of the Roman Church. This latter
rule extended to the Church at Moscow, and by it,
the Catholic communities of both capitals were
secured against any arbitrary acts on the part of
their clergy. But this act had a yet more significant importance. In according entire liberty to
the Roman religion, but certainly without proselytism, forbidding it under severe penalty, and preserving intact the dogmas of the faith, the Empress,
who at this time reckoned several thousands of
Catholic subjects, did not recognise the right of

Rome to nominate the Latin clergy in her dominions. She did not permit the Conclave at Rome
to send superiors to the Roman Church in Russia,
but she sent direct to Germany for priests (she had
directed the Foreign Office to demand the Franciscans from one of the Bishop rectors of Germany),
subordinating them completely to the Ministry
itself. The Catholic community received this
regulation as a benefit which released them from
oppression, thus attesting that, inasmuch as the
dogmas of the Faith were independent of the
temporal power, so much the more should the
clergy submit to this power.

During the first years of the reign of the Empress
Catherine II., the Germans established colonies in
Saratoff, in the south of Russia. These colonies still
exist, some of them Roman Catholic, some of them
Lutheran. The government, at its own expense,
built houses for the clergymen, and churches,
which they furnished with every requisite for divine
service, conferring many privileges on the colonists,
which after experience unhappily did not justify,
particularly if one considers the little benefit these
colonies produced to Russia. The Foreign Office
nominated these priests and the *rapports* between
them, and their parishioners were regulated by the
law of 1760 for the Church of St. Petersburg.

This epoch opened up a certain and regular
organisation for the Catholic clergy in Russia, but
there was no ecclesiastical administration, properly
speaking, until a later date. Apart from projected
ecclesiastical buildings, there was a church at
Moscow, one at St. Petersburg, one at Astracan, and
one to Nirjni. The date of the erection of the
latter is unknown. As to Russian subjects born
Catholic there were extremely few. The greater
part of them were the children of strangers serving
the Crown, or strangers themselves in the Russian
service, and some Armenians converted to Popery
at Astracan. Russia only received a Catholic population after the partition of Poland. Her consecutive
union of the western provinces gave her a solidly
established Roman Catholic hierarchy, with laws,
rights, and traditions of its own, and it is only from
this period that, properly speaking, the history of
Catholicism in Russia begins. To comprehend
and appreciate the acts of the Empress Catherine
concerning Catholic ecclesiastical institutions, it is
indispensable to glance at the state of Catholicism
in Western Russia at the time of the re-union with
the empire. The limits of this work will not
permit us to treat the subject at length, as it
would involve a preliminary history of Romanism in
Poland, but the history of Rome in Poland is

Poland herself. Romanism was inseparable from
her destinies—it created, organised, reversed, and
at last brought about the struggle which terminated the political existence of this unfortunate
country. The reader who desires more detailed
information as to the *rôle* played by the Roman
clergy in the history of Poland, and the fanatical
spirit of the Latin clergy in Lithuania at the time
of the introduction of Christianity into the country,
will find much information in the documents contained in the Archives of the Ministry, " des
affaires étrangers," at Moscow, " Les archives
principales de Moscou," &c., &c. As to what
concerns the history of the Catholic Church in
Lithuania, we confine ourselves to those circumstances merely which relate to the ulterior measures
of the Russian government with respect to the
ecclesiastical administration of the Roman Catholics
in Russia.

CHAPTER V.

APERÇU HISTORY OF CATHOLICISM IN LITHUANIA
UNDER THE POLISH DOMINATION.

The Greek Faith anterior to the Roman Church in the
Western provinces.—Introduction of Romanism.—Difficulties
which it encountered.—Idolatry in Lithuania in the sixteenth
century.—Erection of dioceses and arrival of the Monastic
orders.—Romanism introduces an element altogether new in
Lithuania.—Cardinal Commendoni makes the Council of
Trent accepted in the Grand Duchy, 1564. — Hierarchical
organisation of the clergy.—The Reformation and its progress
in Lithuania.—Arrival of the Jesuits, 1569.—Their rapid
success.—They hinder the march of Calvinism.—Greek
Church in Lithuania.—Conduct of the Jesuits with regard to
it.—Struggle between the Latin and Greek priesthood.—
Introduction of the union at the Council of Brescia, 1596.—
Views of Rome and its plan of action.—Protestations of the
people of the Greek rite.—Means employed by the Jesuits
to effect the union.—Persecution of the Greek Church.—
Polemic between the Latin and Greek priesthood.—Discontent
which the Jesuits excited among the Roman Catholics in
Lithuania.—King Vladislas IV. opposes the Peares to the
Jesuits.—Influence of the Jesuits.—Jesuit almanacs.—State
of the Clergy.—Dissensions between the Clergy and noblesse.
—Rôle played by the Jesuits in the State.—Precautions taken
against the accumulation of riches by the Clergy.—The
Roman Clergy contribute to the downfall of Poland.—State of
the Reformed Church from the seventeenth to the eighteenth

centuries. Progressive Romanisation of the united Greeks.
—Political phase of the union.—The Jews oppressed by the
Latin Clergy.

THE History of Western Russia is generally
enough known. With the exception of Lithuania
proper, which comprised the governments of Wilna
and of Grodno, Samogitia and a part of Courland,
the other provinces of that country were of Russian
origin, and formed a section of the different appan-
age principalities. One of them was even the
cradle of the Empire as well as the birthplace of
the religion of Russia. Lithuania itself, though the
population belonged to another race than that of
Russia, was no stranger to her, as it was from this
latter country that the Gospel had been brought
at a period when Latinism was completely unknown.
In the convent of the Holy Spirit at Wilna repose
the remains of the first martyrs of the faith,
Anthony, John, and Eustace, killed by the Lithuanian
idolators; and an old church, now ruined, formerly
dedicated to Saints Boris and Gleb, still exists at
Nowogroudek, an antique testimony of the early
religion. It still confers the title of Metropolitan,
as the See of the Russo-Greek prelate. The
Lithuanian Metropolitans afterwards removed their
seat to Wilna. It contained in the fifteenth
century the Preczistenska Cathedral, known as the

Spaska; and the Greek Metropolitan resided beside it, while the adjacent houses belonged to the clergy of this confession. The two countries were also intimately united by royal marriages, and the refuge found there by the Greek priesthood who fled from the devastations of the Tartars. The Russian dialect penetrated with the Russian faith, and became the idiom of the Legislature, as proved by the Lithuanian statutes and other official acts.

The efforts of the Teutonic Knights to introduce Latinism by violence into the country, in the hope of conquering it, and the missions of Franciscans and Dominicans towards the same end, were failures. According to the testimony of Western writers, the Lithuanians were at the close of the fourteenth and the commencement of the fifteenth centuries either idolaters or followers of the Greek Church. It was not until after the union of that country to Poland under Jagellon that Romanism was imposed on the people. Jerome of Prague visited these regions in the latter century, when Latinism first found some success. It took root with difficulty as it was introduced by violence, and was preached in a language unknown to the people; the conversions were consequently slow and insincere. The Latin monks sent by Rome knew nothing of the common language, and preached through interpreters, so that they could scarcely be comprehended. At the same time they endeavoured to augment the number of their parishioners for the interest of their Order; but they did not succeed with the population, and notwithstanding 'the zeal of their Grand Dukes this doctrine made little progress until the middle of the sixteenth century, or even later. Latinism entered this region at a period when, undermined by the selfish and mundane considerations and calculations of the priesthood of the papacy, it had decreased in other parts of Europe. It was not the pure doctrine of the gospel, nor did it contain the elements of Christian fervour that pervaded it during the first centuries of Christianity. It was tottering and falling, enfeebled by the vices and ignorance of its preachers, their cupidity, their dominating spirit, their ignorance of the duties of their ministry, and their unbounded arrogance. Cardinal Commendoni himself said: "In Lithuania there is no ecclesiastical civilization and no true priesthood, if we except those of Poland. The priests who arrive there are individuals, for the greater part, incapable and ignorant, who cannot find places in their own country." With respect to the erection of ecclesiastical dioceses, they did not at all correspond with the requirements of the Roman Church, but were laid out, not because of the number of parishioners, as the people generally speaking belonged to the Greek confession, but as a basis for future operations. Samogitia and Kamienec were erected at the commencement of the fifteenth century. The Monastic Orders arrived progressively in the country ; the Dominicans and Franciscans in the fourteenth, and the Bernardines following them at the end of the fifteenth century ; and in the sixteenth the Carmelites established themselves.

With Romanism an altogether new class appeared, with a new language, new inspirations, new traditions and quite another canonical legislation ; an element, in short, which completely modified the social body. The canon law legislated the civil tribunals, the language of the Church insinuated itself in every form into all classes of the people, into literature, and into the affairs of the State. Besides this a new and independent power, that of the Pope, sprang up which was often in direct contravention to the interests of the country. Rome arrogated to herself the nomination of the bishops, confirming them even without the preliminary consent of the King. The clergy mixed themselves up in judicial affairs, often interfering with the civil tribunal, and meddling with the privileges of the aristocracy in order to enrich themselves, at the expense of all classes of Society, so that in the sixteenth century they were already engaged in a struggle with the government and the noblesse, not for the purity of their faith, but for their own private interests. They refused to be taxed for the benefit of the State, denied the competency of the civil jurisdiction, and for their own use, levied tithes and imposts upon the peasantry. The King and the nobles did not try to curb their proceedings, as all decisions in such contentions rested with the Nuncio at Warsaw. In war time if they came to the aid of the government by pecuniary donations, it was always stipulated that such assistance should not be considered as precedents for future taxation, but be regarded only as a loan ; and these loans were afterwards made the basis for demands of further concessions—greater privileges. The legislature was obliged to be continually on the defensive in consequence of the boundless influence which Rome exercised over the organisation and discipline of the Lithuanian clergy. But from the close of the fifteenth century the Kings themselves assumed the right of nomination to the Episcopal Sees, and since that period restricted also the sending of first fruits to Rome—a grievance not longer to be tolerated. They denied the right of the Popes to confer certain ecclesiastical functions, while the choice of the Titular was reserved to the sovereign.

The hierarchical organisation of the clergy evinced great disorder as well as little unity of action. The religious orders, being subject only to generals or superiors residing at Rome, did not recognise the authority of the bishops; and the curates and priests struggled very often to reduce their deans to subjection to themselves, questioning their right in the parishes, and appropriating the money destined to the construction and repair of places of worship. Many of them enjoyed a plurality of benefices without even residing in the parishes.

It was in this state that the Reformation found the clergy, when towards the middle of the sixteenth century it entered Lithuania. Society was prepared for it, as well by the preaching of John Huss, well enough known in the country, as by the liberty of the press which, since 1539, legally existed in Poland. The Reformation was accepted with such enthusiasm that in the latter half of this same century, the Lithuanian Senate was almost composed only of Calvinists and Lutherans. In the whole Lithuanian army there was only one Roman Catholic chaplain, who was attached to the

Hetman. The Roman ecclesiastics, contrary to the laws of their church, married. Instead of opposing the new doctrine, the bishops disputed amongst themselves and with the government on the subject of church lands and the revenues they derived. These dissensions, according to Commendoni, exceeded all bounds. "When the Roman Churches pass into the hands of dissenters," he said, "when the glory of God is eclipsed, these bishops are silent; but when a morsel of ground is in question they are ready to fly to arms." It is true that the sovereigns themselves often named incapable persons to episcopal places, sometimes even minors. Thus King Sigismond Augustus, in consideration of a pecuniary subsidiary, nominated the Son of the Duke of Mecklenburg, John Albert, a boy of fifteen years old, to the Episcopal See of Riga.

Profiting by political and religious troubles, Cardinal Commendoni, the Nuncio, endeavoured to make the King, in 1564, and the Senate accept without any restriction, reservation, or preliminary discussion, the decrees of the Council of Trent. These decrees were a chart of Papal omnipotence, against which the Gallican clergy protested. Some Polish doctors tried to prove that this council had never been recognised by Poland, as its decisions had never been ratified by the Diet, and only been accepted by the King and the Senate. This was in one sense true; but dating from this epoch all the Lithuanian clergy based their acts and dispositions on the tenour of these decrees. The Polish government had never opposed them, and the Court of Rome considered, and with reason, that the decrees of Trent were in full vigour as much in Poland as in Lithuania. If they had not been presented to the Diet, it is probably because that at this time the Diet was composed principally of Calvinists. The clergy had accepted them with only one single condition, namely, that the restriction preventing ecclesiastics enjoying a plurality of benefices should be done away with, as well as the injunction requiring them to reside in their parishes. This condition was so stringently insisted on that Commendoni was persuaded that they would rather abandon the faith altogether than accept them without it. "The Kingdom of Poland," he wrote, "resembles a sick man who at first submits to bad treatment, and who at length arrives at such a state that medicines no longer act on him. To-day the treatment but accelerates his death."

Seeing the clergy in no position to struggle against the Reformation, the Nuncio induced Sigismond Augustus to despatch the Jesuits to Lithuania; and with the King's consent, he wrote to Lainez, the General of the Order, to send professors of Theology, Philosophy, Mathematics, and the Sciences to Wilna; but religious discord and the war with Russia postponed the execution of this design to another ôpportunity.

After the death of the celebrated Calvinist Prince Nicolas Radzivill, surnamed the Black, the Latin party took heart; and four years later Bishop Protassewicz called the Jesuits to Wilna, and, in 1569, applied them without delay to the conversion of dissenters and the instruction of youth. The following year they opened their college in a house belonging to the Church of St. John, and, in 1579, it was erected by Pope Gregory XIII. into a university. *" Ad fidei orthodoxæ propugnaculum, civitatis ornamentum felicissimum, totiusque provinciæ decus."* It enjoyed the same rights and privileges as the university of Cracow, and Sigismond III., left it to his library. These immunities were afterwards enlarged by Augustus II. and III. In 1580, Polotsk was founded, the first rector of which was Skarga, the celebrated Jesuit preacher. In 1584, Prince Nicolas Christopher Radzivill laid the first stone of the Jesuitical college at Neswez, which was opened in 1595. In a short

time the whole country was filled with religious
houses and schools of all ~~with~~ sorts. The Jesuits
consolidated themselves everywhere, establishing
seminaries richly endowed in twenty of the chief
towns, besides their numerous missions. The
education of youth was not their principal aim, but
only a means of arriving at the realization of their
ambitious views. Their resources were constantly
increased by splendid legacies and donations, and
King Etienne Bathory, their great Protector,
conferred vast estates on them in the neighbourhood of Polotsk, and these estates were considerably
extended from the time of Sigismond III. The
Radzivills, Sapiehas, Khotkeiwicz and other noble
families left them important legacies. The more
easily to obtain their ends, they influenced both the
aristocracy and the sovereign, and completely succeeded with Sigismond III. During the thirty
years' reign of this prince they disposed, so to speak,
of the affairs of the State, the only desire of the
King being to please them. To proselytise the
lower orders, they translated their liturgy and
religious books into the national language, built
convents, and worked false miracles, so that in the
course of the seventeenth century more new saints
were canonized in Lithuania than in all the preceding centuries.

Soon after their arrival in the country, many of the great families who had abjured Romanism re-entered the pale of the Church; and those who had been the most fervent defenders of Calvinism became the zealous adepts of these priests, whose churches they enriched by splendid offerings. The son of Prince Niĉolas Radzivill the Black, the powerful protector of the Calvinists, at whose expense the Bible had, in 1563, been printed in Polish at Breslau, passed over to Romanism, chased the ministers from their properties of Neswez, Olyka, Kleck, and others, and gave their churches to the Jesuit clergy, together with their printing-presses and libraries. In the course of the reign of Sigismond III., the half of the Calvinist nobility seceded to Rome, and the year of the death of this Prince did not find one single dissenter in the Senate.

The Calvinists were not the only sufferers by this dominant clergy: the inhabitants belonging to the Greek faith were equally persecuted and proselytised. From the time of Jagellon, the Greek Church in Lithuania had been oppressed by the Latin priesthood, who, not content with despoiling the Church, levied tithes upon the parishioners, and afterwards actually upon the Orthodox clergy themselves. But Orthodoxy was widely and firmly rooted in the country, for Heberstein and Guag-

nini inform us that in Wilna there were more
Russian churches than Roman Catholic ones; and
even under Etienne Bathory there were already
thirty Orthodox places of worship in Wilna.
The most illustrious houses of Lithuania, those of
Chodkiewicz, Pouzyna, Tyszkiewicz, Chreptowicz,
Czartoryski, and several others, belonged to the
Greek confession. Even in our own time we
find existing monuments of the days when the
Russian faith was the faith of many of the Lithuanian nobility. In the Greek convent of the
Holy Trinity at Wilna there is a vault belonging
to the family of Tyszkiewicz; and two miles from
Bialostok, rose the beautiful convent of Souprasc,
built in 1506 after the model of St. Sophia of
Constantinople, by Alexander Chodkiewicz, which
belonged to the Greek religion. Many other
monuments of the same kind are to be found in
Lithuania. The acts of the Council of Florence,
1438, which proclaimed the union of the two
churches, here remained a dead letter, as nobody
was disposed to execute it. The Greek Church
maintained itself as before, sustained as it was by
the advice and the personal visits of the Patriarch
of Constantinople, and partly by the influence of
Russia.

The ill success of the Council of Florence in

Lithuania was attributed, without reason, to the marriage of the Grand Duke Alexander to the Princess Helena, daughter of John III., Grand Duke of Moscow. The suite of this princess was composed only of persons belonging to her own faith, and, notwithstanding the exertions of the Polish priests, and of the Pope himself, she remained faithful to her Creed. The Lithuanian magnates, not strong enough to oppose the religious persecution to which they were exposed, ever found a refuge at Moscow; but the people, notwithstanding their convictions, fell in the struggle before the activity of the Jesuits, who, armed with the subtlest theology, influenced by fanaticism, and backed by the King, pushed them within the pale of the Roman Church, and called their violence conversion. Nor was Lithuania the only field they attacked. Not confining their activity to this province alone, they endeavoured to force themselves into the Russian provinces—into the Ukraine, Podolia, Volhynia, etc., and actually succeeded in founding the colleges of Luck, Bar, Kamienec, Winnica and other places where they definitely established themselves. They received gifts of money and of land; collections were raised for them, and all to facilitate the conversion of the peasants to Romanism. Their tactics were to Romanise first the confines of the country, beginning by the frontier of Lithuania and Russia; and it was with this intention they directed their steps towards the Ukraine. White Russia was invaded with the same view, although at the beginning of the seventeenth century they had only carried two points, Polotsk and Orsza.

While everything seemed to promise the Jesuits rapid success for the future, the Greek Church, which defended itself alone against their attacks, had little hope of receiving any solid assistance from any quarter. Constantinople was distant; Moscow, absorbed by her own affairs, could afford no efficient succour against an enemy always in the breach. Nothing therefore remained to Lithuania but her own defence, the patience of her people, and the firmness of the clergy who guided them. Their patience was indeed great, and grand was their faith in this hour of trial; but unfortunately the priesthood did not correspond to the demands of this most critical period. Poor, oppressed, badly instructed, without political rights, they often wanted even bread to sustain their very existence. A contemporary reproaches them, rouses them, and expostulates with them thus:—

"Pastors, you sleep, and the enemy is at your gates! Oh, doctors and guides of your flock, until

when will ye remain deaf? Until your sheep be
devoured? We suffer, not because we want bread,
but the Divine Word. It is not physical thirst
which consumes us, but thirst for evangelical
preaching. We are deprived of our Lord and
Prophet—of chief and pastor. There are pastors,
it is true, but only in name and not in fact. Some
of the pastors of the flock of Christ would make
better shepherds for a troop of asses! Ah, poor
flock! Can he be Pastor and Master, who himself
has never been taught; who does not comprehend
his duty towards God and his neighbour? How
can he offer service for his people, who from his
tender infancy has not studied the Gospel, but has
passed his time in idleness, or things incompatible
with the ecclesiastical dignity? He has entered the
priesthood because oppressed by want, having
neither food nor clothes, without the least idea of
the sacerdotal character, or comprehending the
sanctity of his mission. One comes from the
cabaret, another from the service of the noble,
some from the soldiery, and even from the very
peasantry, without any election or any certificate of
fitness for the Divine Office. Such are the people
we have for guides and pastors. Dying of famine
themselves they know not how to feed others.
Blind, they offer themselves as guides. Lame of

both feet, they would sustain and support others; ignorant they take upon themselves the instruction of the people!"

The testimony of another impartial contemporary, Prince Koursky, fully confirms this picture of the Greek clergy, at the time of the introduction of the Union into Lithuania. He says that the priests often passed their time in the cabarets, and pillaged the churches, and that he tried in vain to find any capable of translating the works of St. John Chrysostom into Slavonian. And Smotricky complains that, "attracted by simony the priesthood is conferred on children of fifteen years;" and again he says, "It is notorious that, contrary to all common sense, we make children priests who have almost the milk of infancy on their lips. They do not know the alphabet, and we send them to preach the Word of God; they cannot manage their own estate, and we give them the administration of the Church! What shall I say," he continues, " of the convents and the monks subordinate to me, who, disregarding the holy rules ot their Order—rules once strictly observed by their predecessors, have trampled them under foot, so that not a vestige remains of this pious profession, of a life vowed to privation and devoted to prayer, to charitable works and to the teaching of the Holy Scriptures? Unfortunate man that I am! How shall I render an account to the Lord in the day of judgment !"

Such pastors could hardly be dangerous antagonists for the Jesuits who, having already destroyed the Reformation, were backed not only by powerful protectors but were seconded by the Polish government. The complete fusion of Lithuania with Poland at a time coinciding with the arrival of the Jesuits at Wilna, drew the country still more towards Romanism, and repelled it from Moscow. Subjected to partial violence—robbed of the churches of the Greek rite—persecuted individually and collectively, the general and open struggle of the two priesthoods burst out at the period of the introduction of the New Calendar.

The people, uneducated and ignorant of science, knew nothing whatever of astronomy, and only saw in this innovation an arbitrary and useless change of fêtes and fasts, and in short, of all their customs. And more civilized people who understood better, looked below the surface, and regarded it as the commencement of the alteration of the rites of their Church, rites as old as their Christianity, which had come down to them from their forefathers, and were bound up with their own social and political life. The discontent was so general and so threatening, that Etienne Bathory, who had introduced it, renounced its extension to the followers of the Greek faith, 1584. It is recounted by a writer of the orthodox creed, who lived at this period, that Prince Constantine D'Ostrog, the celebrated Protector of the Greek Church, arrived at Gorodnia, and had a long interview with the King, who received him very graciously, and informed him that the Pope had sent a brief on the subject of the introduction of the New Calendar amongst the Russians. "He could not do that," answered D'Ostrog, "without a preliminary conference with the Eastern Patriarchs." "That is also my opinion," replied Bathory. "The Russian people aid us in peace as in time of war; it is therefore necessary to leave them in peace. The introduction of the New Calendar among the followers of the Greek rite, subjecting them to the Pope, so far from drawing the two classes together, would only disunite them. I will not therefore introduce novelties. Everything shall remain as before."

Sigismond III. and the Jesuits saw matters in a different light; they only waited an opportune moment to entrap some of the Greek bishops and execute the decisions and prescriptions of the Council of Florence, for a long time forgotten in Lithuania. They fell upon a suitable instrument

in the persons of Ipatius Pocej, Bishop of Vladimir
and through him influenced several others, particularly Terlecsky, Bishop of Luck, and the
Metropolitan, Michael Ragosa. Without consulting
either the Eastern Patriarchs or their co-religionists
in Russia, they called a Council at Brescia, with
the design of submitting their Church to the
Pope. When the people became aware of it, they
surrounded the place, yelled and hooted, and summoned the apostate prelates to account for their
intentions, effectually preventing the opening of
the assembly at the time appointed. But force
and the sovereign authority dispersed the crowd,
and the Council sat hurriedly and carried its
resolutions, fearing the intervention of Russia.
Pocej and Terlecsky set off for Rome and presented
the Pope the Act by which the Greek Church of
Lithuania recognised the supremacy of Rome.
We note here the illegality of these proceedings:
first, that this decision was arrived at without
preliminary consultation with the Patriarchs, the
recognised heads of the Greek faith; and secondly,
that it was despatched to Rome though unsigned
and unattested by the principal bishops belonging
to the country itself.

It was then that the Court of Rome proclaimed
the Union. This union of the two Churches might

at first sight appear advantageous enough for the
Greeks, who still preserved their ecclesiastical
language and ceremonies, and even retained some
of the dogmatical expressions and sacerdotal
practices different to those of the Latin Church.
The priests and bishops remained in their districts,
and the Metropolitan was secured the right of
consecrating bishops without nomination by the
Pope. The Latin priests could not officiate in the
services, even supposing they used the Sclave
language. One might well say at first glance that
the union of the two Churches only consisted in
the recognition of the Pope, and in the prayers
offered up for him in the churches in place of the
Patriarch of Constantinople. The dogmas, the
rites, and the clergy were unchanged; and the
Latins said that the union did not signify the
fusion of the two Churches into one, but that a
species of convention had been concluded between
them. Apparently nothing was changed; the
images occupied their places; the people saw
the same ceremonies and the same priests to
which they had been accustomed. But in
reality the true dogmas of the Greek faith
had been invaded or destroyed by this union;
as according to the bull of the Pope, the rites and
doctrines of the Greek Church could be preserved

in so far as they were not contrary to the Roman Church. At first the execution of this important clause was not insisted on, Rome in this matter displaying an amount of circumspection, patience, and sagacity, rarely met with in the history of politico-religious reorganisations. An official recognition of the Pope was all she exacted, reserving all the rest for a more propitious period. The main object was accomplished, and the consequences would be developed in a peaceful manner, and gradually brought into play as opportunities occurred, while Rome did not infringe the basis of her own peculiar system.

The two Bulls of Rome, published at the same time on the occasion of the Union, evince how she counted on the ignorance of the people in religious affairs, and on the possibility of drawing them over to Latinism in a dishonourable manner. In one of them, destined for public inspection, she permits the united Greeks the celebration of all their rites and ceremonies according to custom; in the other, on the contrary, she discovers a broad programme of the future working of the machinery of the Greek Union. The Pope obliged the Bishops Pocej and Terlecsky to take an oath in presence of all the cardinals, that they believed in the Procession of the Holy Spirit *from the Father and from the Son*, as well as in purgatory—in the communion in one kind—that the sacraments are not really efficacious unless celebrated according to the rites and ordinances of Rome; that indulgences should be recognised as one of the most holy institutions of the Church; that they should adopt the decisions of the Council of Trent, inculcating this doctrine amongst their people. All this they swore by their Maker on the Holy Gospel. Thus there were two doctrines—the ostensible and public for the people; and the other—the private one for the priests, who took an oath on the Evangelists to guide their flocks into ignorance and error. As to the fundamental basis of their faith, both doctrines as if identical were confirmed under the name of the Union by the one who styled himself the Vicar of Christ, that is to say the representative of the God of pity, of justice, and of love.

It was not enough, however, to convoke a council, and draw up acts. Rome must have the Union recognised; and this was precisely the most difficult point of all. When the people of the Greek rite knew the decisions of the Council of Brescia, both ecclesiastics and laymen presented petitions to the Diet and the provincial courts, refusing obedience to the apostate bishops, whom they accused of having arbitrarily sworn to the

Union without previously consulting their co-religionists; of being the allies of Rome, and of having committed acts the most reprehensible, and done things which nobody could have imagined them capable of doing. The Patriarchs of Alex- andria and Constantinople, when they knew what had taken place, exhorted the people by pastoral briefs to remain faithful to the creed of their fathers; and expressed their indignation against the traitors. Melitius of Alexandria wrote to Pocej himself, denouncing the abandonment of his co-religionists, telling him that while leaving his own people he had not even satisfied Rome. "Besides," he argued, "what pleasure can it be to minister to a flock that does not recognise you as a pastor?" The most of the priesthood remained firm. But upon the national soil appeared a force which threatened the Jesuits: it was only one man, it is true, but he was himself a legion. This was Prince Constantine D'Ostrog, whose voice Podolia, Wilna, and the Volhynia well knew. Pocej had tried to induce him to adopt his views. Some time before the Council of Brescia, he endeavoured to gain his good graces, to tranquillise him, and to set the question at issue in another light. But the Prince refused to admit him to his presence, and made his secretary reply to his

letters. The Jesuits had two means of persuasion at their disposal—theological activity and
force; they had even the government to 'fall back
upon; and they used the one or the other according
to the circumstances, or to the classes of society
they desired to act upon. The common people
were driven by means of police agents, deprived of
all civil rights, and "converted" from the orthodox
faith by violence. The Greek churches were meta-
morphosed into Roman chapels. "They deprive
us of our last shirts," cried the pastors of the
orthodox rite. "We give them with pleasure and
remain naked, but our consciences are pure." With
the nobility they acted otherwise; attracting them
with the bait of temporal advantages, employments,
and dignities, and met with great success; these
joined the Church of Rome so rapidly, that in the
space of ten or fifteen years the best Lithuanian
families of the Greek Church—the princes of Sluck,
the Czartoryskies, the Ibarazs, the Sangouszkas, the
Pronskies, Chreptowiczs, and others—had entered
the Catholic faith. Thirty years after the commencement of the Union, the inhabitants were professed
en masse; the parents remaining in the old religion,
while their children were already Catholic! Even
the son of Prince D'Ostrog abjured his faith. But
against force the people sometimes equally employed

force ; they beat and often killed the Latin priests as well as those of the Union, while defending their churches at the risk of their lives.

A pastor of the Greek Church traces the following picture of the state of the Church at this time in Lithuania. After having personified it, he exclaims;—"Alas, I am poor, miserable, and robbed of all my possessions! Pity me, exposed naked to public shame, and laden with a burden beyond endurance. Fetters on my wrists, a yoke round my neck, chains about my body, the sword above my head, my feet steeped in deep waters, fire around me, tremblings, terror, and persecution in and before my eyes. Calamities in the cities, in the fields, in the villages, in the valleys, on the mountains, in no part can I find rest or tranquillity. I pass the days in sickness and sufferings because of my wounds; the nights in tremblings and sighs. In the summer I suffer so much from the heat that I am exhausted; in the winter I endure mortal cold. For I am naked and am cruelly persecuted unto death. Once I was exalted and rich ; now I am poor and maltreated. Of old a queen, beloved of all, now persecuted and ridiculed. Come to me, oh people! Run towards me, ye who stand upon the earth, hear my voice, learn what I have been, and be

astonished. Once I was the wonder of men and
angels; now I am the laughter of the world. I
was adorned above all others; beautiful and adored.
I was like the Aurora of morning; brilliant as the
moon, radiant as the sun. The only daughter of
my mother, I was her darling child, pure as a
flower. Seeing me, the daughters of Sion proclaimed me the blessed Queen. I was among the
maidens of Sion, as Jerusalem in the midst of
Judea! Amongst virgins, I was as the lily; and
the King, more beautiful than all other men upon
the earth, marvelled at my loveliness, loved me
and united himself to me in marriage. Children
were born o⸴ me and brought up, but they have
turned from me, denied me, and exposed me to
laughter and ridicule. They stole my vestments
and chased me from home. They stoned me and
tore the diadem from my brow. Night and day
they wearied my soul, and considered only how to
despoil me. Oh, ye who see me, is there any
sorrow that surpasses mine? Sovereign of the
East, of the West, of the North, and of the South,
in the olden days, here I stand a weeping widow.
I cry night and day, and tears fall down my cheeks
like rain. Yet there is nobody to console me.
All abandon me. My kinsmen are banished from
me, my friends have become my enemies, and my

sons, like hideous reptiles, poison my existence with their venom."

Proceeding by intrigues and insinuations, the Jesuits, though backed by the civil power, had recourse at the same time to the Polemic, which they directed equally against the Calvinists, but after the introduction of the Union, particularly against the Greek Church. The Russian clergy, educated in the harsh school of persecution and adversity, and inferior to them in address and cunning, could not always reply to their theological attacks, as they were badly prepared. Smotricky, indignant at them, thus rebukes them :—

"I ask you, why you are silent before your accusers? Why do you not defend yourselves? Why not refute these accusations? Your calumniators neither honour nor believe you, and you have not one word to say to such infamies. Say at once, What will you do? You hear and you understand nothing. You have eyes and you see nothing. You pay no attention to things which concern you. Tell me, has not nature given you a tongue? Why are you distinguished from other beings by speech? When beasts are maltreated, devoid of reason though they be, they nevertheless defend themselves and show their sentiments by every means in their power. And you? you have reason and language, created in the likeness of God, yet you hear and you see the Holy Truth insulted and humiliated, calumniated and defamed, and you are silent ! "

The Union created a theological Polemic—a thing very little studied until then by Russian savans, but remarkable for various features. In presenting new historical facts, it revealed the state of society of that era, and the respective position and ability of the two priesthoods. The limits of this work will not permit us to enter into details on this subject; we confine ourselves merely to an enumeration of the most important works on both sides. Amongst the writings of the Greek Church we may mention " L'Antigraph " (Wilna: 1608); "Les Doléances " of Smotricky (Wilna: 1610); " L'Apocrisis " and " La Palinodie " (1621), etc., etc. The Catholic and united Greek clergy cleverly sustained their arguments in the " Antirchesis," and in the works of Smotricky after he embraced the Union ; particularly in " L'Apologie," " The Parænisis," " The Exsetesis "(1628-29), and later in " The Hiérarchie " of Donbowicz, 1644, as well as in the writings of some preachers of the Order of the Jesuits.

This wordy war was but an accompaniment to the rencontres in places of public resort ; rencontres

in the streets, in the villages, in the private houses ;
resulting from the pretensions of the Latin clergy.
The writings of some of the Greek party were
certainly not free from inexactness in the explanations of the dogmas of their Church. Many of
them were not even accepted at Moscow; nevertheless the Lithuanians received them with enthusiasm,
regarding their authors as their defenders against
the ecclesiastical tyranny they had to endure ; the
common people kissed the books, considering them
sacred.   But the struggle was not equal.   The
Catholics and united Greeks could with impunity
defame their opponents, publishing the most aggra-
vating and exaggerated calumnies ; but the Russians
could be prosecuted by the police. Nevertheless
some of the anti-Russian writings demonstrate, with
a certain amount of talent and moderation, the
inexactness of their antagonists. The essence of
the Latin polemic consisted in a refutation of the
principal dogmas of the orthodox creed, non-con-
formable to Roman doctrine ; proofs to the contrary
formed the subject of the Russian polemic. Besides
this the Latins and their coadjutors, the united
Greeks, endeavoured to stigmatise the Eastern
Church, and to attract to their own by the bait of
material advantages. These accusations are so
little creditable to the Catholic party, and so utterly

unfounded, that we shall not stop to examine them,
only succinctly deducting some of their gravest
assertions taken from the polemical writings.
They said, for example, that the Greek monks were
permitted to live with the wives of other people;
that they killed and imprisoned their bishops ; that
they did not fear God ; and obeyed neither King nor
authority. The Latins mocked some of the rites
of the Greek Church. To this the Russian clergy
replied: "If the rites of our Church are so
absurd, why then are they preserved by the Council
of Florence, which sought the re-union of the two
Churches. This re-union would consequently be
only a mask and a means of entrapping the lower
classes. If the united Greeks believe that the rites
and dogmas of the Church of Rome be better founded
than those of the Eastern Church, why do they not
entirely abandon the old rites and ceremonies of
their fathers, and freely and openly unite themselves
to Rome ? How can one call one's-self a son of a
mother whom one degrades ? Why swear to keep
and preserve rites which are considered absurd ?

The partisans of the Roman Church endeavoured
to prove its superiority over the Eastern faith by
the argument that, after the conquest of Constantinople by the Turks, the clergy were no longer a
recognised and official body, having been deprived

of their churches, of liberty of conscience, and persecuted, while at the same time the Church of Rome remained independent. The latter must therefore be the Church of God, as the Greeks, having passed under the Ottoman rule, could not preserve entire unity of faith.

The reply was, that the excellence of the Church of Christ did not consist in its freedom from the persecution of the infidels, for that these infidels could neither build up nor destroy that which was founded on the Rock of Christ. Persecution, however, had but rooted it more stedfastly, and it would be unworthy of glory if it flourished continually in repose. He only is worthy who, having intrepidly sustained the combat and repelled the foe, collects his forces and returns in triumph to his home. The Church of Christ is the more glorious, in that she repulsed the masses of infidels who have assailed her. In her internal organisation, if amongst her Patriarchs one was found unworthy his high vocation, he was deprived of his dignity; but the faults of one single occupant of the Patriarchal Chair never prejudiced the whole community, there being besides four Patriarchs, and not one ruler as in the Church of Rome, where the Pope is the visible Head; and once the Head is attacked, the body is prejudiced, and the members suffer also. " But it appears," wrote the Russians, "that the Latins have never understood true faith." If it be a sentiment intimate, invisible, eternal, implanted within us by the immortal God, how can it be destroyed or done away with by mortal man? Christ's words are, " Have no fear of those who kill the body, but rather of that which kills the soul." Faith would be vain; our hopes vain, as well as those of all the elect of God, who through it have endured persecution and death; the Fathers of the Church and the early martyrs, who cruelly lost their lives by the sword and the fire, if the purity of this divine sentiment could be destroyed by man. If the Eastern Church ceased to exist from the moment that the Turks subdued Greece, and Christianity fell under the yoke of the infidel, it is indisputable that there has been consequently no true Church since the time of the Apostles, when the followers of the true God had no religious liberty, but were persecuted and cruelly used, and when there did not exist one Christian sovereign, notwithstanding which the Church of Christ flourished like a rose. Such remarks reflect on the Apostle Peter, whose succession, they say, has descended to the Pope, as he had no temporal power, nor the immense riches enjoyed by his *soi-disant* successors, but was until his death a martyr bearing the cross of distress, persecution, and suffering. Paul, too, the elect of God, the model of all patience and humility, did he not accept the yoke of slavery? His kingdom was not of this world. Did he not pay tribute to the temporal power? And are we not taught that the servant cannot be above his master?

With respect to the accusation of ignorance amongst the Greek clergy, the Roman priesthood was asked if in respect to instruction they themselves surpassed the Lutherans and Calvinists? The ancient philosophers were wise, but their philosophical system was extinguished before the light of Evangelical Truth. "As to ourselves," said the Russians, "we try to be only humble Christians after the example of the anchorites of the first century, who were not learned."

It was announced that in accepting the Union, the clergy and people received political rights, and were eligible for government situations. Replies to such methods of conviction in matters of faith were not difficult.

The Jesuits headed the Latin polemic, though other ecclesiastics helped them. Greek and Roman Catholics devoted their efforts to the same cause, but it was essentially the priests of this famous Order who communicated life and spirit to these controversies. It was, therefore, natural that the Russians should regard them as the real authors of their persecution, and that they applied themselves with energy to study the faults and failings of these men and expose them to the eyes of the public.

"The means which these Fathers employ to multiply and extend their possessions," said the Russians, "are well known. They gain them by tricks, by entreaties, and by violence, and all this under the appearance of right. They ruin the nobles, who believe them liberal and independent, and despoil those of bread who have earned it by the sweat of their brow. We do not hesitate to say that all the local authorities, all the tribunals, not excepting the diet, are filled with complaints against the Jesuits. Nobles expelled and banished from their estates; widows deprived of their dowries; children ruined in their minority, all bear witness against them. "It is for the church," they say, "therefore go and beg. It is for the college; go, father and mother, do what thou canst. It is for religious consolations; therefore, brothers and sisters, go out into the world and earn thy bread amongst strangers. It is for the Holy Father; therefore, man, take thy wife and children, despoil thyself of thine own food, and go and beg with the others." These Intriguants take all, seize all, gather all, and peacefully enjoy their ill-gotten gains, for they depend on Rome only, and it is only at Rome that they can be judged or a decree given against them. " So, poor noble, sell thy last estate, take thy wife and children to protest at Rome, and if thou dost not die of famine on the way, thou wilt return with empty pockets."

These accusations were not the fruit of a blind and bitter animosity; even fervent Catholics soon discovered all the evil which the Order brought to Poland.   They reproached the Jesuits with meddling in State affairs; with using their illimitable influence over Sigismond III., to secure places and appointments for their adepts; and loudly accused their cupidity, the discords and animosities they excited in private and in public life, their egotistic views, their pretended restitution of the privileges of the nobility; so that, in 1606, this spirit of opposition to them was so developed that a project existed amongst the Catholic community to deprive them of the education of the young, and to expel them from Lithuania.   Public indignation was so general and so strong against them, that at length they were forced to defend themselves publicly. It may be guessed without much difficulty, that they termed the accusations brought against them, calumnies; declared that they never meddled in politics; pretended that their integrity and their charity had reduced them to mendicity, as they often refused even what was offered them; that they raised no discords, and only defended and guaranteed the existence of their establishments; that they violated none of the privileges of the nobility, and only supported their own. But even their justification of themselves proved the truth of some of the accusations against them—accusations as commonly found in other Catholic countries into which they have been admitted, and on account of which they have even been expelled. They said, that so far from interesting themselves in mundane affairs, they occupied their hours only guiding the conscience of the sovereign, which is essentially the prerogative and vocation of the clergy, and for which they quoted an antecedent in St. Louis, who consulted theologians on the gravest affairs of the State. Ecclesiastics, they said, were worthy of honour, who, without pretending to nominate to places of trust, recommended honest people; in short, it was only sovereigns, acting under clerical inspiration, who could really prove a benefit to their country; and those who have not followed these counsels had seen their empires and their power decay. These

justifications convinced nobody, and served them
far less than the powerful protection of Sigismond,
who, while he lived, defeated all efforts to put limits
to the power of these priests. His son Vladislas
regarded them in another light. Indignant at their
intrigues in the affairs of the government of his
father, he not only banished them from his court,
but opposed the Peares to them—an order also
engaged in educational pursuits—brought them to
Poland, and introduced them into Lithuania. But
notwithstanding the royal protection accorded to
these latter, the Jesuits triumphed in the end,
and in 1738 compelled them to close their colleges.
Only the power of the Pope could put an end to this
pernicious Order, which had filled Lithuania with
fanaticism and ignorance under the mask of theological civilization. Until 1773. the Jesuits represented the Roman hierarchy in Lithuania ; they
were the most active propagandists and the most
implacable persecutors of all other Christian confessions ; so that really the history of this body
in Western Russia is the most detailed history of
the Roman Church herself in this region, while they
sojourned there. They nominated not only to high
ecclesiastical dignities, but even to the curacies ;
they governed the entire Latin clergy in every sense
of the word, exercising by their wealth an irresis-

tible influence over the people, as well as by their
system of education, their preaching, and their
writings, which were specially destined for the
masses. A curious specimen of the means to which
they had recourse for the latter purpose exists in·
what is called "Les Calendriers des Jésuits," a
sort of monthly obituary of their monks and saints,
with details of their merits, their visions, their miracles performed during life and after death. These
writings are so strongly characteristic, that it may
not be superfluous to quote some extracts :—

1. Cardinal Stanislas Hosius, who first called
the Jesuits to Poland, and is styled the Father of
the Order. He died at Rome, in 1579, in the glory
of holiness.

2. Shirivid, died also in great sanctity at Wilna,
August 23rd, 1631.

3. Guinkewicz died in the same city, August 4th,
1663, in all holiness. He was rector of the College
of Neswiz.

4. The body of Gawronsky, who died April 11th,
1610, at Posen, was found intact.

5. December 5th, 1656, Starocirsky appeared
after death to one of the Jesuits, then a prisoner
of the Swedes, and exhorted him to merit eternal
life by patience.

6. October 3rd, 1591, Warzewicky, the first

rector of the College of Wilna, the tutor of Sigismond III., who had converted several Polish lords and many Lithuanians to Romanism, appeared after death with an areole of glory round his head to the Jesuit Peter Skarga.

7. May 23rd, 1615. It is said of Lasco, that he was a laborious ånd happy missionary; that he drew all the magistrates of Cracow to his church, and was the author of the decree by which dissenters were excluded from the Senate.

8. December, 1652. It is said of Ryninsky, that he was the son of honest but schismatic parents, and the servant of a gentleman belonging to the Catholic Church, with whom he went to Czenstohowo. During Mass, the devil, having perceived him, cried, " Behold our brother, there ; let me enter him also." Nearly frightened out of his senses, he embraced Catholicism, and became a Jesuit.

9. September 27th, 1612. The celebrated preacher, Skarga, was ill eight months before his death, and once saw St. Ignatius, St. Francis Xavier, and Warzewicky, who had died long before, beside his bed. They recommended him to pray to God to prolong his life for his own glory. Before his death, he, with his own hands, made a white wax taper which he sent to the

Convent of Czenstohowo, to be placed before the image of the Virgin. The moment this taper was consumed, he yielded up his soul to God.

10. June 16th, 1619. After the death of Sykoul, he was seen to ascend to heaven accompanied by St. Ignatius, St. Xavier, and St. Louis de Gonzague.

11. August 23rd, 1635. Several persons in the act of prayer, saw Bartilius, who was endued by God with the gift of prophecy, ascend to glory. During his life, he went one day in a shower of rain to Loretto, but not one drop fell on him.

12. July 27th, 1597. The right hand of Wouek, which had written much for the glory of God, was found entire many years after his death!

13. May 3rd, 1597. Brounowsky, Woinicz, Krasnostawsky, and Domagalsky, laborious missionaries, were killed by the schismatic Russians in a forest in Galicia, at a time when they fervently worked with much zeal to draw them to the Union. On the spot where they were buried, there was seen for a whole hour, a lamp which gradually rose towards heaven.

14. Kostha was invited by the Holy Virgin to enter the Order of the Jesuits. He was twice fed by angels with the Body of Jesus Christ, and was caught up to Heaven in 1568.

15. August 17th, 1721. The Swedes themselves recount the miracles made by Loukaszewicz, as for example, that he passed dry through the rivers Willa and Arzica. The particular but doubtful merit is attributed to him, that he never drank anything but beer!

16. Sousliga saw in a vision the Virgin and the infant Jesus, who said to him, "Sousliga, ask what thou wilt." To which he replied, "No other thing than to be eternally with thee." To this Christ answered, "Thou shalt be." But Sousliga replied, "I have no confidence in myself, Lord, I am a sinner." "Take my hand," said Christ, "as a testimony that thou shalt be with me eternally." He caught Christ's hand, and ascended with him to Heaven, November 27th, 1623.

So wrote the Jesuits of themselves, after which it is not difficult to form an idea of how they imposed on the people, on the subject of their Order, in their conversations, their sermons, and in the confessional. Apparently, they were believed by the masses, otherwise one cannot imagine or explain the appearance of such writings so far from truth and the real humility of Christianity.

It was not to Poland but to Rome that the Jesuits rendered effective services in augmenting the number of Romanists, in converting Calvinists, in introducing the Union, and in developing a proselytising spirit with tendencies towards ecclesiastical omnipotence conformable to the instincts of Catholicism. In completely prostrating the fundamental laws of the State, the Latin clergy tended at the same time to aggrandise the ecclesiastical power abroad, and for this purpose employed exterior pomp, which has always an immense effect on the people. With this aim they established dioceses even in countries where other Christian churches dominated, and where Romanism had very little chance of taking root. The senses were besieged by the pomp of the episcopal court, with its canons and its prelates, its solemn processions, its fêtes, and all the grandeur and glitter it could muster, to attract to Latinism. But the interior organisation of the clergy corresponded in nothing with their exterior pretension. The bishops, independent of the civil power, were often powerless in their own administration. The monastic orders were exempt from their authority; their provincials themselves sometimes far from the district if not absolutely out of the country. For example; of the eight convents of the Benedictines in Lithuania, seven were subordinate to the Benedictine congregation of Koulm, while that of Irock depended on the congregation of Cluny. Very few of the religious Orders were exceptions to this rule ; one only may be mentioned, that of Latram, which depended on the bishops. The secular clergy, too, often disobeyed their bishops, and did not act conformably to their vocation. These disorders were not temporary or local ; they existed everywhere, as one can see by the Synodical ordinances of the principal Roman Catholic bishopric of Lithuania, Wilna, and by the episcopal letters of Bishop Wojna, 1601-13, of Eienne Pac, 1682, by the decisions of the Synod of 1679, under bishop Matthew Sapicha. In all these documents the bishops discuss the sorrowful state of the clergy ; but it was difficult to attempt an amelioration, as they did not possess sufficient authority. The High Clergy, who formed the chapter, occupied themselves with the management of their vast estates; and the subject of their deliberations consisted almost exclusively in the sale or exchange of their lands, in economical calculations, in processes, lawsuits, etc., etc. But with all that, the administration of these estates was so defective, that very often their employés did not receive their appointments for years ; and the subsidy which the government claimed from the clergy, commonly called *Subsidium Charitativium* was not paid, while the peasants were often ruined by the Jews who farmed the lands. A still greater evil existed in the relations of the clergy with the government and with the other classes of society, particularly the Noblesse.

In *Status* the clergy were not subordinate to the civil authority; and they lived in constant antagonism with the Lithuanian nobles, not considering themselves, so to speak, a part of the Kingdom of Poland.

In the eighteenth century the animosity between the clergy and the nobility, attained its last limits. The laity refused the interest which the clergy hypothetically laid upon their lands, made raids upon the ecclesiastical property, ravaged it, and often came to blows with the monks and the priests. The influence of the clergy commenced visibly to decline, their weaknesses and their vices were brought before the public, and the Press became the medium of a lively polemic between the civil and ecclesiastical authorities. Then the tendencies of the priesthood first began to be manifest, and it was felt that they had compromised their position in the State. This polemic coincided extremely apropos with the appearance in France of the work "*dé la Borde*," a treatise upon the spiritual power. Benedict XIV. censured it, but nevertheless it spread both through Poland and Lithuania. Wyzicky, archbishop of Livoff, refuted it, and made the following remarks :—

" As in man the soul is more important than the body, so even the power of the Church is above the temporal power : therefore Pope Innocent III. compares these two powers to two celestial stars, that is, to the Sun and the Moon ; and says that the Church, as the principal star, illuminates the affairs of the State, and the civil authority, like a secondary star, lights the clouds of temporal vanities." One may thence conclude that the ecclesiastical power in nothing whatever depended on the civil authority, but, *au contraire*, that the latter was subordinate to the Church. The Archbishop continues :—" What are after all the rights and the obligations of the government with respect to the Church ? Its right—its obligation, is to defend her against heresy, not to tolerate liberty of conscience in the realm, for this liberty is ominous, and contrary to the doctrine of the Gospel and the Saviour who will have only one single Church —one flock and one visible Head. The government has the right and the obligation to spread the honour and the glory of God throughout the kingdom, that the dogmas of the true faith be received without discussion, that there be no judges in this matter which only concerns the superior ecclesiastical authority, acting as the simple agent of the Spiritual power, *executores ministri*. The Almighty God who vouchsafes the true doctrine to sovereigns has confided them to the clergy, as sheep to the shepherd, to be brought and guided. He gives them no authority over the Church, but on the contrary he orders them to obey her, as Esau said 'An infant shall govern kings;' which means that the humble clergy who have converted sovereigns to the true faith, shall govern them." From such logic the following consequences may be deduced :—That no sovereign has any right to meddle in the nomination of the bishops. On the contrary the bishops, as proprietors of the lands, enjoyed every political right, and could even make war, the works of the Dissenters should not be translated into the national language or printed in Catholic countries, as the celebrated Bull " In Cœna Domini " excommunicates those who read heretical works, the excommunication extending of course to the translators and printers.

The writers of this category explained the advantages the State derived from the clergy by the consideration, that it was they who supported the Noblesse, particularly in aristocratic States, where the estates were not entailed, but were divided equally among the children. " That a married noble " said Kowalsky, " may reside amongst us in manner suitable to his rank, it is necessary that he have at least ten thousand florins per annum, and even with such a sum, many complain of the insufficiency of their means.   The same noble becoming cure of even a small parish can live on the half of that sum.   If he enters a convent, even of a princely family, he can live there on less than a thousand florins, and it is both convenient and consistent with his rank.   If in such States all the nobles marry, there would come a time when to every hectare (two acres) there would be two nobles, and even now there are several who are mere artisans and agriculturists.   But look at the advantage that the nobility derive from having its members prelates and the occupants of lucrative ecclesiastical places.   1. Such ecclesiastics can cede, and often do cede, to their parents and relatives that part of the hereditary fortune belonging to them.   2. They assist them by the gifts and offerings which they receive.   3. They pass to them the revenues of their ecclesiastical estates :— it is true they are not permitted to enrich their relations at the expense of the Church; but on the other hand, as they help the indigent in general, they are justified in helping those most nearly related to them, who are poor." The Latin clergy as we have seen, only strengthened their own power by their riches; but the good time for them was passing away, it was exactly their riches and their power which roused society against them.

Already, in the seventeenth century, means began to be taken against their cupidity and their tendency to accumulate riches which would otherwise have been better employed in assisting the exigencies of the country. By the constitution of 1632 it was forbidden to alienate hereditary estates in favour of new ecclesiastical institutions, without the absolute authority of the Republic; but as the clergy constantly eluded this law, it was renewed at the several Diets of 1635, 1669, 1676, 1677, 1726; and in 1768 this measure became a fundamental law as said in the Constitution of 1676 :—"Without it the vital forces of the State are exhausted, the wellbeing and the defence of the State are endangered." Estates acquired by the clergy contrary to this law were confiscated; one half went to the informer, and the other to the treasury. In the second half of the eighteenth century, they limited the right of donation and of the legacies in favour of the clergy, by enacting that three parts of the fortune left by priests who died without a will should pass to their inheritors, and the quarter only go to the Church. As to nuns, the convents should receive nothing of their fortune, it should all return to their relatives. The tithe of sheaves was converted into a pecuniary obligation; the temporary subsidy of the clergy, known as the Subsidium Charitativium was recognised as a fixed tax, and the interest which one paid them in Poland was diminished to one half; but this measure did not extend to Lithuania. The stamp duty was levied upon Church property at the time of the transfer of such property from one priest to another. In short, the Diet of 1789 permitted the confiscation, for the benefit of the State, of Church property and ecclesiastical lands. Some curates contented themselves with fixed emoluments. In 1790, in conformity with the decision of the Diet, inventories were taken of the landed estates and livings held by the priesthood, certainly with the intention of secularising them.

Rome roused herself. Popes Clement XIV. and Pius VI. addressed letters to King Stanislas Augustus full of eulogies as to his piety, but representing all the misfortunes likely to result from the impoverishment of the clergy, through which they saw the decadence of the Church, and centred all their hopes on the King for the preservation of the rights of the Holy See. These briefs were generally sent at the opening of the Diets, as in 1784, at the time of the Diet of Grodno. But when Rome received news of the decision of this body, a decision which struck a terrible blow at the Church, she complained that now the bishops could be pillaged and chased from their estates, and wrote no more to the King, but to the Polish and Lithuanian Marshals and directly to the Diet itself.

These exhortations were of no use; they did not stop the decrees which had gone forth, but the imminent state of Poland left no time to execute them, and they were only realized half a century later by the Russian government. We may attribute these measures to the spirit of the age; to French literature, and the philosophy of the period; to the progress of mankind in liberty of conscience and political liberty—all contributed to the adoption, perhaps, of these measures; but there is no doubt that these were not the necessary causes which provoked them, and that these changes were only the inevitable consequence of a system which no longer permitted the absorption of the State by the Church. The clergy, by their greediness and their intervention in temporalities, had lost their ecclesiastical character; the result of which was that public opinion would no longer tolerate the privileges and riches of a priesthood useless to the Church, and a nuisance to Poland. Indeed, Poland herself was on the point of partition between the three frontier powers, and but a very few years later, her last hour had sounded. And what at this time did the rich and privileged clergy do? They demanded the abrogation of those restrictive enactments regarding landed estates, and the diminution of their taxes by the expiring Republic. At such a moment that their ambition required the confirmation of the political influence of their caste—at such a moment they complained that they were unrepresented in the Diet! This priesthood, after the first and second partition of the country, expressed themselves thus:—"How can we say 'country,' and love a country which, while favouring all other classes of society, only abases us?" The want of a guarantee for property —the constant fear that in a moment it may be diminished or done away with, is a great misfortune for man. Let us once more repeat: the Jesuits did everything for Rome and nothing for Poland; for the Polish priesthood belonged more to Rome than to their own country; they there formed more a caste than a class of society, and were more attached to the interests of the Pope than to those of their Fatherland.

As to the proceedings and acts of the Latin clergy towards Dissenters in the seventeenth and eighteenth centuries, we know that they availed themselves of the powers of conviction through the influence of the government, backed by violence. The pupils of the Jesuitical institutions were frequently employed as a material force against Dissenters. From the seventeenth century, Calvinism began to decline in Lithuania; the Protestant churches were more and more forsaken, and the clergy diminished. This decadence arose from two causes : interior, inherent to the organisation of the Calvinistic Church; exterior, to the influence of oppression on the part of the administration. This Church had no fixed centre. The convocation of the Synod could not supply the loss of a firmly established ecclesiastical authority. The appearance of new Sects, particularly of the Socinians who spread rapidly, weakened it farther. The two principal branches of this doctrine, Lutheranism and Calvinism, having no intimate ties between them, a union was not even possible, as the Calvinists were Poles, and the Lutherans were exclusively Germans. It is true that they had between them a species of Convention, concluded at Sandomir, 1570, afterward renewed in 1669 and in 1719, at Keidanj, but this alliance was, so to speak, merely formal and purely external; there was never an intimate and frank sympathy. Vladislas IV., conceived a project of conciliating the clergy of different confessions, and called the Council of Thorn in 1644, which, however, had a result quite different to what he hoped for; not only did no conciliation follow, but the ecclesiastics returned home more embittered against each other than ever. The Calvinist clergy were themselves the cause why their doctrine did not take deeper root in Lithuania, as they confined their activity solely to the upper classes and to the *Tiers-état* without troubling themselves to spread it among the masses of the people. To this internal weakness was added external persecution; as Dissenters were deprived of the right of sending deputies to the Diets, of holding government situations, and from 1717, from even having representatives in the tribunals, who might judge appeals between them and the Catholics. The Roman clergy, having deprived them of public worship, seized their churches and cited them before the tribunals, endeavouring by force to induce conversions. For example: the Protestant children of a widow should embrace Romanism if their mother contracted a second marriage with a Catholic. The Calvinists very often complained of their grievances to the

Diet, and it must be acknowledged that these assemblies censured the acts of the priests of Rome, reminding them of the necessity of liberty of conscience; but their admonitions and injunctions remained a dead letter. In the seventeenth century, the position of the Calvinists became so insupportable that there remained no other means of self-defence than to demand the protection of the Protestant powers, England, Denmark, Holland, Sweden, and particularly Prussia. The Court of Berlin became for them what the Cabinet of St. Petersburg was for the Lithuanian population of the Greek rite. This priestly intervention in the affairs of Poland carried with it, as its consequence, the catastrophe of this unfortunate land; and the Roman priesthood who disregarded the welfare of the country, and whose solicitude was exclusively confined to their own interests, attained under these circumstances the result they desired. Towards the mid-second half of the seventeenth century there were nearly no Calvinists in Wilna, Vitebsk, Polotsk, etc. At the close of the same century, there were only left forty-eight churches of this confession in Lithuania; and at the end of the eighteenth century there only remained in the entire country twenty-eight churches.

The history of that bloody persecution known as

the "Union," which deprived Poland of Little Russia cannot be detailed in this brief *exposé*. It must suffice to mention succinctly the progressive Romanisation of the United Greeks, as we find them later under the domination of Russia. In the course of the seventeenth century as much as one can find from existing documents, the United Greeks preserved a great part of the dogmas and rules of the Greek Church, conformable to the prescriptions of the Council of Brescia, very few changes being made at the time. At the Council of Nowogrondk, in 1617, it was decided to make some changes in the outward customs of the priests of the united Greek Church, such as cutting the hair very short without altogether employing the tonsure, and shortening the beard, without shaving it entirely, so as to accustom them gradually to Romanism. The theological works of the period, too, urgently advocated communion in one kind, the marriage of the priests was not tolerated, and not legally permitted, and so on with regard to other questions, these new introductions and ordinances all tending openly in the one direction—Rome. The Synod of Zamosc, assembled in 1720, under the presidency of the Nuncio, confirmed nearly all the rites of the Eastern Church, and the autonomic of the united

Greek Church, was recognised anew. The policy of Rome consisted in gradually and imperceptibly introducing Latinism in the Union, without suddenly startling the masses, for fear of producing a *bouleversement* which this court might be unable to cope with; as had already happened in the Ukraine. Nevertheless this same synod instituted among other fêtes that of La Fête Dieu, which is altogether Latin. The united Greeks preserved the Communion in two kinds—the sign of the Cross from the right to the left—the Lents and the Julian Calendar. But already towards the middle of the eighteenth century, the symbol, referring to the procession of the Holy Spirit, was changed; purgatory was recognised, and bells were used in the service. Baptism by sprinkling was introduced, several Masses daily on the same altar, and the priests were absolutely forbidden to marry. Besides this, the Latin priests could receive the confession of the united Greeks, and *vice versâ;* they could even baptize in emergencies, under the condition, however, that the infants so christened should be brought up in the confession of their parents. The Latins would officiate in their churches, but with the sacerdotal vestments of the United Greeks. And with the introduction of Latin rites and customs, the Latins forced

the Union clergy to embrace the spirit of their
caste; pretending that to enter religious orders a
distinguished origin was necessary; that ecclesiastics were in no case amenable to lay tribunals;
that the priest had a right to pretend to royal
honours; and that consequently he should not
occupy himself with the cultivation of the earth.
But the Roman clergy oppressed the United Greek
priesthood quite as much as they did the Dissenters; they deprived them of their rights, of all
education, and even of the proper means of sub-
sistence. While the others took their place
amongst the Polish aristocracy, the United Greeks
were degraded. Was this sound policy of the
Poles under the circumstances? In attentively
studying the struggles of the Union, we certainly
recognise that there was not only a religious
struggle but a decided antagonism between two
political elements totally opposed: the aristocratic
element, to which the Polish Latin clergy belonged,
noble by position, relatively civilised, rich, possessing immense estates, which passed by succession
to the Church, enjoying great political privileges;
on the other hand, the popular element, represented
by the Russian priest, poor as a Russian peasant,
denied of all political rights, uneducated like him,
sometimes trying with difficulty to write, perse-

cuted like him; these two elements, we repeat, are
to be found opposed in the religious struggle which
was the forerunner of the downfall of the kingdom.
The Russian priest, as Prince Koursby tells us,
diverted himself with the peasant in the cabaret,
lived beside him, partook of his joys and shared
his sorrows.   Therefore the people . remained
unchanged in their faith, notwithstanding all
persecutions, while the aristocratic Lithuanian not
only passed quickly and easily to the Union, but
even embraced Romanism.   The Russian element
was, and rested, the national element among the
rural   population and   the Greek priesthood of
Lithuania ; the nobility and the Polish clergy, *au
contraire*, were the personification of the aristocratic element, and with the loss of the privileged
aristocratiques, they lost their ancient political
importance.   " Panska   wiara "   and " Chlopska,
wiara " (religion of the lords and religion of the
peasants), or " Polska wiara " and " Ruska
wiara " (Polish religion and Russian religion),
were no vain words.   They exactly express
our thoughts and our convictions, that the *lutte
acharnée* of the Union was as much political
as religious ; and that therefore this privileged
class in repulsing the Greek clergy, left them
in the opposition, even in the. very essence of

their nationality, their identity with the nationality Russe.

In speaking of the Roman priesthood, and in closing this chapter, one cannot pass over their acts with regard to the Jews, acts which appear incredible, if authentic documents did not confirm them. In the latter half of the eighteenth century they forced these people to shut themselves up in their houses during the Roman processions, as well as during the Holy Week ; and the Jew who rented or owned house, cellar, or shop, was obliged to pay a fixed sum to the curé of the parish ; for the plausible reason, that if this house, cellar, or shop, were not in his possession, it would be in that of a Catholic who makes offerings to his Church. In short, the Jew had to pay tithe to the Latin priest, on the score that, according to the Books of Moses, their own recognised law-giver, they were enjoined to render to the Levites the tenth part of the fruits of the earth and of the animals !

CHAPTER VI.

APERCU HISTORY OF THE DIOCESES IN LITHUANIA.

I. Diocese of Wilna.—Its extent.—Propagation of Catholic-. ism in this diocese.—The Greek faith had preceded the introduction of Catholicism in this country.—Division of the diocese into deaneries.—First Bishops of this diocese.—Religious intolerance.—Successive arrivals of the Monastic Orders.—Legates of the Pope.—The principal qualifications for nomination to the Episcopal chair.—Influence of the Jesuits upon the Bishops. Position of the Bishops vis-à-vis the Chapter.—Composition of the Chapter.—Opposition of the Chapter to the Bishops.—Estates and jurisdiction of the Chapter.—Seminary.—Its management given to the Jesuits, 1588.—The Jesuits abandon the Seminary, 1652.—This school regulated by the Secular clergy.—The Seminary, shut for some time, passes into the hands of the Missionaries.—State of this institution.—Diocesan synods.—Eclat of the See of Wilna.—Creation of new dignities in the Chapter.—That of Vicar of the Bishop and Vicar of White Russia.—Dissensions between the Clergy and the Noblesse.—Contests between the Clergy and the Army.—Open struggle between Brzostowski and the Hetman Sapieha, 1693-98.

2. Diocese of Samogitia.—Its extent.—Violent introduction of Catholicism in the country.—Foundation of dioceses, 1417. —Propagation of Romanism in this bishopric.—Return of the Samogitians to idolatry in the sixteenth century. Seat of the diocese.—Relations of this diocese with that of Wilna.—Composition of the Chapter.—Division of the diocese into dean-

eries.—Bishops of Samogitia.—Their connexion with the Chapter.—Seminary.—The direction taken by the Jesuits.— Process between the Bishop and the Jesuits on the subject of the Seminary, 1624.—The Seminaries confided to the Piares, 1741.—The same institution restored to the Jesuits, 1760.— Jesuitical system of education.—Later arrival of the Monastic Orders in Samogitia.—Oppression of the Secular Clergy by the Monks.—Provincial Synods.

3. Diocese of Kamience.—Foundation of the See, 1414.—. Dependence of this bishopric upon the Metropole of Livow.— The See of Kamience little esteemed.—Composition of its Chapter.—Establishment of its Vicarage, 1730.—Abuses by the Religious Orders.—Seminary.—Efforts of the clergy to free themselves from obligations towards the State.—Division of the diocese into deaneries.

4. Diocese of Luck.—Foundation of the See.—Its extent.— Composition of its Chapter.—Seminaries.—Diocesan synods. —.Division of the diocese into deaneries.

5. Diocese of Kiew.—Supposed epoch of its foundation.— Mission of the Dominicans and Franciscans in the thirteenth century.—Extent of the diocese.—Erection of convents in opposition to the progress of the Greek Church, eighteenth century.—Division of the diocese into deaneries.—Transfer of the Episcopal chair to Zytomir, 1724.—Erection of the cathedral, 1751.—Creation of the dignity of Archdeacon of Czeringow.—Composition of the Chapter.—Establishment of the Vicarage, 1740.—Seminary, 1762.—Diocesan Synods.

6. Diocese of Smolensk.—Foundation, 1638.—Chapter.— Vicariat.—The diocese composed of only four churches.

7. Diocese of Inflandt.—Its formation.—Vicariat, 1743.— Chapter.—Seminary, 1755.—Aperçu général.

AFTER having thus presented the Tableau Historique as it were of the propagation of Romanism in Western Russia, and detailed succinctly some of the acts of the Latin Clergy, it may not be unnecessary to give some historical sketches of the different dioceses. These details, as a complement of the preceding, confirm our former impressions.

The bishopric of Wilna at the period of its dependence on Polish domination, extended from the actual limits of Wilna and Grodno, to the eastern part of the government of Kowno, that is to say to the east of the district of Poniewesz and Kowna, to the districts of Wilkomir and Nowoaleksandrowsk, to the governments of Mohilew, Vitebsk, and Minsk. We have only one means of following the propagation of Romanism in these districts, namely by fixing the epoch of the construction of different churches, although this method is itself defective, as after the formal introduction of Romanism into the country, the Grand Dukes of Lithuania built churches at the expense of the State in certain localities where there were no Catholics and particularly in those towns which were the centre of administration. In the course of time, the Magnats, having joined the new religion, built splendid temples on their own estates, notwithstanding that the peasants on these lands belong to the Greek Church. Be this as it may, churches, as the exterior expression of an established religion, indicate if not the general establishment of Catholicism, at least the centres from whence it sprang. In examining from this point of view, the chronology of the Roman churches, we find that in the diocese of Wilna the Latin Church had passed the confines of Wilna and Grodno in the fifteenth century. But it is certain that she there met the Greek Church already in possession, as when Jagellon baptized the people of Wilna, one half of the population refused to be christened, as they belonged even then to the Greek Church. The greater part of the Latin churches built in the eastern section of the government of Kowno, belong to the sixteenth century; towards the middle of this era a great number of churches were built in the province of Bralostock. Queen Rose, Sigismond III., the Radzivills and other aristocratic families during this century erected many churches on their demesnes; nevertheless Catholicism did not extend beyond the confines of the above-named governments, with the exception, perhaps, of some churches in the government of Minsk upon the frontiers of Wilna, and five or six more in White Russia, but as a whole the general number of these churches was inconsiderable. One of the great obstacles to the establishment of Romanism, was the ignorance of the clergy in the idiom of the country, for in the sixteenth century we find whole localities in Lithuania where Christianity had not yet penetrated. Bishop Woicech Radzivill, in 1508-19 pulled down with his own hands the idols he found on some of his estates, as well as in other places; and Sigismond I. ordered a church to be built on his own private estate of Krijnki, as the people had not then embraced Christianity (1522). In the act authorising the foundation of a church at Jassianowec in 1553, it is said that since the introduction of Romanism into Lithuania, the population of this locality had not seen a priest, that they lived and died without confession. In 1589, Anne, Queen of Poland, founded a church at Ponemoune upon the Nieman, twenty versts from Grodno, "to recover the inhabitants of this place from infamy and diabolical idolatry." Even in the seventeenth century we find Nicolas Sapieha founding churches in the district of Trock at Niemonvitzy. "As the people, not having a priest, lived without marriage or confession," coercive and severe measures were often resorted to. Sigismond I. in authorising the construction of a church in the royal demesue of Wysoki Duor, assigned an annual stipend to the curate, under the express condition that he should constrain his parishioners, through the power of the police, to frequent the church, and should· they not attend divine service to fine them a certain sum. But such measures were little favourable to the spread of Catholicism.

In the fourteenth and at the commencement of the fifteenth century there were already four Greek dioceses within the limits of the Roman diocese of Wilno, namely Pinsk, Mohilew, Minsk and Polotsk. It is evident that the more Greeks there were, the fewer Romanists could there be, and this goes to explain the extremely slow march of the Latin Church in the other governments of Mohilew, Vitebsk and Minsk. It was not introduced, properly speaking, until the seventeenth century, when it entered in conjunction with the Jesuits, under circumstances not very favourable to its dissemination. For example : when Sigismond III. ordered a Roman church to be built at Mohilew, this city already contained seven Greek edifices ; and many other localities of the same governments presented an analagous proportion. Therefore, even in the eighteenth century, the deaneries found in this government, though covering an immense extent of country, contained very few churches. The deanery of Vitebsk, from north to south, crossing the deanery of Orsza, embraced nearly all the government of Mohilew, as far as the town of Bieliza and Borisow, government of Minsk, a distance of nearly a hundred versts, in which there were only eight churches. The deanery of Polótsk, which comprehended the districts of Polotsk and Lepel, with Disna in the government of Vitebsk, and a part of the district of Wileika, government of Wilna, had only thirteen churches. The deanery of Orsza, occupying an immense extent, embraced five districts of the government of Mohilew, viz., Orsza, Mscislaw, Czaoussy, Mohilew, and Bychow, and possessed only seventeen Roman Catholic places of worship, eight of which belonged to the convents. The deanery of Rodoscow, which was comparatively limited, enclosed the districts of Borrisow, and Wileika, with thirteen churches. The deanery of Bobrouisk stretching over more than the half of the actual government of Minsk had also only thirteen churches. Thus properly speaking the Latin diocese of Wilna was circumscribed within the government of Wilna, Grodno in its eastern quarter, and of Kowno, with isolated churches dispersed over the whole extent of the governments of Vitebsk, Mohilew, and Minsk, artificially united into deaneries for the convenience of ecclesiastical administration. Even in the centre of this diocese, a great many religious edifices for worship were erected towards the close of the sixteenth and the beginning of the seventeenth century, through pure antagonism to Calvinism which was then spreading itself widely.

The diocese of Wilna, at this period definitely constituted within marked boundaries, was divided into twenty-six deaneries; containing, in 1717, four hundred and thirty-five, in 1779, four hundred and four churches, and in 1744, three hundred and sixty-four.

The bad state of the roads and the extent of this diocese made its administration extremely difficult. Bishop Masalsky therefore divided it into three parts—Trock, Grodno and Luck—with a separate consistory for each of them. These consistories placed under the presidence of an official, and composed of several assessors, had a very extended authority, the members of which were called to the consistory of Wilna. This partition lasted for ten years, but after experience did not justify such a division; as, so far from promoting a better order of things in ecclesiastical affairs, it only engendered new disorders. The local consistories commenced to correspond directly with Rome unknown to the Bishop; so that it might be expected that in course of time they would throw off the episcopal authority altogether and form themselves into three dioceses. In 1781 these consistories were abolished, and the ecclesiastical administration was concentrated at Wilna. This diocese was, as we have seen, instituted in 1388, and subordinated to the Archbishop of Gnezo. Its first two bishops were of the Order of St. Francis, but, dating from 1407, the bishops were no longer selected from among the regular clergy. This fact explains the antagonism existing at nearly all periods between the regular and the secular priests, which early showed itself in this diocese. The Chapter constrained Bishop George Plichta to take an oath that he would augment the number of curacies in which he would place secular clergy, and at the same time diminish the number of convents, and that the churches of such establishments should be placed at the disposal of the same priests. Of the four first bishops, three were Poles, but from 1421 no more Poles were elected to this See. It belonged exclusively to Lithuania, and its rights were preserved long after the fusion of this country with Poland; so that after the death of Bishop Prince George Radzivill, 1590, the Bishop of Luck, who had been nominated by Rome and was protected by Sigismond III., was not accepted, because he was by birth a Pole and not a Lithuanian. The first bishop was a native of Poland, but this selection was explained by the fact that at this epoch Lithuania did not possess a national secular clergy.

Hardly was Romanism introduced into Lithuania when its intolerant spirit showed itself towards other Christian sects. Jaquellon in 1387, having entered the Latin Church, promulgated a law forbidding Lithuanians to contract marriages with members of the Greek confession, at least without change of religion. With the first Roman Catholic bishop in this country, appeared also the ecclesiastical sword. In 1391, Bishop Andre assembled the prelates and canons, and in accordance with the Papal sanction gave them the permission to compel all those who refused tithes or pillaged the estates of the church, to appear before ecclesiastical tribunes, and to place them beyond the pale of the Church. But these tribunes, and the anathema of Rome, were not enough for the Roman Clergy; therefore in 1492-1507, Bishop Tabor obtained authority from the Pope, both for himself and his successors, to oblige them to serve in arms against the Tartars, the Armenians and the Russians. Not seldom did the bishop himself take up arms. The first preachers in Lithuania were the Franciscans. In 1469, the Bernardines arrived at Wilna, and towards the close of the fifteenth century the Dominicans fixed themselves at Trockej.

The Legates of the Pope came from time to time to visit the diocese, and Rome derived from it considerable sums of money. In 1501, the Grand Duke Alexander forbade the sending of the money obtained at the Jubilee to Rome, ordering it to be employed for the benefit of the troops in campaign against Russia. The Nuncio who afterwards arrived in Poland made severe remonstrances on this head to Bishop Tabor, but it was already too late.

Dating from the sixteenth century when the number of the churches and the clergy and the extent of their revenues had considerably increased, the episcopal chair of Wilna had become, so to speak, the exclusive property of the Lithuanian aristocracy. "Since this epoch," writes an ecclesiastical contemporary, "the protection of the Magnats is of more value than real merit." It was Prince Worcech Radzivill who inaugurated this series of ecclesiastical lords; then came John, the natural son of Sigismond I., and after him Prince Paul Holszanskej; these three lords filled the See of Wilna during nearly the first half of the sixteenth century. Once the episcopal dignity is looked at in a pecuniary point of view, pastoral qualifications become rare exceptions. Of this one may be convinced by analysing the circumstances which accompanied an ordinary elevation to this See. John, the son of Sigismond, was already designated as successor to the bishop when he should attain the age of seventeen years; at the age of twenty he was diocesan bishop. His mother collected the revenues and often interfered in the affairs of the diocese. This bishop conducted himself in such an unseemly manner, that one day in a quarrel with the young Stanislas Radzivill, he lost a finger of the right hand, which Radzivill cut off with a blow of his sword. But in reality he was only a bishop in name, his father Sigismond regulating the See instead. Notwithstanding all this, John pleased the Polish aristocracy as he forced the Polish language amongst the Lithuanians, and commanded his curates to explain the Bible and the Acts of the Apostles to their flocks in that tongue. The ravages of the Reformation in the country at this era was not considered of as much importance as the Episcopal dignity. Again in 1574, George Radzivill, being only nineteen years old, was named Bishop-Vicar of Wilna, *with future succession*; and it was only after his nomination to this place that the Jesuits sent him to Rome to complete his studies and become a priest. At the age of twenty-three he was not only sub-deacon but diocesan bishop and a Cardinal!

These premature distinctions turned the head of the young man, who knew perfectly well that he was unfitted for the priesthood. His diocese mattered little to him, he took no care of it, and attended to only some of the more important matters. Instead of living at Wilna, he, in 1582, accepted the post of Lord-Lieutenant of Livonia, where he remained three years. This governor, bishop, and cardinal was not consecrated until his removal to Riga, the capital of his lieutenancy. He afterwards went twice to Rome to the conclaves, and was nominated by Clement VIII. his Legate to Poland. Later he played the rôle of peace-maker between Sigismond III., and the Emperor Rudolf, and was transferred to the See of Cracow, so that he hardly ever resided at, or administered, his Lithuanian bishopric. He wished however to enjoy the emoluments arising from the dignity, and succeeded, but only for a time. A year and some months later the Chapter named another adminis-trator, and this administration which passed from hand to hand under the surveillance of the Pope's legate, lasted ten years. Bishop Wollowicz, 1616-30, being Vice-Chancellor of the kingdom, only visited his diocese twice during the term of his episcopate; once to be solemnly installed in the See, and a second time, 1620, to assist at the

conference of the Chapter. Bishop John Dowg-
wiallo Zawisza, 1656 to 1661, did not even enter
upon the administration of his diocese, passing all
his time travelling, or in assemblies general and
provincial. Towards the end of the seventeenth
century, the great family Sapieha having commenced to decline in Lithuania, and desiring to
rebuild its fallen fortunes at the expense of the
Church, destined one of its members, Alexander,
to the ecclesiastical profession. He was initiated
at an early age, and afterwards from 1667 to 1672,
he was bishop of Wilna. Sapieha was succeeded
by a married priest, Nicolas Pac, 1672-84, Woje-
woda of Trock, governor of Wilna, who had formerly
distinguished himself in war, had spent his fortune,
and like Sapieha, would recruit it at the expense of
the See of Wilna. He was protected by King
Michael Korijbutt, who had named him a canon
when but a clerk, and confided the administration
of the diocese to him. Pac rarely remained in his
See; he went sometimes to the Diets at Warsaw,
sometimes to Jaworowo, where the King liked to
reside, often to his estates, or he travelled to
Rome and in Italy. Such a system of nomination
to the episcopal Sees lasted till the last days of the
political existence of Poland. Prince Massalsky
was elected on the sole consideration "that he

could be useful to the Church, as he belonged to a
great family." From the time of their first
appearance in Lithuania the Jesuits endeavoured
by every means to influence the bishop of Wilna,
as chief of the most extensive diocese in the
country, and in this they very often succeeded. The well-known predilection of Protassewicz for them is notorious. It was he
who had called them to Wilna. Prince George
Radzivill, Benedict Woyna, Wollowicz, George
Tyszkiewicz, Alexander Sapieha, and Ancuta,
their first pupils, became afterwards their warmest
protectors. The weaker the bishop, the more
incapable he was of fulfilling his charge, the more
could he rely on this Order, providing only that he
belonged to a powerful family.

If on the one side the election of bishops from
purely mundane considerations was an evil and a
disgrace to the Church, on the other, those prelates
who were zealous and faithful to their trust, finding
their power limited by the Chapter, found it
impossible to do all the good they would under
other circumstances have done, through the
defective hierarchical organisation. The members
of the Chapter, that is to say, the prelates and the
canons were, according to the canon law, considered the most zealous coadjutors of the

bishops; in reality they were very often useless, negligent and mischievous in their systematic opposition to the bishop, their constant efforts being to limit his authority as much as possible, and at his expense enlarge their own rights and importance.

When the diocese of Wilna was first founded, it was enacted that it should have ten canons and two prelates; afterwards new capitulary charges were added, and the number of members considerably increased. To these were later attached titulary or honorary members, who enjoyed the revenues of the estates of the Chapter, but rarely assisted at the conferences. The Grand Dukes of Lithuania and, at a later period, the Kings of Poland were the hereditary collators of this See; that is, they distributed the dignities of the Chapter, and the bishops were compelled to accept every member named by royal authority. These dignities were therefore mostly given to people of rank, or to clerks of inferior grade who had not yet become priests, to foreigners, to medical men, to professors, and even to alchymists. Protection and birth were the sole qualifications to obtain them. It was not surprising to find young men, nearly youths, invested with these responsibilities. Several bishops of Wilna, like Brzostowski and

Massalski, were canons at the age of sixteen;
Wallowicz and Abraham Wojna at twenty, and
they were not consecrated till after their promotion.
Such canons were considered as the vassals of the
episcopal chair; they did not reside at Wilna, but
passed their time at Court, or on their estates, as
they pleased. The prescription of the Council of
Trent, "*Omnes canonici divina per se, non per sub-
stitutos, compellantur obire officia,*" was little
thought of. Twelve vicars filled the functions of the
Cathedral in their place; and these were the true servants of the Church, who received for their labours
only a moderate salary, while the members of the
Chapter lived in idleness, debauch, and luxury, enjoying their large ecclesiastical incomes. The priest,
Przyalgowsky said:—" These men think only of
the acquisition of benefices, dignities, and cures;
so as to occupy a certain position, and to be
distinguished in society. They have each, more
or less, two or three charges, and enjoy the
revenues of several curacies." How could such a
priesthood come to the aid of suffering humanity?
Thus, when some misfortune happened Wilna, such
as an invasion, or the passage of the enemy's
troops affected the city, the canons, the prelates,
and the bishop flew away, as if the pest had
appeared, and the members of the Chapter followed

their example. This took place in 1602, 1625, 1631, and in 1656. "There existed a custom," said the same priest, "that for a long time the clergy, principally the higher clergy, took great care of their health and their existence, not daring to look death in the face." Who remained therefore to console the suffering, to succour the indigent, or to bury the dead? Always the simple and poor vicars. The high ecclesiastical functionaries were more necessary for Episcopal pomp, for Roman Catholic ostentation, than for the requirements of the Christian Church. Naturally the masses sympathised little with such shepherds; they saw in them no father, no consoler, no adviser, only lords and magnates robed in the vestments of the Church, driving in sumptuous equipages with many horses; "so that," as the priest goes on to say, "the sinner has not even the hardihood to approach them."

Under these circumstances, the Chapter formed neither a senate nor a consulting assembly, according to its own regulations, when constituted; it was more a Diet, and still more a Polish Diet. Polish politics passed also into the sphere of the Church, but it was even more disordered than the Diets. "Just as the King without a Diet," says this same priest, the historiographer of the diocese of Wilna, "so a bishop without a Chapter has no signification. Such was the spirit, the Polish customs, and the time, that while the Church accorded the Bishop superior authority, it was only a divided authority, so that dissensions broke out frequently, and he encountered so many obstacles to the realization of his most benevolent intentions, that to contend with them was almost an impossibility." Already in the time of George Plichta, the second Bishop, 1398-1407, the Chapter considerably limited his power, and obliged him to sanction by oath his *pacta conventa* ; and the day of his installation he had to swear to preserve in all their force the privileges of the Chapter, or in other words, they compelled him to conform to the will of the prelates and canons. Alexander Sapieha tried to fulfil this ceremony *privatim* in the sacristy, but he was not permitted. The dissensions of the Chapter and the Bishop began under the Episcopate of John, 1519-36; and later on we find the Chapter appealing to the Primate, Archbishop of Gniesno, against Bishop Protassiewicz, 1556-80, and fastening copies of the appeal upon the doors of the Cathedral. In 1629, they opposed the creation of the post of Chancellor, by Bishop Wallowicz, although the estate for the support of this dignitary came from private funds. The Chapter based their opposition on the ground that the Chancellor, having all the capitulary documents in his hands, and owing his appointment to the bishop, could inform him of all that passed at the conferences, and direct affairs according to his inspiration. "If," said the Chapter, "this project be carried out, the Chancellor should be subordinate to two authorities, and then the injunctions of either party would be useless; as, according to St. Luke, *deficit enim ambobus qui vult servire duobus.*" It is here necessary to remark that every member, on entering the Chapter, took an oath not to divulge what passed during the sittings. A canon once recounted to Bishop Biallozor, 1661-67, the discussions which had taken place, but only after the bishop had absolved him from his oath. This oath forbade the member under any pretext to reveal, either on the demand of the bishop or even of the Pope himself, what passed at the sitting; and it was enacted in 1633, "that if any one of the members, through any considerations whatever, implored the interference of the bishop, to the detriment of the Chapter, he should be subjected to a severe penalty." It is related that George Tyszkiewicz, when nominated to a bishopric, approaching Wilna, was met on the road by one of the envoys of the Chapter, who came to present

him beforehand with the form of oath. The
bishop, a man of firm character, astonished at the
pretension which would limit his episcopal power,
would not accept it, and drew up another, which
he signed and handed to the messenger, telling
him that he would fulfil this oath and no other.
His memory appears to have been little honoured
by the chapter, for his body remained for nearly a
century in the vault of a Lutheran Church at
Kœnisberg, where he died, and when afterwards it
was transported to Wilna, it was not interred in
the Cathedral Church, as customary with respect
to bishops of the diocese. Never were the dissensions between the chapter and the bishop of the
diocese so violent and so prolonged as under Pac,
1672-84. The episcopate was the theatre of
continual struggles, the sources of which were
cash accounts. It was the custom that, during
the interval between the death of a bishop and the
installation of another, the episcopal revenues
were divided between the members of the chapter.
This took place also under Pac, who being only a
simple clerk when charged with the administration,
went to Rome to be consecrated, and for the two
years intervening could not receive or profit by
the revenue. A bad feeling between chapter and
bishop was the result; the canons carried their accu-

sations against him, both to the Primate and the King, demanding from the Nuncio that he should be deprived of all episcopal power and suspended, and sent a most insolent writ to the bishop himself. Tearing it up in the presence of several ecclesiastics, Pac called them all rebels, declaring that if any member of the chapter presented himself there, he would imprison him in the donjon. He then left for Warsaw, to complain personally to the King. But the mediation of John III. did not result in peace. The chapter despatched delegates to Rome, to support a protest against Pac. At length, after some concessions, the bishop was about to be reconciled to the chapter, when his cousin, Casimir Pac, Bishop of Samogitia, arrived, who was himself intriguing for the chair of Wilna, and who interrupted the proceedings. The Bishop of Wilna was afterwards obliged to go to Rome, where he found the *manditaires* of the chapter. He tried to conciliate them, but in vain; he fêted the cardinals, presented sums of money to the different chancellories, but did not succeed. In the mean time, Casimir Pac had taken up his residence in the palace of Wilna, and when the Bishop of Wilna returned from Rome, the chapter refused to appear before him as customary, declaring that they did not require his

benediction. They excited the peasantry on the
Episcopal estates against him, and the struggles
recommenced. New complaints were addressed to
the King, to the Pope, and to the Nuncio. Pac,
however, continued his administration, but was not
consecrated until 1682, two years before his death,
and it was only then that he was reconciled to the
chapter. No doubt that the habit of command
which he had acquired in his different administrative functions, united to a very energetic character,
as well as his sudden transition from a lay to an
ecclesiastical position, contributed greatly to excite
these scandals between bishop and chapter. But
these circumstances were not the only result.
The principle of disorder engendered itself into the
grain and spirit of the chapter, which personified
truly all Polish anarchy. Under Bishop Zien-
kowicz, 1730-61, another disagreeable dispute
occurred with the chapter, relative to the subject
of the Archdeaconry and the revenue attached to
that dignity; there was even a quarrel between the
two stewards of the parties, one of whom had
been named archdeacon by the bishop, and the
other had been raised to the same dignity by the
chapter. The King decided in favour of the
bishop, the Pope on the contrary for the chapter;
the dispute lasted eight years, and time only put

an end to it, as in the case of Pac, without either party being the winner.

The Chapter of Wilna possessed considerable property in the city. Many workmen, mechanics, and others, only acknowledged its authority, and were exempt from the judicial tribunes as well as from all duties and imposts. Criminals were confined in the Episcopal palace. The occupations of the same tradesmen were regulated by the same Chapter. In 1607, when a complaint was made of the dearness of some stuffs, the Chapter found that it was because they were sold in a quarter of the city thinly inhabited, and that they were exported. They therefore restrained the license, and prohibited the exportation abroad. Municipal corporations of these tradesmen were forbidden, that they should not be subjected to lay interposition ; and, among other obligations, they were expected to take part in the processions of the *Fête Dieu* and other cathedral ceremonies. The bishop did not dare meddle in the affairs of this class, though he himself owned nearly a third of the town. He had his burghers, who did not enjoy municipal privileges of the law of Magdabourg, which extended only to the workmen of the corporations ; but Bishop John ceded his rights jurisdiction to the provosts of the city.

As to the position of the lower clergy, the state of the seminaries at different periods sufficiently prove how the priests were prepared to interpret the Divine Word and become the true teachers of the people. Towards the middle of the sixteenth century, when the Reformation had already entered Lithuania, no seminary existed at Wilna. The young men destined for the priesthood, had to study at a parochial school, and were ordained priests when they knew only how to write and read a little Latin. The seminary of Wilna was not founded until 1588, by Prince George Radzivill, for the instruction of twelve clerks, whose education was confided to the Jesuits, while the Chapter defrayed the expense of their physical support. The following were the conditions of guardianship appertaining to each party :—1. The management of the landed estates held in trust for the seminary, belonged to the Chapter, without any interference whatever from the Jesuits. 2. The Jesuits received annually from the Chapter, a fixed sum for the support of the seminary, without being subject to any inquiries as to how this sum was disbursed. 3. The Jesuits undertook the education and moral training of the young, and might guide the consciences of the pupils without any one having a right to interfere. In 1613, Nicholas Pac, Bishop of Samogitia, demanded access to this school for the clerks of his diocese, which was arranged conditionally that he should pay at once a certain sum towards the repairs of the building, and that the new pupils should assist at the cathedral service on fête days. The Jesuits having an Academy in Wilna, and several schools elsewhere in Lithuania, attached very little importance to this seminary; and the Chapter managed the income derived from its endowment very badly, giving only very limited sums out of the receipt for its support. Thus, morally and physically, it was a failure owing to the double authority exercised by the Jesuits and the Chapter. It may be inferred, that in founding this establishment, Bishop Radzivill had more in view the carrying out of the prescriptions of the Council of Trent, than to furnish the diocese with a proper priesthood. The number of pupils never exceeded twelve, as preliminarily fixed, generally there were only six, and *never* eight. There was only one master who acted as governor at the same time. The pupils were badly fed, their clothes had to last them two years, and when the revenues of the estates were not forthcoming, they received no new ones, so that sometimes, even at Divine Service, they were literally in tatters. Young men were not received, but only children, who were taught rhetoric. When they left the seminary, they received no assistance, but were presented with a breviary. In 1628, the possibility of leaving this school longer in the hands of the Jesuits was discussed; and ten years later the Chapter endeavoured to withdraw them altogether, and take the direction of the instruction themselves, attributing the dreadful state in which it was, to want of proper attention and care. The Jesuits, on the other hand, fell upon the Chapter, blamed the shameful administration of the estate, and replied to an accusation brought against them of accepting only very young children, and not instructing them in the sciences. Their answer was that these children had powerful protectors, and that they did not consider it necessary to instruct them in the higher branches, as the pupils did not demand it. In 1652, there was a definite rupture between the Chapter and the Fathers, on the subject of the nomination to the curacy of the church of the Order at Wilna. The Jesuits were dreadfully irritated, and in revenge chased the pupils from the seminary during the night, carried off their books and effects, and declared that from that moment they would never speak of or about the establishment. It afterwards reverted to the management of the diocesan bishops, who, how-

ever, did not ameliorate its condition. Very few
pupils cared to enter it, as once the studies were
completed, those who were ordained had no actual
curacies, but were attached to the churches as
vicars ; while younger clerks, not having any
ecclesiastical degree, were named through patronage, canons. With such a system, it was only
natural to see young men show little predilection
to enter it, and the number considerably diminished
afterwards. In 1668, there were but four pupils ;
and in the time of Pac and Brzostowsky, eight.
In 1724-30, Casimir Ancuta, the favourite of
Bishop Pancerzynsky, appropriated the revenues
to his own use, so that the establishment fell into
the most deplorable state. Two prelates, who
were named inspectors of the school at the demand
of the Chapter, found that there were only seven
clerks supported ; that they knew nothing, learned
nothing ; and that those who desired real instruction, must visit other institutions, as the pupils
here were not taught anything. Their education
consisted in chanting during the day two litanies,
and reading, morning and evening, a chapter of
Thomas à Kempis—nothing else ! They were
passably fed, but had little light in their cells, for
during the long autumn evenings, they had only in
the whole edifice, two tallow candles ! Under

Massalsky's Episcopate, the estates of the seminary were in such a dilapidated condition, that the house was altogether shut. It was again opened, when the administration passed into the hands of the Missionaries, who conducted it till 1800. Under them, the number of clerks amounted to thirty, but the interior arrangements were no better. As to qualifications, up to 1792, the pupils were received without any preliminary examination or attestation of ability; they were not given the necessary dress, and were only taught purely ecclesiastical routine. Their residence at the establishment was not subordinate to a fixed course of study, and depended only on the arbitrary will of the superior. A regulation required that every year two inspectors should visit it, one deputed by the bishop, the other by the chapter; but they were of little real use, as representing two distinct authorities, they often quarrelled and presented contradictory reports. The estates in trust for the school, upon which there were two thousand peasants, fell into such decay, that not only were they insufficient for the support of the pupils, but they did not even defray the interest of debts contracted on them. The four masters were miserably paid, and the building fell into ruins. As to the education of the clerks, it was altogether defective, owing to the economical considerations of the administration. "Can such an education," said a canon who visited it at the close of the last century, "suffice for young men destined not only to fill the places of vicars, curates, etc., but also the position of preachers, canons, and bishops? This object merits serious attention, that the system of instruction for the seminary be determined in a stable manner; for, I say it loudly, it is actually totally neglected, and, as it appears to me, is absolutely vicious."

Provincial synods were convoked at different times to ameliorate the condition of the diocese and the clergy. These were held at Wilna, in the years 1526, 1555, 1582, 1604, 1607, 1613, 1628, 1631, 1635, 1654, 1669, 1685, 1717, and 1744. The considerations for which these synods were called varied according to circumstances. The three first were convoked because of the rapid strides of the Reformation in Lithuania; that of 1635 took place because of the restriction put upon the right of the clergy to acquire landed property. The synod of 1654 discussed, among other things, the different taxes on the clergy, but the greater number were summoned merely for form's sake. The Council of Trent enjoined the assembling of all the bishops at these synods, but in reality, they could be of little importance, as they sat only two days, and different religious ceremonies took up the larger part of this short time. Further, the resolutions of these meetings were not seldom prepared beforehand, and were not even signed sometimes, until the assembly had dispersed. They were often called to fulfil some formality; as we find in the case of Bishop Abraham Woijna, 1631-49, who convoked a provincial synod the day of his elevation to the See. Kotowicz, 1685-86, did the same, and announced his installation the next day at its meeting. It is evident that the most of the ecclesiastics who attended these synods, were those who were then at Wilna on especial affairs, or for the consecration of a bishop; and in most cases they had little time to examine the affairs of the diocese, as it was impossible to discuss them seriously in the space of three days. The ordinances, therefore, of most. of these assemblies consisted often in admonitions, which as they were really obeyed, were as often renewed. The synod of 1717, for example, reproved the curates that they quarrelled among themselves as to the limits of their parishes. The Monastic Orders were rebuked at different times because they did not recognise the power of the bishops; and the synod commanded their obedience, reminding them of the prescriptions of the Council of Trent concerning the relations between bishops and curates. Some of the Orders, as we see by the enactments of these synods, tried to emancipate themselves from the Episcopal authority, especially the Benedictines. The priests also not unfrequently appropriated the money destined to the construction or repair of the churches; and the curates levied *honoraires* for interments, and on occasions refused ground necessary for graves to inter the dead. It is evident that these admonitions were a dead letter, if one may judge by the posterior state of the clergy. Some of the bishops wrote epistles to their subordinates, containing instructions and commands, and in this style of admonition, Benedict Woijna distinguished himself; and there is a mandate from Pac still extant, of the same description.

Interior organisation was sacrificed to exterior pomp. The Bishop of Wilna, who was rich, powerful, a Senator of the Republic, and surrounded by a splendid Chapter of canons and deans, exalted the éclat of his See by the creation of new honorary places. Bishop John, 1519-37, created the dignity of Vicar of Wilna, associated with which office was very often the title of Bishop of Metonene; and Wollowicz instituted the Archdeaconry

of White Russia, the mitre with the title of Archdeacon of White Russia being afterwards attached
by George Tiszkiewicz, 1650-56. This functionary did not reside in the country from which he
derived his title, but lived at Wilna, where he
officiated as one of the canons. In the seventeenth
century, the bishops of Smolensk, later bishops of
Livonia, having no diocese, were only superior
prelates of, and their Chapters were identical with,
the diocese of Wilna, where, on great occasions,
they, together with the Bishop of Samogitia and
his Chapter, assisted the bishop in the grand
solemnities. This pomp and magnificence of the
Church flattered the national vainglory as much
as the vanity of the Polish nobles and the Latin
clergy. Altogether the richness of the priesthood,
their cupidity, and their exceptional position in the
social scale, attracted, for a considerable time
before, attention ; the first symptoms of the general
discontent showing itself in contests as to titles,
and later, the nobility raising themselves against
their excessive privileges. In 1612, the Chapter
of Wilna moved that it was necessary that the
bishop should protest against some of the enactments of the Grand Duchy of Lithuania, which
tried to extinguish the rights and privileges of the
clergy ; and in 1614 it was resolved to request the

bishop not to tolerate that the noblesse threw obstacles in the way of the members of the Chapter, expressing their opinions at the Diet which was about to be held at Wilna. In 1620, the Chapter elected the Bishop-suffragan to the general Diet at Warsaw, charged him to defend the rights and privileges of the clergy, and in con-junction with all the bishops of the realm, to take measures against the projects of their adversaries. We find a resolution of the Chapter in 1629 thus worded :—" Seeing the difficulties of the times, and the wickedness of men, particularly of those who have charge of the welfare of others, and what is more, of the welfare of the Church, that they, instigated by the Devil, have done away with the estates of the clergy and appropriated them, we resolve, in order to defend ourselves against such acts, to appoint a special agent to attend the royal tribunals with a salary of 100 florins a year, to be paid from the treasury of the Chapter." The Diet of 1635 passed a law which forbade the clergy accepting all donations or landed estates without the direct consent of the Diet. This measure excited them exceedingly. Bishop Woijna called an extraordinary synod, at which all the priesthood, Polish and Lithuanian, drew up a collective pro-testation. Ossolinsky was despatched to Rome to

entreat Pope Urban VIII. to mediate between the
nobility and the clergy; and the year following,
the Chapter having elected delegates to the royal
tribunal, invited the bishop to order the diocesan
clergy to make a collection in their favour, "that
they might attract (bribe) their lay colleagues,
assessors of the same office, to act in favour of the
ecclesiastics." Abraham Woijna, in 1643, entering
the Chapter then sitting, declared that in several
districts of the kingdom and of the Grand Duchy,
when the election of the deputies to the approaching Diet was going on, those who had been elected
were furnished with instructions which enjoined
their action against those who would infringe the
rights of the priesthood; and further, that prayers
were ordered to be said in all the diocesan
churches, "that the Lord might confound' the
enemies of the Church and the clergy." In 1647,
the Chapter and bishop together resolved to
register their protestation against the decision of
the Diet of the 2nd May, in the acts of the Court
House.; and in the instructions given, in 1654, to
the delegates of the Chapter to the Diet of Warsaw,
they were commanded to assist at all conferences
of the ecclesiastical envoys, and to advise with
them on all affairs concerning the Church. They
were also to influence the bishops *in faciem*

Reipublicæ, to protest publicly against every ordinance contrary to the privileges of the clergy, and at the same time to send memorials to the minor Diets of Trock, Kowno, Polotsk, and Samogitia, as well as to Prince Stanislas Radzivill, Chancellor of the Grand Duchy of Lithuania, upon the absolute necessity of preserving the liberties of the priesthood; and in 1673, the Chapter expressed its gratitude to the deputies to the lesser Diets for having protested against the decision of the Diet *générale précédente* by which lay creditors should pay seven and not eight per cent. interest to the clergy, commanding also a new duty upon wine imported into Lithuania. Existing documents sufficiently explain the relations which existed between the noblesse and the clergy; the latter upholding their exemptions and privileges, the nobility trying to subordinate them to general laws, and to oblige them to take an active part in the taxation of the Republic, that they might become useful members, and assist as reliable citizens, of the same. We believe it superfluous to enumerate posterior facts illustrative of the same tendencies; it suffices to add that these relations changed in nothing till the eighteenth century. We know that in 1736, Bishop Zenkowicz, returning to Wilna from Prussia, declared to the Chapter,

that passing through Warsaw, he had assisted at
the Diet, where he had heard strong recrimina-
tions on the part of the noblesse and other classes
against the richness of the convents and the ecclesiastics, and that the clergy were menaced with
the confiscation of all their estates.

The clergy were held to come to the aid of the
Republic in time of war, by payment of a subsidy
called *subsidium charitativium*, and, besides this,
their estates were subject to dues in the shape of
supplies of provisions and military lodgings. The
weight of all these charges fell upon the peasants,
as the clergy, having discharged the obligation,
levied it again upon their lands. This, however,
did not prevent them trying to liberate their properties from all duties to the State ; as in 1650,
they declared themselves in no position to sacrifice
what they had for the benefit of the government,
and that the delegates of the Chapter of Wilna
had never consented to such an impost. In 1662,
the bishop and Chapter of this above-named city,
protested to the commandant of the troops that
the clergy refused contributions without the special
authority of the Holy See, not considering themselves subject to extraordinary dues ; that if they
tolerated them this time it would only serve for a
precedent for future demands of the same nature.

With respect to military quarters or lodgings, the bishop entered into an arrangement with the Hetman of the Grand Duchy for the ransom of this duty; but very often, at the general diets, the clergy entirely liberated" their lands from military levies. On these occasions they did not think it beneath their dignity to have recourse to underhand means to carry out their intentions. Thus there were everlasting complications between the clergy and the army, which were particularly manifest in the struggle between Constantine Bryostowsky and the Hetman Sapieha. Bryostowsky forbade the peasants of the ecclesiastical estates to furnish provisions to the troops in the cantonments, as, according to his ideas, the clergy were free from all imposts and fiscal obligations, by reason of the Subsidium Charitativium. They complained to the tribunals in 1693, and afterwards to the King, against the Palatine of Wilna, Cassimir John Sapieha, the commander of the Lithuanian corps, but without success. Bryostowsky then invited the bishops to commence an open war against the temporal power, and not obtaining their adhesion, he decided to act alone. He levied on the peasantry the money destined for the troops, kept it himself, burned the hay and oats on the estates that it should not fall into the hands of the troops, and ordered a crusade to be preached by his curates against the army and its chief. The Nuncio Santacruce, mediator and arbitrator between the bishop and Sapieha, sided with the former, and gave a decree against Sapieha which he published. The latter replied that the licence of the troops depended on the government and not on the ecclesiastical authority, still less on the Legate of a foreign power, and that it was quite impossible to withdraw the soldiers at a time so very difficult for the country. Sapieha was accordingly excommunicated on the 18th April, 1794, along with his principal officers, the rest of the army excepted; and Bryostowsky, who had done it, ordered him to be cursed in all the churches, he himself pronouncing the anathema in the Cathedral; he also at the same time stopped the celebration of divine service for some days, to mark the mourning of the Church. The nobility and inhabitants of Wilna assembled at the head-quarters of the commander-in-chief, and unanimously decided that such a proceeding of the Bishop was tyrannical; and the monastic orders, too, found the act illegal, and refused to execute the sentence in the churches. The same day Sapieha gave a ball at his palace, and published his protestation, which excited the murmurs of the people. Bryostowski considered himself ruined and disgraced, put off his gold cross and put on one of tin instead, threatening to retire to Riga. But these manœuvres were useless, and only rendered him absurd, without attaining his desire of passing for a martyr. The Archbishop of Gnięzno to whom he was subordinate, reprimanded him as having exceeded the limits of his power, of having acted arbitrarily, and of being too precipitate. He said, "As the Khan of Tartary is on the march against Poland, it is no time to excommunicate the chief of the Polish Army." "Ostentanda sed non emittenda erant hæc jacula, juxta continuam et stabilem meam sententiam. Roma quamvis suprema fruitur potestate, nihilominus nunquam præcipitanter descendit ad similes excommunicationes, quæ status convellere possent; providet namque ne sit medicina pejor morbo." Further on he says that the bishop had no right to do it without the preliminary consent of the Synod. " Excommunicare namque generalissimum ducem exercituum, non est excommunicare aliquem ex vulgo, et quidem ob rationes publicas in quo negotio requirebatur alia cognitio et authoritas non vero privata solius D. vestræ." The archbishop absolved Sapieha from the anathema, and published his decision the 26th April, 1694, against which the bishop protested, denying that the prelate was his superior, and said that he himself had the same powers in Lithuania as the archbishop enjoyed in Poland. The King and Court and the Senate condemned the act of the bishop. There was a popular tumult at Warsaw, and the most influential people expressed in writing their sympathy with the Hetman. In revenge, Bryostowsky anathematised the monastic orders, in his own cathedral, which had not obeyed his commands. He shut the churches of the Dominicans, the Franciscans, the Carmelites, and the Bernardines, sealed the door with his own seal, and even imprisoned some of the monks. The people loudly said that the bishop was not a Pastor, but the enemy of God and man! And this was not all. He unsuccessfully tried to incite the army against Sapieha, but the officers demanded the same treatment as their chief, and desired excommunication with him. The army sent a deputation to the King, informing him of the affront which was paid to their commander, and which they took as personal, saying that they would lose the last drop of their blood with him. Sapieha was soon after victorious over the Tartars of the Crimea, and returned with a rich booty. On this occasion a Te Deum was chanted in all the churches, but Bryostowsky, from hatred, would not permit it to be performed in any of the churches of his diocese. He continued his intrigues against the Hetman, and later tried to incite the noblesse and the commons against him, but did not succeed. At last he proposed to absolve him from the anathema, on condition that he would no longer canton his troops on the Episcopal estates, and pay him three thousand florins indemnity. Sapieha thought as little of the absolution as of the anathema. After that Bryostowsky demanded permission of the Pope to levy upon his diocese a certain sum of money, pretending that his estates had been ruined, and for the greater glory of God; to which the Pope replied:— "Desiste, frater charissima, a fastu et litigiis, sufficiunt tibi reditus episcopales, qui aliis episcopis sufficiebant et sufficiunt." These dissensions lasted nearly five years, and at length Bryostowsky decided to be reconciled to Sapieha.

2. The diocese of Samogitie consisted of the Western part of the actual government of Kowno, containing the districts of Rossiene, Telsz, and of Szawly, and part of the districts of Poniewicz and of Kowno; from this side, the line of demarcation extended between the dioceses of Samogitie and Wilna, the river Niewiaja, which empties itself into the Nieman; but this frontier was inexact, as

beyond the river there were several churches belonging to the bishopric of Samogitia, and what is more, some churches in Prussia made part of this same diocese, as well as some churches of Courland, at an epoch not very remote.

The Crusaders were the first who introduced Catholicism into Samogitia, but the preaching of these armed apostles had no result. In 1413, when this district was re-united to Lithuania, the Grand Duke Witolde arrived with an army, and by force baptized the inhabitants; but no sooner had this force quitted the country, than the people returned to their ancient faith. But in 1416 another army returned, and the following year the diocese was founded, with the intention of spreading Romanism. But Witolde departed for the Volhynia in 1418, and the people abandoning the faith so violently imposed on them, massacred some of the fanatical preachers, chased the others, and set fire to and pillaged the churches. Witolde returned the third time to preach the Gospel in his own fashion; he assembled a strong army, put several apostates from Romanism to death, and forced the remainder to become or take the name of catholics. A general outbreak of the Samogitians was the result. The people killed not only the priests but the noble partisans of the Grand

Duke, and Witolde appeared among them the fourth time, to punish the obstinacy of the idolators. These violent measures had only one result—that the Samogitian people did not with sincerity, but only through constraint and persecution, adopt the Christian religion, and for two centuries it was not solidly established among them. Although called Catholics they remained for a long time idolators. The construction of Latin churches among them, indicates, as in Lithuania, the points from which this clergy spread their faith, but offers no proof of the conversion of the inhabitants to Catholicism in the localities where these churches were built.

In examining the geographical propagation of Romanism, so to speak, as traced by the foundation of ecclesiastical structures, we find that the greatest number of churches in this diocese were constructed in the fifteenth century, in the district of Rossiene, and later in those of Szawly and Telsz. We believe that this march of Catholicism may be explained by the fact that this district was contiguous to the kingdom of Poland, where Romanism was the established religion, whereas Lithuania was, at this epoch, only a Catholic country in name. In the districts of Pomewicz and Kowno, we find no Catholic churches in this century; but following the same direction in the sixteenth century, we find that the greater part of the churches were then built in the district of Rossiene, Szawly, and Telsz. These three districts were the centres from whence Catholicism advanced and directed itself east and south-east. During this era, a church was built in the district of Pomewicz, and two in that of Kowno. It is remarkable that the Church in the first-named district was built upon the confines of Szawly, and the two churches of Kowna were erected not far from the frontiers of Rosiene, where, till the middle of the sixteenth century, there was neither church or priest, and the people lived in idolatry. They also built two churches on the coast of the Baltic. Again, in the seventeenth century, the greater number of Roman chapels were erected in the same districts; Catholicism extended itself further east, in Kowna and Pomiewicz, and even afterwards still farther. Thus the Church of Smigelska was nearly twenty-five, and Poszolotska forty, versts from the frontiers of Szawly. Sigismond III. built here many churches, and endowed them with rich estates.

At the period of the Reformation there were only to be found in Samogitia thirty-four Latin churches in all. In 1551, the first church to the

south-east was built at Massiady, but the doctrines of Rome were little received by the
people. This explains the immense progress of
Calvinism, as in all the diocese there remained
only three Latin churches and six priests. But
what was still more extraordinary, is that the mass
of the people did not become Calvinist, but
returned to idolatry. There is little sincerity in
the adoption of any religion imposed by violence ;
and the exterior expression of Romanism in the
organisation of its hierarchy and in the construction
of its churches, corresponded little with its interior
progress and reality, in the consciences of men,
who were nevertheless considered as Catholics.
Stanislas Rostowsky, a Lithuanian Jesuit, reports
that the Samogitians rekindled the sacred fire in
honour of Peroune, recommenced to adore the oak
and to offer sacrifices ; and in the year 1587, Prince
Melchior Gedroic, the Bishop of Samogitia wrote
to the Jesuits of Wilna :—" In the greater part of
my diocese, there is not a single person who once
in his life confesses or takes the sacrament ; there
is not a single one who knows how to make the
sign of the Cross, recite a Pater Noster, or has any
idea of the Christian religion. The Samogitians
do not think it sinful to offer sacrifice to Peroune,
to worship the oak and consider some forests as

sacred temples." Even in the diocese of Wilna, different coercive regulations were enacted, to constrain the parishioners to religious duties, and in one locality, in 1644, there was even a penalty imposed on those who did not frequent the Church or did not have their marriage blessed.

The bishopric of Samogitia was founded, as we have seen. in 1417, and like Wilna, was subject to the Archbishop of Gniesno, its Episcopal capital was at Wornia or Miedniki, from which the bishops and the diocese were often called Miedniki. Canonically speaking, this bishopric was entirely independent of Wilna, but in reality, in some respects, stood with regard to it, as a vassal. The See of Samogitia very often devolved on the canons, prelates, and suffragans of Wilna, and the bishops were sometimes, promoted as a mark of distinction, to the same See, as occurred three times during the seventeenth century. The Samogitian clerks at this period were educated at the seminary of Wilna. It not unfrequently happened that the bishop and Chapter of Samogitia assisted at the solemnities of the Bishop of Wilna; and there was even a case in which the Chapter carried a complaint against their diocesan bishop to the bishop and Chapter of Wilna, so that in reality the Bishop of Samogitia was but a sort of superior prelate, and his Chapter but a consistory of that diocese. Such dependence, neither legal nor recognised, which was established of itself through force of circumstances, explains the immense difference in the social position of the high clergy of the two dioceses, and even the extent of the bishoprics. The bishopric of Wilna comprehended several actual governments; that of Samogitia, *au contraire*, only a part of the government of Kowno. The Bishop of Wilna was four times as rich as he of Samogitia, and, comparatively, speaking, the Chapter was equally so; while in the Senate, the former had a higher vote than the other, and, in short, carried himself in all things as the superior.

The Chapter of Samogitie was first composed of six canons, which, for more than a century, were considered sufficient, " but afterwards," said Wollonczewsky, the actual bishop, " it was found that the See had not enough pomp and eclât, and they therefore augmented the number." Later, eight charges were added, so that it was at last composed of fourteen members, and in 1621 they created the dignity of vicar.

This diocese was divided at the close of the sixteenth century into three deaneries — under Stanislas Kiszka into four; in 1636, into six; in 1752, into ten; under Etienne Gedroic, 1778-1801, into eleven ; these deaconries were Wornia, Olsiady, Szidlow, Retow, Szkoud, Janisz, Szadow, Krokow, Velone, Wekszniane and Botock.

As this was a poor diocese, having only a few churches and few estates, its see was generally occupied by bishops belonging to the *petite noblesse;* but when the number of the estates and churches augmented, the aristocracy did not disdain it either; and during the seventeenth and eighteenth centuries it was principally in the hands of the great families—of the Gedroics, the Pacs, the Sapiehas, &c. During this period these houses gave eight bishops, who administered the diocese for one hundred and sixteen years. Although the relations between the bishop and the chapter were usually the same as those of Wilna, nevertheless, the prelates being less independent and much poorer, comported themselves with more propriety towards their head. But the bishopric did not altogether escape dissensions and disputes, as we find in 1514-22, that Prince Nicolas Radzivill defended the episcopal rights against the chapter ; and farther, Bishop Victor Werzbycki 1565-67 solicited and obtained another diocese only that he might escape the arbitrary acts of the Chapter.

In fulfilling the prescriptions of the Council of Trent with regard to the education of the clergy, Bishop George Petkewicz, 1567-74, sent twelve clerks from Samogitia to Wilna, to study at the Academy of the Jesuits. After remaining there ten years and receiving consecration, they returned to Samogitia as curates. Prince Melchoir Gedroic, in 1581, built a house for his pupils in Wilna, and in 1601 a seminary was established at Wornia, and was confided to two Jesuits, but it did not exist long, and was closed in 1614, the pupils having been placed the preceding year at the Seminary of Wilna. After several years, however, students ceased to be sent to the Academy of Wilna. Nicolas Pae, 1609-19, proposed to give the Jesuits of Kroz some estates, on condition that they built and supported a seminary at Wornia, to which they willingly consented. After receiving the lands, however, they troubled themselves little about the seminary, but built one for themselves at Krozy, sheltered under the inspection of the bishops, and concerned themselves as little about it as they had done at Wilna. In 1624, Bishop Stanislas Kiszka demanded the restitution of the estates which had been given for the support of the seminary, and a process ensued between the Bishop and the Jesuits. This lawsuit was carried to Rome, where the Jesuits gained it, kept the estates, and the right of supporting the diocesan seminary of

Krozy. "They behaved themselves," said Wol-lonczewski, actual bishop of Samogitia and its historiographer, "as real mercenaries. Showing decided disdain for the secular clergy, they represented the priests and the clerks as so indigent and ignorant in every respect, that some of the best pupils refused to become a part of them. The seminary is full of young men little inclined to study; and the Jesuits intentionally neglect to develope their intellectual faculties, so that in future they should not eclipse the members of the Order." The higher Samogitian clergy constantly insisted on the transfer of the school to Wornia, so that they might more easily observe the teachings of the Jesuits. In 1635, 1691, and 1694, they expressed their opinions that if such a transfer did not take place, the instruction of the secular clergy would be in a deplorable state. At last Bishop Count Antoine Tyszkiewicz, in 1741, built a wooden house at Wornia and removed the seminary there, under the guardianship of the Piares, as the most instructed Order of that period. This school educated eight students, of whom six were supported at the expense of the establishment, and two at their own cost. The humiliated Jesuits could ill support such an affront, and in revenge intrigued to such a degree, that they succeeded in obtaining the banishment of the Piares and the complete control of the seminary, which they continued to manage till the abolition of their order. Wollonczewski thus describes their system of education :—To learn by heart the obscure Alvarius (Jesuitical Grammar) ; to speak good and bad Latin ; to imitate the national idiom by a *mélange* of Latin locutions ; to write entire volumes on the merits of their protectors and other powerful people ; to fill every work with periphrases and metaphors ; such were the characteristic traits of the savants of this period. With such trash the Jesuits filled the heads of the youths confided to them, which they taught in the school until a late date ; and it was they who spread that general ignorance, coupled with the decline of the sciences which we find in Poland under the reign of the house of Saxe." In 1774 the missionaries were called from Warsaw to Wornia, and the seminary was confided to their direction.

Such an educational system could certainly not produce instructed priests, but the lower Samogitian clergy were in general a pious class who greatly developed the religious sentiment amongst the people ; notwithstanding the masses did not act so much from conviction as from fear of punishment. What the system of coercion was may be judged by the fact that there was found in the churches an instrument called counitza, a sort of yoke, one end of which was fixed to the wall near the door of the church, and the other terminated in an iron ring which would admit the neck of a man. It was in this ring that they placed the sinner. Wollonczewski says, that in his time not very long ago,. a counitza was found in the church of Rosiene. The diocesan authority proceeded also severely against culpable ecclesiastics, they confined them in a prison built at Wornia for this purpose.

It was at a later date that the monastic orders appeared in Samogitie ; we do not find them there until the middle of the seventeenth century, and they arrived only to assist in arresting the progress of the Reformation. They spread themselves very rapidly in the following directions : 1st. The Jesuits, who first arrived, selected as their centre the city of Krozy district of Rosiene ; 2nd. The Benardines who fixed themselves at Kretengen, on the frontier of Prussia—at Cytowiany, at Telz, and at Datnow ; 4th. The Carmelites at Lincow, at Kejdany, at Rosiene and at Khwaloine. It was only in the eighteenth century that they founded their convents in the three last localities ; 5th. The Piares,

who also built their convent at Rosiene in the
eighteenth century; 6th. The Benedictines erected
their monastery at Posztoune in the end of the
eighteenth century; 7th. The Franciscans at
Zogniny; 8th. The Basiliens, fixed at Podoubisse
in the middle of the eighteenth century; 9th. The
Rockites at Wornia and Kenstacy and the
Mariaites at Krozy at the same epoch, and the
nuns of St. Catherine at Krok. The number of
the monastic orders which arrived displeased the
secular priesthood who soon found themselves
exposed to various inconveniences; the monks
relieving them of part of their charge and officiating in the parish churches without the consent
of the curates, so that in 1627 Bishop Abraham
Wojna was obliged to command that such monks
should be arrested where they showed themselves,
and conducted to the episcopal palace. Bishop
George Tyszkiewicz, the zealous protector of the
monastic orders, roused the indignation of both
the secular clergy and the noblesse, for having
dared, in 1642, to take the church of Rosiene from
the secular clergy and give it to the Dominicans.
The provincial synod of 1643 forbade the monks
to attract the people from the parish churches to
their convents, to preach in the pulpits tirades
against the secular priests, or to celebrate the

Sacrament in the parish chapels without the permission of the incumbent.

In accordance with the prescriptions of the Council of Trent, provincial synods were con-voked in the diocese of Samogitia as in that of Wilna, more for form's sake than for any real utility to the Church. It is a known fact, that the ordinances of the second Synod which took place in 1636 were drawn up without the synod being convoked. The bishop, George Tyszkiewicz, 1633-49 showed himself extremely partial to these assemblies, of which there were four under his episcopate. In all there were in Samogitia seven provincial synods between 1555-1636 at which the clergy were forbidden to wear the beard, and were commanded to cut the hair : and at which the priests were enjoined, in fact had no longer the right, to absolve those who did not pay tithes. The seventh and last synod, sat in 1752.

About the year 1414 the diocese of Kamience was founded, the Dominicans and the Franciscans being the first Roman priests in this district. At this period the population professed the Greek faith, and a Greek bishopric had already been established, so that here Catholicism did not introduce Christianity, which was disseminated far and wide before its appearance. As it contained a small number of priests and churches, it was subordinate to the metropolitan of Livow. The bishops of Kamience never convoked provincial synods like other dioceses, but sent their delegates to the synod of Livow, whose ordinances regulated it; thus one sees that this subordination to the Metropole of Livow was of much the same nature as the dependence of Wilna on the Archbishop of Gniesno. The town of Kamience was the seat of the diocesan chair, but at the time of the domination of the Turks it was transferred to Prague, to Lublin and other cities of Poland.

This diocese was not rich in ecclesiastical estates, so that the Polish Magnats did not grasp at it as they did at Wilna and Samogitia. It was, on the contrary, but a sort of preliminary step to richer and more important appointments, the occupants of the episcopal church being almost always transferred to the See of Chelm. The chapter was at first composed of sixteen prelates and canons, but in the course of time, the number augumented of itself without necessity and without authority to twenty-three. In 1712 this number was reduced to its primitive amount, but it again augumented, notwithstanding the remonstrances of the bishops. The Vicarage was quite useless because of the limited number of Catholic in-

habitants; it was established in 1730 by Adam
Oranski, the chancellor of the diocese, in an
arbitrary manner and only to serve his own views
of, as he expressed it, spreading Romanism; he
assigned it a considerable income hypothetically
upon his estates, but conditionally that the
members of his family should by preference be
appointed to this dignity. The consent only of
the bishop was considered necessary to sanction
such a creation. Oranski was himself the first
Vicar, and after attaining his end, he refused to pay
the sum promised for its endowment, began to dispose tyrannically of the diocese and the clergy, and
completely ruined the estates of the Chapter. The
High Clergy, headed by the bishop, complained to
the Pope; nevertheless the Vicarage remained as
it had been constituted until the annexation of
Podolia to Russia. The canons and prelates living
an idle life on their lands, entirely ceased to be
united in Chapters, so that in 1709 it was enacted,
under pain of a fine, that at least one part of the
members should meet every month; but this command, constantly repeated, was never executed.

The monastic corporations could still less contribute to the regular organization of the hierarchy.
Their opposition to all the measures of the bishops,
and their systematic antagonism to the secular

clergy, was evinced more openly in the diocese of Kamience, than in other bishoprics. In nearly all the epistles of the bishop to his flock, he directly mentions the disorders of the convents, and the insubordination and irregularities of the monks. In 1742 the bishop complained that under pretext of immunity and privilege they disregarded his authority, sixteen years later the secular clergy accused them of trespassing on their rights. In 1760 Bishop Krasinsky at his installation repeated the words of his predecessor concerning the abuses in the convents. Such admonitions, unsupported by a stedfast authority could hardly be otherwise than vain. The monks, living in idleness and luxury, following the impulses only of their own cupidity, defying and eluding the statutes of their orders, robbed the secular clergy of their revenues —principally those derived from interments— usurped the place of the curates, and even in occupying these places refusing obedience to the bishop. The erection of new convents was no exception to this rule. The monks assembling two or three near a church, gave it the title of a monastery, though they themselves following the statutes of another order; and one can imagine that these abuses were frequent enough, as Bishops Sierakowski and Krasinsky adverted to

them constantly in the epistles they published.

More than three centuries after the diocesan
seminary was founded, but only in name. In 1721
Etienne Roupnewsky, Bishop of Kamienec, assigned
700 florins yearly for the foundation of the school,
and the support of four pupils. Such a small sum
could not assure the existence of the institution,
and the number of pupils did not promise to increase the priesthood of the district, but in a
general way, this was but a secondary object.
Stanislas Hosius, bishop in 1727, published a
broadly enough defined regulation, for the administration of the diocese, containing the most
minute details of the different branches of ecclesiastical science, but does not mention the seminary.
No one ever visited or inspected the establishment,
and an Act of the Chapter of the year 1737 says:
"the clerks of the seminary are nearly naked." It
was only in 1742 that the age at which pupils could
enter the establishment, as well as the duration of
the course of study was determined on; and the
same year the bishop commanded that an annual
collection should be made for the benefit of the
school, but the priests would not pay even a trifling
sum to defray the support of their own instruction.
A legacy was left in 1752 by one of the canons for

the construction of an edifice for a seminary, but the Chapter who had the outlay of the money, so prolonged the works, that the house was not finished till 1791, and it was only in this year that the school was opened for instruction. This establishment presented a remarkable peculiarity, that neither the missionaries nor the Jesuits could ever obtain possession of it, but the Jesuits tried by a ruse to attract the pupils towards their institutions, and not unfrequently succeeded.

The dominant passion of the Latin clergy was riches. Not contented with estates they levied tithes under pain of anathema upon the poor parishioners, but from all their own revenues they sacrificed little for the public good. So far from this, the members of the Chapter in 1767 demanded exemption from all taxes, on the plea of their poverty ; and in 1773 when the republic had need of money all the clergy of this diocese refused the due called *subsidium charitativum*, pretending that they were impoverished in consequence of an epidemic which had scoured the country. Even at a period as critical as the invasion of the Turks, and the subjugation of the country by the infidel, the Roman clergy, forgetting their duty as citizens, only thought of their own interests. The Trinitarians to whom Count Potoki, Palatine of Coujuvie sent a sum of money for the benefit of the prisoners, appropriated it so that the Chapter was obliged to constrain them annually for their accounts.

Until 1742 the diocese of Kamienec was divided into four deaneries, but the same year two more were created. These deaneries were :—Jazlowiec with seventeen churches; Dounajgrod with eleven; Sharogrod with eight; Medziboz with six; Satanow with nine, and Czar-no-cosène with seven churches. At the time of the annexation of Podolia to Russia there were in this diocese more than fifty churches.

It is supposed that the bishopric of Luck was founded in 1375, beside Vladimir in Volhynia; in 1428 the episcopal chair was transferred to Luck. This diocese was very extensive, comprising Volhynia, Podlachei, Braclaw, Bresch, Litewski, and Polessie.

Volhynia was the cradle of the Orthodox Church in Russia; even in the tenth century the Greek bishopric of Vladimir existed, and at the commencement of the thirteenth that of Peremyszi was founded. Luck was erected in that of the fourteenth century. At the time of the establishment of the Roman Catholic diocese of Luck, all the population belonged to the Greek Church, so that it is evident that the Propagand instituted it exclusively for its own interests, that is to say, for proselytism. In 1340 the Volhynia submitted to Poland, and dating from this epoch, persecution commenced. The Greek clergy were oppressed, their churches were converted into Catholic chapels; so that, in 1343, the Greek population in this country implored .the assistance of the Tartar Khan to deliver them from this dreadful religious yoke. At last to promote more rapid conversions, Pope Gregory XI. established a Latin diocese, and the most efficacious and active arm of Romanism in the land consisted in Missions, whose only aim and end was the conversion of the Rutheniens to Romanism.

To avoid repetition, we shall not here speak of the interior organization of the different classes of the clergy of this diocese, amongst whom were many of the nobility, referring those of our readers, who desire more lengthened details, to the ample reports on this subject of the ordinary synods of the diocese, published in 1726 under Bishop Roupnewski.

The chapter of Luck was composed only of six canons; in 1755 Bishop Kobeilsky erected the vicarage. The bishops of Luck were often transferred as a sort of advancement to Wilna. This diocese had three seminaries :—Luck founded by Alexander Wychowski; Olyca founded in 1631 by Prince Radziwill, the Grand Chancellor of Lithuania, and at the expense of Zajerski, prelate of Olyca, who left a special sum to establish a school for eight pupils. This institution took the name of Collegium Zajerscianum; at the close of the last century it was transformed into a lay school. Janow, founded by Bishop Wytiwicky, in 1685; this seminary was confided to the Communist priests, and in 1782 to secular ecclesiastics. At their most flourishing periods these seminaries had only a very limited number of pupils, and their general state differed in nothing whatever from analagous establishments throughout Lithuania. Six provincial synods were held in this diocese, viz.:—1607, 1621, 1641, 1684, 1720, and 1726.

In the eighteenth century Luck had one hundred and eighty-three churches, and was divided into fourteen deaneries, namely, 1. Vladimir, with nineteen churches; 2. Doubno, with nineteen; 3. Kremenitz, ten; 4. Zbaraz, nine; 5. Zaslaw, nine; 6. Braclaw, where there was no church but had mission services; 7. Janow, nineteen; 8. Wengrow, nineteen; 9. Bielsk, sixteen; 10. Shereszow, fourteen; 11. Briansk, fourteen; 12. Droguiczine, eleven; 13. Lositza, thirteen; and 14, that of Kamience-Litewsky.

The date of the erection of the Roman Catholic

diocese of Kiew is not exactly known; some report it as in the middle of the fourteenth century; others in the year 1433; others again in the year 1471. This difference of opinion is thus explained: that the dignity of Latin bishop of Kiew was instituted before the real erection of the diocese for the purposes of proselytism. The first seven Latin bishops of Kiew were only honorary, and cannot be considered as such; and the first real incumbent of the diocese was Clement, who died in 1473. Just as many European monarchs wished to derive their lineage from the Emperor Augustus, and aristocratic families from ancient Rome, so the Roman Catholic clergy were pleased to trace the origin of Catholicism in different countries to a questionable period. Such an historical error, once adopted, passed from generation to generation, and without being impartially criticised, was converted into a pretended truth generally recognised. In our days such fictions are impossible by reason of conscientious investigation. They are only retained by some Catholic fanatics, who, contrary to truth and probability, support them; and thus it is that in the works of some contemporaneous Jesuits one reads such assertions as this,—that the Russians originally acknowledged the Popes, differing from the Roman Catholics only in the

Liturgy and not in the dogmas; and that during
several centuries the supremacy of Rome was
recognised, &c.

The constant efforts of the Popes during this
same epoch was to induce the Russians to acknowledge them as chiefs of the Church; proofs are
not wanting, however, to show that the Russians
never committed such apostacy, but this did not
prevent the Roman priesthood building deductions
and conclusions more erroneous still. There were,
it is true, some united Greeks, ignorant apostates
from orthodoxy, who in the seventeenth century
were particularly distinguished for their misplaced
zeal; there were even those who spread this fable,
that in the first half of the eleventh century the
Cathedral of St. Sophia at Kiew* had been a Roman
Catholic Church, and was afterwards transformed
into the Cathedral of the Latin bishops of that
diocese. These inventions, contrary to all historical evidence, passed into the works of some
Poles, and were re-copied by foreign writers. Such
was the favourite source from which modern Ultramontanists argue, who know little of the history
of Poland, and still less of that of Russia. The
Roman priesthood wished to base the history of

* Built by the Grand Duke Jaroslaw Wladimirowcz in the
first half the eleventh century.

their Church in this country on that of this illustrious cathedral, such a foundation being analogous with a recognition of the antiquity of Catholicism in the land; the Chapter of Kiew, in 1731, therefore, begged the Pope's permission to use a seal with the image of St. Sophia engraved, and, in accordance with their demand, Rome, in 1744, published a Bull, authorising the members of the Chapter to wear an octangular cross, with the eagle between St. Sophia and St. Joseph depicted on either side.

When the Grand Duke Vladimir embraced the doctrines of the Greek Church at Kiew, the inhabitants soon followed his example, and the Church became definitely established. This could not, naturally, be pleasing to the Popes, who, at the commencement of the thirteenth century, under Innocent IV., instituted a Russian mission composed of Dominicans and Franciscans, under the title of Societas Peregrinantium, the principal aim of which was the conversion of the orthodox to Romanism. About this epoch, the Dominicans built a cloister in the quarter of Kiew, called Podol; it was magnificently constructed, and was for a time the only Latin church in the government of Kiew, or in the eastern district of the Volhynie.

The Catholic diocese of Kiew having been definitely constructed, embraced the districts of Zytomir and of Ovroucz, and some churches in the district of Zwenigorod, as well as the meridional part of the government of Minsk. Founded like the dioceses of Kamience and Luck, for the purpose of conversions, in the middle of a population belonging to the Greek faith, this bishopric had for a long time but few churches. Niessecki says that in the fifteenth century there were only seven ; in the middle of the eighteenth, and even later, but nineteen, of which eight were monastic churches ; but when the Empress Catherine II. interfered efficaciously in the affairs of the orthodox Church in Lithuania, the Roman clergy united all their zeal to erect Latin places of worship in this country bordering on Russia ; so that, in 1777, there were already twelve, and the total number elevated the same year, in the district of Kiew, amounted to thirty-one, in a population of 27,459 souls. The parishioners lived in villages and towns remote for the greater part from the churches. Of the nineteen monasteries of different Orders, thirteen were built during the second half of the eighteenth century, and some even as late as the close of the same, that is, at an epoch when the taste for a monastic life was on the wane. This is another proof that the construction of such retreats was not based on real necessity, but sprung from the ambitious desire of proselytism. The monasteries on the right bank of the Dnieper were, so to say, the entrenched camps of Rome against a country lying on the opposite side of the river, the population of which was exclusively Greek in religion, and amongst whom there was not one Latin edifice. In the greater number of the convents the number of monks was very limited—three or five; and the monasteries were, as one may say, rallying centres for Propagand activity. In the year 1793 this diocese contained forty, divided into three deaneries, Zytomir, Ovroucz, and Faustow or Zwenigorod. The parish churches on the right bank of the Dnieper were all built in the second half of the eighteenth century, in the direction of North and South. These churches were, Iwankowska, Makarowska, Moszwenska, and Slimouska. Catholicism in this country advanced according to strategetic rules—to meet orthodoxy on the shore opposite the Dnieper. The Latin clergy hastened to cover all this district with churches; a short time before its annexation to Russia it was decided to build twenty-four parish churches on the royal lands of the Palatines of Kiew and Brescia, on spots selected by the bishop of the district. Every church was assigned a certain extent of land, with three thousand florins a year for the support of the building and the curate; but this decision of the Diet was not executed. We therefore see that, at the end of the eighteenth century, the Propagand had at least succeeded in laying out an insignificant bishopric, but that in reality this bishopric existed in name only.

The Bishop and Chapter of Kiew lived a life nearly nomadic. They were never in the cathedral, but officiated in the convent of the Dominicans. In the middle of the seventeenth century this city commenced to draw towards Russia, and in 1686 its union was an accomplished fact. Two years before the chair of the bishops had already been transferred to the Dominican convent in Lublin, where it remained till 1724. In this year it was placed at Zytomir, and during war time or periods of political disorder it was temporarily transported to other places;—to Sokal in 1743; in 1743-68, to Czoudnowo, fifty versts from the town of Zytomir; to Berdiezew to the convent of the Carmelites; to Serbinowka, to Faonstowo (district of Wassilkow), which was episcopal property. The cathedral of Zytomir, which Bishop John Osga commenced to build, was only consecrated by his successor, Güetan Soltyk, in 1751. Since the time of Bishop Alexander Sokolowsky, 1636-45, the bishops of Kiew appropriated to themselves the title of Bishop of Czernigow, styling themselves from this date bishops of Kiew and Czernigow, in imitation of the title of the orthodox bishop of Kiew and Czernigow, though in the whole of the latter district there were absolutely no Latin churches. This, however, did not hinder the Roman bishop from creating the dignity of Archdeacon of Czernigow.

The Chapter of Kiew only commenced to organise itself in the beginning of the seventeenth century. Bishop Christopher Kazymirsky (1618) founded six canonicates and Radoszewski four prélatures. In time the number of the Chapter considerably increased, so that towards the close of the eighteenth century we find eight prelates and twelve canons. The Chapter was not rich in landed property, therefore the prelates and canons may be said only to have borne an honorary title. They paid little attention to their duties, did not reside near the Episcopal See, and passed their time at Warsaw and elsewhere. In 1726 Bishop Osgar wrote to the Chapter that for a long time he had not seen one of them, or even heard of them, so that he was in ignorance as to their location. He thus terminates his epistle, "Scit enim quisque ex personis capitularibus esse cathedram nostram ad Boristhenem, non ad Vistulam."

Fresius, the historian of the diocese of Kiew, thus characterises the epoch of the episcopacy of Bishop Osgar :—" Hoc pessimum malum ex eo precipue hanc occuparat diœcesin, quia longo tempore antistitum nullus suas cognoverat oves, nec istæ suum cognoverant pastorem. Capitulum erat extra diœcesin, diœcesis extra sacerdotas." Such a position of the diocese and the chapter even later varied not, notwithstanding all the admonitions of the bishops. Thus, for example, in 1746, of all the prelates and canons there was not a single one at his post. The Roman diocese of Kiew existed more, as we have said, in name than in fact; but it had all the exterior appearances of a real and even an important bishopric to such a point that in 1740 it was found necessary to establish a vicarage, which consisted then of eighteen churches. Antony Tyskiewicz, the Secretary of the Grand Duchy of Lithuania and canon of Wilna, assigned in 1739 a sum of twent thousand florins (Polish) for the foundation of the Vicarage of Kiew, for which he mortgaged his estates, and which, according to the most ample and reliable information did not belong to him.

Notwithstanding this the Vicarage was created, and Tyszkiewicz named vicar.

The Seminary founded at Zytomir supported six students, and was confided to the Jesuits, 1762.

This more imaginary than real bishopric had also its Provincial Synods, one held in 1640, but where is not known; the other in 1762, at Zytomir.

The diocese of Smolensk was created in 1638 at the request of Abraham Wojna, Bishop of Wilna, in a country where for centuries the population belonged to the Greek rite, and where, as early as between the years 1128-37, there already existed a Greek bishopric. The pretext for the foundation of this diocese was the extent of that of Wilna, a part of which formed the new see The excuse, given out before the actual erection of the bishopric that Wilna was too extended, was certainly not valid, but the true intention of its institution was to propagate Romanism amongst a people essentially and originally Russian. The Jesuits entered Smolensk in the suite of Sigismond III.; this city, during the seventeenth century, passed from hand to hand, sometimes belonging to the Russians, sometimes to the Poles. It was not definitely restored to Russia till 1686. The Latin bishop of this see did not reside in the city, but lived at Wilna or Warsaw. In reality the bishops of Smolensk, although they had a seat in the Senate, and bore the title of "Vicar of the Metropolitan of Gneisno," were only the superior prelates of Wilna. Thus Bishop Prince Jerome Sanguszko— the first of his name who renounced the Greek faith—and Gothard John Tiesenhausen were at the same time vicars of Wilna; Cassimir Pac was Arch Priest and Kotowicz was *prelat custos* of the see of Wilna. The bishops of Smolensk were purely nominal, but distributed with prodigality the honorary title of Canon of Smolensk, so that in a short time all the Chapter of the bishopric assembled round the chair of Wilna. It exalted the *eclât* and the pomp of the bishops of the last named See, who loved to pass themselves off for Primates of Lithuania, as the Archbishops of Gniesno were in reality for Poland. This same Kotowicz erected the vicarage of Smolensk. In all this diocese there were only four small Roman Churches; but, notwithstanding this see and its Chapter of eight canons continued to exist till the end of the eighteenth century. There were in all fifteen bishops, although this city had for a long time before ceased to belong to Poland. ' The Roman bishopric of Smolensk had neither a sufficient Catholic population, Latin churches, nor an episcopal capital.

The bishopric of Inflandt or Livonia was founded on the ancient archbishopric of Livonia. In 1561 this country was annexed to Lithuania, and in 1569, at the time of the re-union of the latter to Poland, Livonia, Courland, and Semigale were equally incorporated with this kingdom. In 1582 Etienne Bathory, the king, replaced the archbishopric of Livonia by the bishopric of Wenden, and gave its bishop a seat in the Senate after that of Kamience. A Provincial Synod, held, in 1621, under the presidency of Laurent Guembicki, nominated the Bishop of Wenden, vicar of the archbishop of Gneisno, although he was always in reality vicar of the bishop of Wilna. This see, however, was by the treaty of Oliva, in 1660, under King John Cassimir, entirely abolished, though the title of Bishop of Livonia was retained. This bishop's authority extended over, in all, twenty-four churches and chapels—fourteen in Livonia and ten in Courland. For such a limited administration a vicarage was founded in 1743, under Pouzyna. At the same time its bishops having a fixed residence went from one town to another—from Dunaburg in Livonia to Kraslaw, the property of the Counts Plater; from thence to Tanow, not far from Kowno, but invariably forgetting and abandoning their flocks. Like the bishops of Smolensk, those of Livonia had no cathedral, but this did not hinder them from surrounding themselves with a Chapter of twelve canons. A seminary was founded at Kraslaw in 1755, which was superintended by the missionaries. Count Plater and Bishop Ostrowsky presented the institution with four thousand thalers, on condition that four students should be educated for the diocese of Inflandt. Guilsen, the Bishop of Smolensk, also gave them two thousand thalers, for the support of two clerks for his see. Besides this the missionaries were bound to render him yearly a mission.

From this glimpse of the history of the Roman Catholic bishoprics of the Western Provinces at an epoch when they belonged to Poland, one sees that in reality there were only four dioceses—Wilna, Samogitia, Luck, and Kamience. As to those of Kiew, Smolensk, and Inflandt, they existed only in name.

RESUMÉ OF THE FOREGOING CHAPTERS.

WE have confined ourselves to an aperçu History of Roman Catholicism in the Lithuanian provinces under the Polish *régime*, and we resume, generally, the state of the Roman Church in these countries at the time of their annexation to Russia.

After the definite partition of Poland four Catholic dioceses entered the new limits of Russia. Wilna, Samogitia, Luck, and Kamience-Podolsk. It is easily understood that we do not include those of Kiew, Smolensk, and Inflandt, which existed only in name. The extent of these dioceses did not correspond either with the number of parishioners or religious requirements. The revenues and the landed estates of the clergy were also very unequally divided. The Bishops of Wilna and of Samogitia, for example, enjoyed great riches, while those of Smolensk and Livonia were poor. Those bishops whose nomination depended on the king, were not only the first senators, but the

presidents of the different Councils of Finance
and War. They occupied the first place in the
Diets convoked within the limits of their clerical
jurisdiction, and not unfrequently they were also
captains in the Polish cavalry. Such an amalga-
mation of civil and ecclesiastical functions did not
permit them to apply themselves to their spiritual
obligations, so that they selected suffragans and
vicars to fulfil their duties.

The relations of the bishops and the chapters
were not always the same, the latter often limiting
the authority of the bishop, and absolutely opposing him ; and sometimes they in turn had only the
name of an Episcopal Council, the bishop acting
independently. In all cases the relations were
unsteady and unstable, depending on persons and
circumstances. The members of the Chapter generally confided the administration of the churches,
of which, in their capacity of ritular curates, they
enjoyed the revenue, to poor vicars, *clerus inferior*,
for a moderate salary, reserving to themselves the
easiest offices.

The Roman Catholic clergy enjoyed in general
great rights and privileges. Nomination to the
posts of Chancellor and Vice-Chancellor of Lithuania depended on the secular clergy, while the prelates and canons filled the position of secretary,

referees, &c. Ecclesiastics encumbered the tribunals, were exempt from all civil jurisdiction, and
depended only on the ecclesiastical bench, which
regulated all processes on the subject of tithes,
legacies, and wills; and this ghostly legislation,
founded on the canon rite, was usually accompanied
with menaces of anathema and excommunication.
They held the exclusive right of censorship on all
religious books or any work on morality; and in
emancipating themselves from the power of the
State, they dabbled in civil and political affairs.
Such were their immense resources by means of
which they fortified their position in Church and
State !

But while the high clergy, through the influence
of Rome, through intrigues, through their riches
and their domineering spirit, obtained the finest
livings and wielded to their own advantage the
power of the Church, the lower clergy were in a
state of penury, and were oppressed and put upon
by their rich *confrères*. Ecclesiastical endowments,
constantly augmenting, were often made in favour
of convents and brotherhoods, while no attention
was paid to the country curates. Indigence is the
parent of ignorance, and many of the village priests
were not in a position to explain the dogmas of
their religion to their parishioners. The Catechism

and the Creed were not even the same in many of the parishes, so that the peasant who moved from one parish to another found there different doctrines to those taught him by his own priest. The establishment of missionaries who travelled in an itinerant way from one parish to another resulted from the ignorance of the parochial clergy, who were themselves deficient in the instruction necessary for their flocks, and obliged them to permit it to be grasped from others. These missionaries travelled through the country from village to town, and from town to village, as they would do in a land into which the light of the Gospel had not yet penetrated.

Directing our attention to the state of the seminaries, we there discover the cause of the ignorance of the priesthood. The students were educated either at the expense of the seminary or at their own cost ; the former only received instruction and board ; the latter being educated at their own expense, were mostly the scions of the *noblesse* destined to occupy the higher ecclesiastical dignities; they were therefore privileged, had better food, and were not constrained to fatigue themselves with scientific studies. The free scholars were obliged to provide themselves with clothes and other necessary articles, and destitute of all means, they often found it impossible to remain and finish the course, quitting the establishment without finishing their education.   These two classes were rigorously separated during their residence at the seminary; and just as the rich and poor were divided in their youth so were they also distinguished at the period of their nomination to curacies—the poor settling down as country pastors, forming what is termed parochial clergy; the rich exclusively reserved for prelacies, canonries, abbeys, &c.   Their families and even the bishops retained these young men in the clerical career, nor was it at all uncommon for them to be nominated canons while yet on the school bench.   When they left the seminary these young men went to Rome to solicit lucrative places from the Holy Father, who had the right during certain months of the year to nominate to the richest curacies depending on the episcopal sees and colleges.   In this way poverty on the one hand, and riches on the other, hindered their intellectual development.

The religious orders were very numerous in Lithuania, and constantly increased even at a time when the penchant for a monastic life was dying out.   The Head of the Church however did not cease to think that he had too few.   It is worthy of remark that the major part of the convents on

the western side of the actual government of Kiew,
and of eastern Volhynia, a country in which the
populations were almost entirely of the Greek
faith, were only founded in the latter half of the
eighteenth century. This is a significant fact,—
they were in fact the Latin forts built upon the
confines of the Russian Church, not for defence
but for attack,—they were the head-quarters of
Latin proselytism.

The same thing appears in White Russia, where
the people were either of the Russian or the United
Greek faith. The number of Latin convents in
this country, compared to the Catholic population,
exceeded ten times the number of the Lithuanian
monasteries, or of those of Samogitia, where nearly
all the inhabitants were Roman Catholics. The
monastic orders acknowledging little subordination
to the authority of the bishop or the government,
struggled perpetually with the secular clergy about
.the curacies; and with the exception of the men-
dicant orders, were much busier about mundane
affairs than the moral education of the people, over
whom, however, they exercised a delusive exercise
in the name of religion. The Monastic Schools
were only nurseries for religious intolerance, and
for centuries rested in a state of complete stagna-
tion. Even at the time when the lay establish-

ments were withdrawn, in the reign of Augustus III., from the Jesuits, and confided to the
superintendence of a Commission of Education,
which considerably ameliorated them, they, not
depending on the government, preserved their
old organisation. • Science, for example, physic,
mathematics, &c. were totally excluded, as the
monks said they had nothing in common with religion.   As to the convents of the nuns, the women
were forbidden even to learn to write.   The provincials who had the inspection of the schools of
their Orders, prepared the pupils not for good
Christians, honest citizens, or enlightened servants
of the Altar, but to grasp at new riches, to propagate their society, and by all and every means
augment its influence.   Their attention was only
directed towards the attraction of new novices,
without inquiring whether these pupils were of a
suitable age to permit them to choose the profession.   Not unfrequently even children of a tender
age pronounced the vows, without any idea of what
they meant or what they related to.   The civil
authority was at last constrained to limit this
abuse, and quoted the articles of the Council of
Trent relating to the subject; and to the great
displeasure of Rome, the Diet of 1768 determined
the age before which the vows could not be admin-

istered—for the men twenty-four, and for the women sixteen years. In case of infraction of this enactment the superiors of the convents were fined.

CHAPTER VI.

STATE OF THE LATIN CHURCH IN RUSSIA DURING THE REIGN OF THE EMPRESS CATHERINE II.

Institution of the hierarchy in White Russia.—The Papal power in Russia limited.—Selection of Monsieur de Siestrencewitz as Bishop of White Russia in 1773.—Biographical notice of Siestrencewitz, 1731-1826.—Subordination of the regular and secular clergy to the Bishop.—Ameliorations introduced by Siestrencewitz in the Convents.—Establishment of a Seminary at Mohilew, 1778.—Plan of education for the Seminary.—Opposition of the Jesuits to Siestrencewitz.—After the abolition of the Order of the Jesuits, the Empress Catherine accords them an asylum in White Russia.—Utility and inconveniences of this measure.—Siestrencewitz elevated to the dignity of Archbishop, 1782.—Benislawaky, a creature of the Jesuits, nominated coadjutor of the Archbishop, 1782.—Relations of the Government with the Holy See.—Mission of Archetti, the Nuncio, to Petersburg, 1783.—Organisation of the Chapter of Mohilew.—Changes in the formula of the oath taken by the bishops introduced by the Empress Catherine.—Steps taken by the Empress to obtain for Siestrencewitz a Cardinal's hat, 1785.—Spiritual powers accorded to the Archbishop by the Pope, 1786.—Permission to bring foreign priests to Russia.— Church of St. Louis at Moscow, 1790.—Construction of churches in the South and in Saratoff.—Measures concerning the landed estates of the monastic orders.—Establishment of the dioceses of Inflandt, Pinsk, and Leticzew, 1793.—Project of limiting the number of Convents, 1795.—Armenian Catholic Church in Russia, and Doctrine of the Primitive Armenian Church.—

Latin Propagand among the Armenians.—Galanus, 1650-59.
—Marquis de Serpos, eighteenth century.—Mekhitar, 1676-
1749.—Catholic Armenian Academy at Venice.—Introduction
of Romanism into the Armenian Church.—Armenians in the
Volhynia and in Podolia.—Bembus and his proselytism amongst
them, 1630.—Torrosowicz, named in 1626 Armenian Bishop of
Livow, passes over to Romanism, 1631.—Conversions by violence of the Armenians of Livow to Latinism, 1631.—The
Order of Theatins arrive at Livow and found the Collegium
Pontificum.—Latin Propagand among the Armenians at Kamience-Podolsk, 1666, and at Mohilew upon the Dniester.—
Catholic Armenians in meridional Russia.—Latin Propagand
in Georgia.—The Armenian Catholic clergy subordinated to
the authority of the Archbishop of Mohilew, 1784.—The
populations of the Western Provinces belong in greatest part
to the Greek and United Greek Churches.—The Greek people,
persecuted by the Latins, continually implore the protection
of Russia.—Intervention of the Empress Catherine in their
favour.—Pope Clement XIII. engages King Stanislas-Augustus
to do nothing in their favour.—The Empress Catherine
decides to employ armed force, and obtains liberty of conscience for the Russians.—Situation of the United Greek
Church in the Western provinces.—The Basilians.—Their
violence against the United Greek secular clergy.—Antagonism
of the Lower Clergy and this Order.—The Empress Catherine
establishes a United Greek bishopric in White Russia.—
Heraclius Lissowsky named Archbishop of Polotsk, 1784.—
The Basilians subordinated to the authority of the Archbishop.
—The United Greeks return to the Greek orthodox faith in
White Russia, in the Volhynia and in Podolia.—Measures
taken against the Basilians.—The union denuded of all
vitality, falls of itself.—Mixed marriages.—General considerations upon the measures of the Empress Catherine for the
ecclesiastic administration.

WE have detailed the hierarchical organisation in
which the Russian Government found the Roman
clergy at the time of the successive incorporation

of the Latin dioceses with Western Russia after
tho partition of Poland.

By the first partition in 1772 Russia acquired
White Russia, which formed only a part of the
diocese of Wilna, excepting some parishes belonging to the diocese of Inflandt, and four curacies
appertaining to the see of Smolensk. The first
act of the Russian Government solemnly guaranteed liberty of religion in these provinces, and
organised the hierarchical administration of the
Catholic Church. Before the chief of that Church
had thought of its future destinies in Russia, the
Empress Catherine spontaneously constituted for
the churches of White Russia, and the other Latin
parishes existing in her empire, the dignity of
Roman Archbishop, to whom she confided their
administration by virtue of the Act of 1769,
published and promulgated for the Church at
St. Petersburg, by the terms of which the Archbishop was not subject to the interference of Rome,
but to the Russian Minister of Justice, as we
shall see.

In uniting to Russia a Roman Catholic population recognising as its spiritual chief a Pontiff,
not only independent of herself, but actually the
sovereign of another independent country, Catherine found it necessary from the commencement to

determine exactly the position of the Pope, *vis-à-vis* the State, in her empire, and to fix the limits of his authority. Far from attacking the dogmas and the rights of the Latin population in White Russia, she but confirmed them by instituting a hierarchy, but would never recognise in Rome the right to interfere under pretext of religion in the discipline of the Roman clergy in Russia, nor in the affairs of the Government. Following the example of the principal States where the Catholic faith predominated, she declared, in 1772, that no Bull or brief of the Papacy, no ecclesiastical ordinance of foreign fabrication should be published in White Russia without the authority and sanction of her Government. This important measure, which completely changed the position of the High Polish clergy towards the executive, as well as towards Rome, the regulation of whose affairs had been until then carried out through a Nuncio residing at Warsaw, became a fundamental law of the empire. The successor of Catherine constantly confirmed this enactment, notwithstanding variations which sometimes took place in the administration of the Roman Church. It exists until the present, and it is to be hoped that in future times it will not be abrogated.

Having resolved on creating an ecclesiastical

hierarchy for the Roman Catholic population of White Russia, and unable herself to select a bishop for such an important function, the Empress begged Monsigneur Massalsky, Bishop of Wilna, to name one worthy the position. His choice fell upon Siestrencewicz, canon of Wilna, who was consecrated, in 1773, Bishop of Malles *in partibus*. This remarkable man administered the affairs of the Catholic Church in Russia for more than half a century. He served four sovereigns, and became the object of the respect of some and of irreconcileable hatred to the others ; attracting these sentiments because distinguished from other Polish priests of this period, as much by his character and capacity, as by the cultivation and enlightened tendencies of his mind. He had been educated in quite another sphere, under different aspects and circumstances, and for these reasons it is indispensable to dedicate to him a special chapter. He was born September 3rd, 1731. His parents belonged to the Lithuanian gentry of the Reformed Church, who placed him at the Protestant school of Sluck, which had been founded by Prince Radzivill at the time of the struggle of the Reformation against the Catholic Church in Poland, and which still remained the centre of the Polish Reformers. This school exists till the present time, under the name

of the Gymnase. His intelligence, and his pre-
disposition for science, attracted the attention
of his superiors to Siestrencewicz. Finishing the
course at Sluck, he was sent to complete his
studies at Frankfort, where he remained three
years, from 1748 to 1751. He then travelled
through Europe, visited London and Amsterdam,
and acquired several languages. The profession
of the Church for which he was destined little
suited a young man full of life, in whom the
passions kept pace with the thirst for knowledge;
so that, instead of becoming a theologian of the
Reformed Church as intended, he became a Prussian huzzar, and afterwards entered the guard of
Lithuania as ensign, from which, after ten years'
service, he retired in 1761 with the rank of captain.
Having no private fortune, and no other prospect
of support, he entered the family of Prince Radzivill as tutor. The ardour of youth having calmed
down, the profession he had adopted exactly suited
him. The position of the Radzivill estates near to
Wilna, then the centre of Romanism in Lithuania;
the frequent visits of the bishop to the Prince, as
well as of other Catholic ecclesiastics, initiated
him into the doctrines of their faith and decided
him to adopt it. He then commenced with energy
to study the dogmas; and in 1762 finished a course

of theology at the chief college of the Piares at Warsaw. The following year the missionaries instructed him in the rites of the Church, and the same year he was consecrated a priest. One cannot suppose him actuated by other motives than the profession he had entered, as neither he nor any other person could then imagine the dignity he should attain. On the contrary, had he remained in the Protestant Church, and become a theologian of that Confession, he was sure of an existence if not of advancement, the professors of Sluck knowing and appreciating him. In their School he had been educated gratuitously, and it was at the expense of the same establishment that he afterwards continued his studies abroad. A certain career was therefore open to him; but, till the end of his days, the enemies of Siestrencewicz reproached him for having been born in the religion of Calvin, as if it depended on himself to select a confession of faith prior to his début on earth! In all the administrative measures as local head of the Church, which diverged ever so little from habitual routine, they saw only the shadows of the darkness of Calvinism. Far from that, he retained from his early education neither the subtle theology or the polemical spirit against Romanism, but a cultivated mind which the system and the

rules of the Jesuits purposely uprooted in their
pupils, by whom nearly all the ecclesiastical contemporaries of Siestrencewicz had been instructed.
It was this which so justly placed him above them
and excited their envy and indignation. Zealous
for religion, he nevertheless preserved his love of
science to the end of his days ; and, to the great
astonishment of the fanatical Latins, did not dissimulate his sympathy for a wise civilization. He
occupied his leisure hours with history, literature,
and even medicine. All this was so new and so
strange in the clerical character, that those around
him attributed this tendency of his mind to secret
apostasy from the faith he had embraced, as in
their opinions Science was incompatible with
faith ! They reproached him, as with a crime,
that he had translated the works of Mackenzie,—a
work on health and the means of preserving it,—
from English into Polish ; yet this translation
procured him with the consent of King Stanislas
Augustus, the Priory of Homel. He was even
satirised for his little respect for the Latin language, which he called a skeleton. But his spirit
was superior to all such criticism, and only required an occasion to prove itself so. This opportunity presented itself at the time of the departure
of Massalsky, Bishop of Wilna, for abroad. Filling

the functions of Canon, he administered the diocese *ad interim*, and in a short time had re-established the episcopal authority amongst the disobedient clergy. He regulated the affairs of the bishopric, put down abuses, and proved himself not only a man of spirit and of extensive knowledge, but of a firm and determined character. This qualification, however, contributed in the end to multiply the number of his enemies. Such was the pastor recommended by Bishop Massalsky for White Russia. He was personally unknown to the Empress, and she had only heard of him through a sermon which he preached at Wilna the 13th of November, 1771, on the occasion of an attempt on the life of King Stanislas Augustus, whom the confederates under Poulawsky had nearly made prisoner close to the walls of Warsaw, when the King escaped with a sabre cut on the head. This enlightened bishop appreciated his sovereign, and seconded all efforts for the amelioration and welfare of his Catholic subjects. Catherine herself, when she knew Siestrencewicz, respected him, and testified this appreciation by deeds.

An imperial ukase of the Empress, dated November 22nd, 1773, named him Bishop of White Russia, his chair and residence being at Mohilew. He received appointments suitable to his dignity :

ten thousand roubles per year, with three benefices
—viz., Dean of the See of Wilna, Prior of Homel
and Bobrinsk, with the estates appertaining to
them in the different governments; so that his
entire income amounted to something like 60,000
roubles per annum.

In 1774, the administration of the diocese of
White Russia was organised by the Empress without any preliminary understanding or communication with Rome. In White Russia, properly speaking, there were few Latins, the greater number
being United Greeks, or Russians of the Greek
faith. Nevertheless, it was necessary for the wellbeing of the Roman Catholic Church, and of the
people of this confession in Russia, to put an end
to the crying disorders which had crept in amongst
the clergy under Polish domination. The chief
abuse consisted in, as we have seen, the gross
ignorance and dissolution of the monastic Orders,
who refused to submit to episcopal authority. A
change was also made in the jurisdiction of the
bishops with regard to the right of patronage in
connection with the secular clergy, as they only could
nominate to the parishes instituted and supported
by private funds the priest selected by the founder
or his heirs. These parishes were numerous enough
in Lithuania. Some belonged to the King, as

founded by the kings, the curates being named by
royal authority. This change subjected the monastic
clergy to the authority of the bishops, and the
secular clergy were at the same time rendered independent of them in what concerned nomination
to curacies. Such an organisation would engender
much disorder under Roman Catholic government,
and under the Russian administration it was next
to impossible, especially in what concerned the
religious orders. The provincials of the different
fraternities which had existed in White Russia,
remaining subject to Poland, where they continued
to reside; they consequently were beyond the
limits of the empire, and the superintendence of
the convents was not confided to them. To give a
solid base to the hierarchical organisation, it was
necessary to extend the authority of the bishop,
and place him in a position to administer properly
the requirements of his diocese. This is exactly
what the Empress had in view in completely subordinating the regular and secular clergy to Bishop
Siestrencewitz, and prohibiting all direct relations
with foreign authorities.

Having taken in hand the administration confided to him, and thinking little of exterior pomp,
the splendour of the Chapter, or the arrangement of
the episcopal palace, Siestrencewitz devoted nearly

the whole of the year 1777, to a most detailed
revision and a personal inspection of the churches
in White Russia. He was not more pained at the
decadence of the monastic life, than by the ignorance and dissolute conduct of the monks, and the
bad state of the monastic schools. There was no
other remedy than to re-organise the convents,
notwithstanding their ancient statutes, otherwise
they would continue to be little else than a scourge
for the country and disgrace even religion itself,
as had already been the case in Poland. The
bishop based his plan of re-organisation upon the
necessity of civilising all the orders in general,
whatever their regulations or privileges might be,
but evading that which was contrary to Catholic
doctrine. To teach others, it is necessary to be
oneself instructed. So before ameliorating the
condition of the monastic schools, it was necessary
that the monks should receive sufficient education to
act as preceptors in these schools. From this point
the bishop started. He enacted as a standing
order, that every monk learn professionally, elocu-
tion, history, geography, and the literature of the
country, French, mathematics, and even physiology.
To afford them time for these acquirements, he
simplified and abrogated several monastic customs
—dispensed with processions and other religious

ceremonies during lessons, and forbade them to
absent themselves from the monasteries in the
hours appropriated to study, dividing their occupations, and arranging the time for recreation and
repasts. He took this opportunity to recommend
them to abstain from the use of strong liquors, and
resolved on the inspection of the monastery every
year. He commanded a wing to be added to every
religious house for a school, or else that a part of
the building should be assigned for it. In publishing these ordinances, Siestrencewitz addressed
the monks as follows : " Our brethren shall not
regard civilization as a scourge, but shall endeavour
to prepare their pupils to be honest citizens, to develope in them dispositions of pity and mercy
towards all humanity without regard to religion, to
country or social condition. They must teach
them to prefer truth to dignities, to cultivate
the heart, and habituate them to the world and the
faithful service of the empress and the country."
After delivering these precepts for the reform of the
monastic retreats, he addressed the clergy, " At
our epoch when it is complained with justice that
the monastic classes are corrupt and falling into
decay, and that none of them consider how to
be useful to his country, Providence has ordered
that in this golden age the immortal Catherine

makes them contribute to the welfare of her other
subjects."

It was scarcely to be expected that the civilization of the monks could be promptly effected. This
was a work of time, as it was no easy matter to habituate to scientific pursuits men who were already of
an advanced age and accustomed for the most part
to idleness. But the Church imperiously demanded
pious and enlightened servants. To prepare such
pastors, Siestrencewitz, in 1778, formed a seminary at Mohilew for fifty clerks, confining the
superintendence to the priests of St. Vincent de
Paul. A part of these were lay students; others
came from the monastic schools, and were intended to enter holy orders later. This foundation was indispensable, considering the complete
decadence of the monastic schools, from which the
bishop expected nothing good. The seminary of
Mohilew was endowed with an estate, and a small
house which had belonged to the Carmelites—its
first endowment consisted of half the revenues which
the missionaries received for the support of a small
seminary founded in 1756, at Kraslawl, by the
Counts Plater, in the district of Dunaburg, government of Vitebsk, upon the confines of Courland.

Siestrencewitz conceived a vast and enlightened
plan of education diametrically opposed to the in-

tellectual slavery inveterate in the Latin schools.
"Above all," said he, "it is necessary to teach the
pupils to reflect and reason otherwise than they
have hitherto done, and to unlearn many things
they have hitherto learnt. The aim of their education is to fit them for the ecclesiastical profession,
which means, that they must prepare themselves
to celebrate the Divine services according to the
dogmas and the rites of their church. They must
learn to preach and to inculcate Christianity and
loyalty in their flocks, deserving their confidence
and respect by their own good conduct, kind-
heartedness, and useful knowledge. To this end
the sciences must be taught in the seminaries, not
only in a scholastic sense, but in a practical, com-
prehensible, and sensible manner." The ecclesiastical courses which they taught in the seminaries
were:—Moral theology, professional eloquence,
Church history, the Canon Law and its rights.
The ideas of Siestrencewitz on the Sciences, and
the spirit in which they should be taught, deserve
particular attention. He said, " The principal
study in the seminary is theology. Monastic
theology merits at least its name; it is only a
science of syllogisms. One can only comprehend
it by a peculiar course of logic and metaphysical
reasoning worth no attention. In our enlightened

century we unite dogmas to reason, and teach
theology to render man better and happier. To
give such an education it is necessary to find enlightened and capable teachers. Another science,"
he afterwards says, " which should make a part of
the first is moral theology. Unfortunately it has
been separated from dogmatical theology in order
to inspire more respect for the moral yoke which
they (the priesthood) preach, and which they en-
velope in clouds, notwithstanding that moral theology, even in its spirit, should be the enlightened
guide of man's existence. If this division of a
pure science must be tolerated, it is at least desirable that a Professor teach the two parts. In
deducing moral precepts from dogmas, and apply-
ing them as the foundation of the welfare of man,
the Professor should not be arrested by frivolous
and supposititious points, such as, for example,
What is the language of angels? or the biography
of Jesus Christ from his twelfth or thirteenth year,"
&c. He thus expressed himself on the subject
of professional eloquence :—" The priest must
learn this science, not only to assist his own
meditations, when with crossed arms he sits at his
own fireside, or in his cell; but to use it in his
pulpit, at the Confessional, or at the bed of the
dying. Massillon and Bourdalone have left us

works from which to draw rules and examples, and which have before now formed great preachers. The history of the Church should be taught according to Fleury." As to the canon law, and the obligations and relations of the clergy, with respect to lay and ecclesiastical authority, he gives the following definition:—" Unfortunately," he says, " reason does not guide everybody. With some it is necessary to employ constraint. The law relating to such individuals has been prescribed and laid down. The ecclesiastic owes obedience and fidelity to his sovereign, in return for his daily bread and the security he enjoys in the empire, and need not imagine that difference of costume exempts him from such duties. He is naturally not bound to know all the laws of the empire, but only those which concern and serve to maintain the clergy and the Church. Consequently they shall teach the canon law in the seminaries, *as laid down by the Sovereign for the Catholic Church of the empire, which enjoys her protection.*" Besides ecclesiastical sciences, the following subjects were part of the programme for the education of theological students. Physique, philosophy, hygienics, history, geography, the Russian language, with judicial explanations, Latin which should be taught, not according to the corrupt idioms of the canonical books, but after classical models; German, French, and Italian, all indispensable in different parishes where there were individuals of mixed nationalities. This plan of education, already applied in the seminary of Mohilew, from the time of its foundation, developed itself gradually in proportion to the means and the men prepared for the important position of preceptors—preceptors, not of the dead sciences, which generally fatigue the memory and obscure the intelligence of pupils, but professors of sciences based on good sense, and destined to form true ecclesiastics, and not a caste; a class of men useful in their parishes as well as in society; not inimical to the State, but desiring to be active members of the same.

In instituting these reforms Siestrencewitz necessarily met with great obstacles; but he had sufficient firmness of character to execute and carry out his projects despite of ignorance, opposition, and prejudice. Not sympathising with the fanaticism and grasping ambition of the Jesuits, he found himself in antagonism to this order, which refused obedience to any authority but their own. At the time of the annexation of White Russia the Empress sent the following command to the governors of these provinces:—" Make a list of the convents and schools of the Jesuits. You will parti-

cularly watch these priests as the most perfidious
and pernicious of the Latin fraternities. See that
they are subordinate to and undertake nothing
without the authority of their superiors." The
year following Pope Clement IV. abolished them,
and the sovereign who had dictated these lines
preserved them in White Russia, gave them an
asylum, and prolonged the existence of their order
until a time when, thanks to a change of circumstances, Rome re-established them. We know not
truly at which to be astonished—the disobedience
manifested in their opposition to the ordinances of
the Pope, whose faithful servants they termed
themselves, or the protection which the most
enlightened sovereign of this period accorded them,
to the detriment of national civilization—a protection which even forbade all polemical discussion
against the Jesuits. The only explanation of this
policy of Catherine II.'s which appears likely, is
her desire to conciliate and consolidate her authority in the newly annexed provinces. Certainly
she could hardly have chosen better instruments
than these priests—people, *sans patrie*, shut up
within the strict limits of their order in every sense
of the word, " *Status in statu*." White Russia
contained individuals from different nationalities—
Italians, French, Germans, Poles themselves forgot

their nationality when once enrolled in this order. Sustained and protected by the Government, the Jesuits have been, without contradiction, useful as the secret police agents of Russia during the first years of the annexation. But this utility, shadowy and secondary as it was, resulted in a prolonged and grave evil—it hindered all reasonable civilization. They recruited and strengthened the United Greeks who were at this period less firm in their religious convictions than when they had been violently converted to Romanism, and even proselytised some Russians. Thus they may be said to have deprived Russia of a considerable population which but for the influence of the Jesuits, would have preserved, as in the past, the Greek Orthodox faith.

It was a grave mistake of the Government this preservation of the Jesuits in Russia, priests who, by their intrigues, made the country dearly pay for their services as police in the Polish provinces. And besides the evil which they worked towards the State, they hindered the regular organisation of the administration of the Roman Church. According to custom they emancipated themselves from the authority of the bishop, at a time when this authority was indispensable to the Church, pleading the statutes of their order—at a period

when the friends of civilization and progress endeavoured to create an ecclesiastical hierarchy, and to
reconstruct the clergy. It was at this moment that
all sorts of cabals and intrigues commenced against
Siestrencewitz, amongst the great dignitaries of the
Court. Instead of quietly carrying out the functions of his high calling, he was obliged to defend
himself against the Jesuits; and in order to live
in peace was constrained to give them full liberty,
and not to interfere in their affairs. This freed
them from all ordinances concerning the monastic
orders. In 1777 they opened a noviciate, with the
intention of recruiting their numbers. Those who,
in pursuance of the Papal decree, had quitted the
society, came from all parts to Polotsk, and there
established themselves. In passing through this
city in 1780 the Empress Catherine visited the
College of the Jesuits, and was received by the
Provincial, who addressed her in a speech in Italian.
She inspected the house, and was very gracious
towards them. Besides some insignificant schools
they possessed also six colleges with considerable
estates, which they also retained in White Russia
when that part passed to Russia Proper, that is the
part situated on the right bank of the Dwina,
which then formed the frontier line of Poland.

In 1782 these priests endeavoured to throw off

the episcopal authority altogether; but even at
this time the power of the Bishop was merely
nominal.   They were permitted to select from
their own body a Vicar to whom the provincials
should be subordinate.   The ukase authorising
this change says, "Although the Order must hold
itself obedient to its pastor, the Archbishop of
Mohilew, the said Archbishop must see that all its
rules be maintained without the least infringement,
inasmuch as is consistent with the laws of the
empire."

Though Siestrencewitz was a dangerous enemy
for the Jesuits, as much by his ability and by his
intellectual capacity as by the firm nature of his
character, they could nevertheless oppose him and
turn aside his direction of the affairs of the Church.
But while placed beyond his influence he was not
curtailed of the right of administering the affairs of
the clergy according to his views.   In 1779 it was
decided that all the monastic orders, the Jesuits
excepted, should be subordinate to the bishop, and
that in future no other ecclesiastical strangers,
under the name of Provincials, visitors, &c., should
be permitted to reside in White Russia, still less
to interfere in the direction of the monasteries. No
one could change the superiors, or transfer the
monks from one monastery to another, "such

acts," says the ukase, "being injurious in many
respects." The following year, 1780, another decree was promulgated. "As liberty of conscience
is tolerated in our empire, the principal ecclesiastical authority of the Roman Catholic Church in
Russia is conferred by us on Stanislas Siestrencewitz, Bishop of White Russia; and we command
our Governors-General and other civil functionaries
to see that our commands be strictly executed, and
that all the Roman Catholic churches and convents
in Russia render him due obedience."

With a view to raise the Latin hierarchy and its
representative, the Empress, in 1782, transformed
the bishopric of Mohilew into an archiepiscopate,
and created Siestrencewitz Archbishop, in which
position he acquitted himself with even more ability
and power. The Ministry of Justice was forbidden
to interfere in the affairs of the Latin Church.
Appeals against the archiepiscopal decisions should
only be made to the Senate; the clergy should
remain in complete subordination to the Archbishop who alone should nominate priests to the
parishes, so that the right of patronage was abrogated, and his superintendence and directions of
the monastic orders was confirmed. Further it
was interdicted " to recognise any spiritual power
beyond the limits of the empire,—to send the

revenues, or any part of them, away, or to have
the least relation with foreign ecclesiastical authorities, under pain of secular judgment for contravention and disobedience to the supreme power." A
coadjutor was nominated to the Archbishop, and
the Jesuits seized this opportunity to turn the
creation of this dignitary to their own advantage,
and procure it for one of their own adepts, Canon
Benislawsky. Siestrencewitz did not oppose this
nomination, or perhaps would not, wishing to quiet
them with a view towards reconciliation, which
was, however, never a sincere one on their part.
This nomination afterwards completely paralysed
all the prerogatives conferred on the Archbishop.

In re-organising and raising the Roman Catholic
Church in her empire, the Empress held strictly
to the plan she had traced, not to permit the Pope
to interfere, and to limit his power in Russia. In
promulgating the aforesaid ordinances which evidently tended to the welfare of her Roman Catholic
subjects, she added:—"We confirm our former
ukases on the prohibition of the receipt of bulls or
briefs of the Pope, or any epistles written in his
name, and command that on arrival here they be
sent to the Senate, where, their contents having
been examined, and it being apparent that they
contain nothing incompatible with the existing

laws of the empire of Russia, and the prerogative which God has conferred on us, they shall be submitted to us, and on the recommendation of the Senate these bulls or briefs may be promulgated with our consent."

The ukase, on the institution of the Archbishop, was exposed in the churches that everybody might see it.

It was thus that Catherine, without the direction of Rome, protected and cared for the Catholic Church in her empire; and she never met with opposition in carrying out her benevolent intentions. Without consulting the Pope, she named Siestrencewitz to White Russia, and made him a bishop a little later. She then elevated his authority to that of Archbishop, and he enjoyed these titles without the sanction of Rome. She called him from private life to one of the highest stations in her empire, and organised an administration for the Roman Church which she confided to him, according to the inspiration of her own judgment as she considered the requirements of her Catholic subjects demanded. Without paying any attention to the bull of the Holy Father dissolving the order, she protected the Jesuits in White Russia, and by instituting the Noviciate at Polotsk, opened out a future for them; in a word she consulted or

accepted no disposition of the Court of Rome contrary to the law of her empire. Rome could not
deny that the principal ' measures laid down by the
Russian Government for the Roman Catholic body
of the empire, were effectively wise, benevolent,
and extremely adapted to the circumstances of the
Church, and showed this appreciation by sanction-
ing them herself. But this sanction was a diplomatic move necessary for Rome. She did it to
save appearances, and to make believe that nothing
could be done in the administration of the Latin
Church without her concurrence. Russia, however, put her projects in execution, without asking
or waiting their confirmation by the Holy See.
When Siestrencewitz was installed in the episcopal
chair of White Russia, all the regular clergy were
subordinate to him, though contrary to the usages
of Rome ; and it was only in 1778 that a brief of
the Pope conceded this point, with a limit of three
years. The welfare of the Church demanded that
this rule should be executed without infringement
in future times, and the Empress, when the three
years had expired, renewed it for the Bishop—then
Archbishop in 1782.

The authority thus confided to Siestrencewitz,
and the subjugation of the monastic orders to him,
served Rome with a pretext for discontent, espe-

cially as it was based on the brief by which, according to the will of the Empress, the Jesuits were permitted to noviciate. The Pope regarded it with rancour; but Catherine, at this very time, elevated Siestrencewitz to the dignity of Archbishop, and demanded canonical confirmation of his functions. The letter addressed to Pope Pius VI. in 1782 by Catherine on this occasion displays with what frank dignity this sovereign recognised the rights of the State, and in what light she regarded the relations between the Government and the Latin Church; we also see the caution she preserved in these relations :—

" We do not refuse, illustrious sovereign, to accede to each of your demands in that which is expedient; but your own experience will tell you that the duties of the throne sometimes prevent sovereigns following their impulses. As to what concerns Bishop Stanislas Siestrencewitz, whom you accuse of having controverted your intentions, and abused the powers you confided to him, we cannot and we will not leave this accusation without reply. In tolerating all religions without exception, and amongst others the Roman Catholic, through the vast extent of our provinces, as our ancestors did, we cannot consent, nevertheless, that those who profess a strange doctrine should

depend on a foreign power. The bulls emanating
from the Papal chair, therefore, are not published
in our empire without our order. As the bull of
Pope Clement XIV. concerning the Jesuits has
never been promulgated in Russia, that part of the
Society of Jesuits which from time to time settled
in White Russia, has been preserved intact, consequently the question of their abolition or reform has
never been raised in our dominions. As the above-
mentioned prelate furnished with your rescript on
the subject of the visitation and the reform of the
convents, carries out our will by opening the noviciate of the Jesuits, can he, by accomplishing the
duties of his oath, incur your displeasure, and render himself unworthy to receive the dignity of Archbishop and the Pallium on your part? This dignity,
as a degree in the ecclesiastical hierarchy, has
everywhere, from time immemorial, depended on
the sovereign power, even on those potentates who
themselves profess the Roman Catholic faith, and
consequently depend, up to a certain point, on the
Papal chair, in that which concerns the Church.

" Such a sovereign prerogative is incontestable,
especially in our empire ; and we, moved by his zeal
for the perfect administration of the Roman Church
in our empire, by his care for his flock and his efforts
for public unity, have resolved to elevate the afore-

said Bishop Siestrencewitz to the dignity of Archbishop of Mohilew, and to name as his coadjutor
John Benïslawsky, Canon and Prior of Dunaburg,
and to confide to them all the convents and parishes
of the Roman Church, situated in the provinces of
Mohilew, Polotsk, as well as in our two capitals,
and in all the empire of Russia; and we beg you,
illustrious sovereign, to preserve the usages of the
Roman Church by furnishing the new Archbishop
with the Pallium, and to consecrate his coadjutor.
We shall consider this an agreeable condescension
on your part, which we shall not refuse to acknowledge on another occasion.

"We unite our wishes to those of our Orthodox
Church, which prays for the re-union of all."

This profession of political faith requires no
comment; it suffices to state that on the 18th
January, 1784, the Bishop was solemnly invested
with the Pallium, and consecrated Archbishop in
the Roman Catholic Church of St. Petersburg,
according to canonical rules, and Benislawsky was
anointed Bishop. To confirm the ecclesiastical
organisation introduced by the Empress, Rome
delegated Monsigneur Archetti, the Nuncio at
Warsaw, to St. Petersburg, who, on the 8th Dec.,
1783, promulgated, in the name of Pope Pius VI.,
the bull concerning the elevation of the Bishop of

Mohilew to the dignity of Archbishop, appointing
him a Chapter composed of four prelates, eight
canons, and six vicars, of whom five should form
the consistory, and the others make, so to speak,
an honorary suite for the Archbishop, without any
functions whatever. It is necessary to observe
that, according to canonical rules, the number of
the members of the Chapter was not positively
determined; it depended more or less on the
revenues assigned to this effect; therefore they
were sometimes augmented and sometimes diminished, to the detriment of the ecclesiastical administration. At the time of the erection of the
diocese of Mohilew; that is to say, at the period
of the annexation of White Russia, eight parochial
benefices were assigned for the support of the
Chapter of this see; so that the half of the revenues
of each of these benefices went to support the
curates of these parishes, and the other half was
converted into appointments for the members of
the Chapter. This was also confirmed by Archetti.

The measures of the ecclesiastical administration introduced by the Empress having been confirmed according to the forms required by Catholic
customs, Archetti prepared to consecrate the new
Archbishop; but objection was taken to the form
of oath supplied on this occasion by Rome—a form

which did not correspond with the sovereign's prerogative, or to the position which a religion, itself
tolerated, should observe *vis-à-vis* the religion of
the State. The following is the formula of this
oath :—" I shall pursue, as long as my powers
permit me, all schismatics, and those who, having
apostatised, are cast aside by Christ and his successors "—meaning the Popes. A clause in this
same oath indicated that all episcopal property
should be dependent on Rome ; the true meaning of
which was, that the Bishop should swear not to
alienate the property belonging to the see, and in
general not to dispose of it without the Pope's
consent. The Empress exacted that these two
clauses should be excluded, and that instead it
should be added—" I shall so much the more
faithfully adhere to the several articles of the oath
I am about to take, as I am convinced there is
nothing contained in them contrary to the oath of
allegiance which I have taken to my legitimate
sovereign and her successors." It was intimated
to the Nuncio that if these changes were not made
in the formula, the Empress would find it possible to dispense with him, and invest Siestrencewitz with the Pallium, as a distinctive mark of the
archiepiscopal dignity, particularly as he had already
taken an oath to the Pope when he was conse-

crated bishop. The will of the Empress was all-powerful. Siestrencewitz was not only consecrated by the Nuncio, but he took an oath to the Pope according to the form prescribed by Catherine—an oath which the dignity of the Church and the sovereign's power considered necessary. This was not all. At the audience *de congé* the Empress felicitated Archetti on the occasion of his own nomination through her intercession, to the dignity of Cardinal, an honour of which the Nuncio was still ignorant.

By the institution of the archiepiscopate the Catholic hierarchy gained in importance; and this was the result the Empress desired, not certainly for the sake of the exterior pomp of the Church of Rome, or for the assistance of the Propagand, but that the Archbishop could—in obtaining through his exalted position greater powers—carry out the organisation of the clergy, and render them effectively useful, being no longer compelled to stop at every step and temporise for want of the necessary powers to execute his reforms. One cannot doubt that this was the principal aim the Empress had in view in trying to obtain for Siestrencewitz a Cardinal's hat, when she charged Archetti, who had already received his new dignity, and who was then about to start for Rome, to take steps towards this

object ; and, independent of this, she desired
Prince Youssoupoff, her minister at Turin, to proceed to Rome to thank the Holy Father for having
acceded to her request, and elevated Archetti to the
dignity of Cardinal ; her real object was, however,
to obtain the same distinction for Siestrencewitz.

Pius VI. received Youssoupoff very graciously,
who, at the first audience broached the subject.
The Pope replied, " You are not ignorant that we
only nominate Cardinals in those countries whose
sovereigns profess the Catholic religion ; otherwise
the King of Prussia would make the same demand,
which would very much embarrass us.   Be assured
that we shall always be happy to prove our respect
for her Majesty."   Youssoupoff observed that the
elevation of a man protected by the Empress would
serve to draw still closer the ties which united the
two Courts ; and finding no satisfactory reply, he
waited two months, and then demanded an audience, reiterating his solicitations.   The Pope
answered as before, but gave no absolute denial.
" This is an affair that demands time," said he ;
" we must first be convinced of the principles of
the Archbishop, and that cannot be done quickly."
In reality the Pope was inclined to accede to the
wishes of the Empress, but the Courts of France
and Spain opposed it.   Meanwhile news of some of

the measures of Siestrencewitz arrived at Rome, of which we shall afterwards speak, which irritated the Pope, as having been effected without his authority; and it was this which principally hindered the success of Youssoupoff's mission. The true reason or pretext for the refusal was the fact of the Archbishop's having been baptized in the reformed religion, and that till a rather mature age he had remained attached to it. After stopping six months at Rome, the Minister returned to Turin without having succeeded in his aim.

If the Government of the Empress did not succeed in elevating Siestrencewitz to the dignity of a Cardinal, it at least enlarged his authority; for, on the 28th August, 1786, the Pope accorded him extended spiritual powers, to the number of twenty-nine clauses for a term of ten years. The more enlarged these powers, the more complete the independence of the administration became, so to speak, of Rome; and we must acknowledge that they were much more extended than usually accorded by the Holy See. The Archbishop, on receiving them, immediately presented them to the Senate to be confirmed. The decision of this body was delivered as follows:—" The Archbishop is permitted by the Senate to accept the above-named brief, basing its permission on the paragraph therein contained, which gives him the absolute right of absolution in all cases of appeal to the Court of Rome ; and in future all correspondence and all relations with Rome must be avoided by Archbishop Sicstrencewitz, especially as these powers are accorded for ever, and not for ten years, as stated in the brief. For this particular reason the Senate approves of the act in question." The Senate only excluded a single paragraph of this document, the publication of which it interdicted—that which permitted the Archbishop, as a special favour, to read heretical books. The Senate forbade this as containing a certain constraint for the mind, and a sort of disdain for other confessions. In 1790 and 1795 it was reiterated that the bulls of the Papacy could not be executed without having been previously examined by the Government.

When White Russia was reunited to the empire, strangers were not eligible for nomination to curacies in Russia without the special authorisation of the bishop, a regulation confirmed on several occasions, particularly by the ukases of July 3rd, 1779, January 2nd, 1780, and November 4th, 1783 ; but, as among the clergy of White Russia there were not many to be found who knew foreign languages, the Archbishop was, in 1784, permitted to allow strangers residing in the country to have

foreign priests, conditionally that such priests took
the oath of allegiance. The Archbishop trans-
mitted this right to the syndics of Moscow and St.
Petersburg, which highly displeased the Roman
Catholic congregation. The chief grievance of
this body dated from the time when the Empress,
in consequence of the complaints of the parishioners
of the Church at St. Petersburg against their clergy,
permitted them in 1769 to send for, through Government sources, their priests from abroad, by
which they were relieved of all dependence on the
Propagand. The Court of Rome threw obstacles
in the way of these priests departing for Russia, till
at last, in 1770, the Russian deputy at the Diet
of Ratisbon demanded four Franciscans. These
priests were refused until the Propagand should
be reinstated in all its rights, and until which they
withdrew the priest Frankenberg from Russia, to
whose intrigues they imputed impressions unfavour-
able to the Propagand. In Russia this section of
the Catholic party made all sorts of concessions to
preserve their ancient privileges, particularly on the
subject of the control of articles for the Church.*
No result, however, followed these steps. The
Archbishop made his arrangements without consulting the Propagand, and consequently stirred up
anew the displeasure of Rome.

* Arch. pr. de Moscow.

The French Revolution drove a great number of strange priests to Russia, who, for the most part, found a support not as curés, but as tutors and teachers amongst the high families and schools. In the year 1790 a church for French emigrants was erected at Moscow, which received the name of St. Louis. After the conquest of New Russia Siestrencewitz visited the country at the request of Prince Potemkin, when he restored the ruins of the Catholic temples built by the Genoese, and founded a new one at Kherson, which city, at that period, had considerable commerce with, and was constantly filled by, foreigners. He nominated priests for the different churches ; and the colonies of Saratoff and New Russia were equally endowed with religious edifices and clergymen.

The attention of the Government was more particularly directed towards the monastic orders, endeavouring only to render them useful to society and give them the true spirit of Christianity. They were therefore prohibited from accumulating riches as they had done in the time of the Poles, through illegitimate and underhand means. The Polish Government had, in fact, already limited their rights of possession ; and when White Russia was annexed to the empire, the estates of the monks who had not sworn allegiance were confiscated, as well as those convents which remained in Poland, or were beyond its frontiers. As to other monasteries they preserved the administration of their landed properties *until a new order.** There is no doubt but that Catherine intended to confide the regulation of these estates to the lay authorities, as she had practically done with regard to the properties of the Russian clergy, but political circumstances and the ultimate partition of Poland, which took place a year before her death, left her no time to arrange these affairs. But the right of convents to acquire landed property, as authorised by the Polish Diets of the 17th and 18th centuries, was entirely withdrawn, so that the bishops and the secular clergy of noble descent were by this act entitled to leave their estates, not to ecclesiastical communities, but to their legitimate heirs. As to monastic discipline, it was enacted in 1784 that the monks would not be permitted to pass their days in idleness or mendicity.

The close of the eighteenth century brought a considerable increase to the Catholic population of Russia, by the re-union (at the request of the Diet of Grodno in 1793) of the provinces of the *Volhynia, Podolia,* and *Minsk,* and at the end of 1794 of the Government of Lithuania, Grodno, as far as the Nieman, and of Courland. For the ecclesiastical

* Recueil des lois, t. 19. No. 13808.

administration of these provinces the Empress instituted in 1795 three new dioceses :—1st. Inflandt, which replaced the ancient diocese of Wilna for Lithuania with the episcopal capital of Wilna. 2nd. Pinsk, instead of Luck and Kiew. This diocese comprehended the Volhynia, which formerly belonged to the Bishopric of Luck, and the Government of Minsk, formerly a part of the see of Wilna. 3rd. Leticzew replacing that of Kamienec for the Government of Podolia, of Braclaw and of Wosnesensk. Kossakowsky was named Bishop of Inflandt ; the Count Sierokowsky, Bishop of Leticzew and Cecieszewski, Bishop of Kiew, passed to the see of Pinsk. This Bishop, having sworn allegiance to the Empress, preserved the estates of the see ; the episcopal properties of the two other dioceses were confiscated like that of Wilna, as that of Wilna remained vacant after the assassination of Messalsky at Warsaw, and because that Krassinsky, Bishop of Kamienec, not submitting to the Russian Government, remained in Poland. The revenues of these were given to the bishoprics which had no landed endowments. Inflandt received 4000 roubles, and Leticzew 3000 roubles per year.

The bishops of these three dioceses exercised the same authority over the regular and secular clergy as Siestrencewitz did in the Archbishopric of Mohilew. They were independent chiefs in their administration, and not mere lieutenants, obliged to execute the orders of the Archbishop. It was they only who ruled the monastic orders in their respective dioceses. All the regulations concerning the Roman Church in Russia extended equally to these sees; the clergy were not compelled to submit to any foreign authority beyond the empire; foreign ecclesiastics were forbidden, and priests who had not taken the oath of allegiance to the Government could receive no clerical appointments.

In 1795 the Empress, wishing to preserve for her Catholic subjects a number of the monasteries in these provinces likely to be useful, and to close those which were a burden to their parishioners, commanded Prince Repnin, the Governor-General of Lithuania, to request the Catholic bishops to forward him a list of all these houses, and to mark those which were distinguished for works of charity or instruction, and to indicate those where the inhabitants lived idly, "without any utility for this life or the next, and which were only a burden on the community." Convents of the first class were to be preserved. As to those of the second a list was ordered to be submitted to the Empress, "so that we can," says the ukase, "take and concert measures for the glory of God and the welfare of

our subjects in so far as shall appear to be useful
and convenient." *   The estates of the convents
were recognised as belonging to the Empire, and by
that act preserved from the ruin to which they
were exposed by the arbitrary sects of the *religieux*,
who, considering them as private property, often
mortgaged them for their personal debts.   The
death of Catherine prolonged the existence of
several of these useless convents, which, to the
detriment of the public good, enjoyed exorbitant
riches in Western Russia.   There can be no doubt
that such convents were positive nuisances, and it
was for this reason only that the government would
abolish them.   It is a well-known fact that the
Ultramontanists, the partisans of the Pope, attributed these measures to the revolutionary tendencies of the government, to liberal institutions,
and the desire for ungovernable liberty.   Such an
opinion was quite out of place in this case; as it is
notorious that Catherine, the liberal friend of the
philosophers and learning of the time, entirely
changed her political convictions after the French
Revolution, put a curb on literature, and abandoned
several projected re-organizations; in short, was
very far from being liberal in 1795.   This desire
to save the Church, and deliver the clergy from
abuses and vices patent to everybody, was an ab-

* Recueil des lois. No. 17380.

solute State necessity—new, certainly, to all political systems—which caused Catherine to desire the reduction of a pernicious class of monks, idle, lazy, inactive, steeped in luxurious opulence, who, far from being an ornament to the Church, were absolutely its disgrace.

The memory of this great sovereign is reviled for having ended the political existence of Poland. Calumnies are heaped on a name venerated in Russia. But it was Catherine, and she only, who in the Polish Provinces supported tottering, rotten, and degraded Catholicism,—Catholicism already condemned by public opinion. It was she only who called it anew into existence, reformed and civilized the clergy, gave it a strong local ecclesiastical authority, and regularly established its dioceses. It was not Rome which saved the Catholic Church in Poland and Russia, but a sovereign not of this creed : not with the aim, it is true, of preserving a Propagand, but for the welfare of several millions of her Catholic subjects. Of her own inclination she erected several churches in Poland, even where there had formerly been edifices of the Greek Confession, and laid out new dioceses; whereas in Poland the Russian bishoprics, which were centuries old, had been in the days of Polish domination uprooted and abolished. The clergy of the Roman Church were placed upon a proper footing and received proper treatment; while the Polish clergy, in the days of their power, had snatched from the Russians everything they possessed. The great Catherine founded seminaries and schools for the Roman clergy; whereas in Poland the Russian priesthood had always been condemned to ignorance, misery, and public misrepresentation. They had been persecuted and insulted with the hope of extirpating the Greek faith. But political grudges often distort and conceal the real facts of history.

The Roman Catholic population of Russia comprehended among the rest the Armenian Catholics converted at Astracan. Their number considerably increased under the reign of the Empress Catherine up to the time that Georgia accepted the Protectorate of Russia. When the western provinces were annexed, there were many Armenians in some of the cities who had joined the Roman religion. It may not be superfluous to mention here the principal differences between the Armenian and other Christian Confessions, as well as the doctrines which separated them, to be later mentioned.

The Armenians, as well as the Greeks, recognised the three first Œcumenical Councils, but at the Council of Chalcedon separated from the Universal

Church in 451, where it was enacted that Jesus Christ had two distinct natures, divine and human, but at the same time indivisible and inseparable. The Armenians did not recognise this decree, and reproached the Council for asserting that our Lord must consequently have two persons and not two natures in one single person. They therefore seceded from the rest of the Church, assisted no longer at the Œcumenical Councils, and formed a Christian Church apart, which received the name of Armenio-Gregorian, after St. Gregory, an Armenian pontiff, and which is governed by a patriarch named " The Catholic," who resides at Eczmiadzine. The word Catholic has the same signification in the Armenian Church as the word Pope in the Church of Rome. The three Armenian Patriarchs—Constantinople, Ispahan, and Jerusalem—are subordinate to this See. The Armenian Turks, Persians, Hindoos, and Russians, recognised the bishop as the chief of their Church, and the Holy Chrism was sent from Eczmiadzine throughout the East, serving, as we may say, as a distinctive mark of the superior ecclesiastical authority, to which was attached in this Church the exclusive right of consecrating the Chrism. In conforming strictly to the religious precepts and the traditions of the first centuries of Christianity, the Armenian

Church preserved several rites and dogmas recognised by the Greek Confession, but which were
changed in the Roman Catholic Church at different
periods.   Like the Greeks, the Armenians believed
that the Holy Spirit proceeded from the Father,
and not from Father and Son, as taught by the
Latins.   They baptized by triple immersion. They
communicated in two kinds, like the Greeks.   They
rejected the doctrine of Purgatory, and Divine
Service was celebrated in the ancient Armenian
idiom, but the sermons were delivered in the
modern tongue.   Like the Greeks, again, the
regular clergy conformed entirely to the rules of
St. Basil the Great, and the priests could marry,
but only once.   The great resemblance between
these two Churches is at once perceived, as well as
the difference of both from the Roman Catholic,
and therefore the re-union of the Armenian and
the Roman, so long projected, never succeeded.
From the time of the Crusades the Court of Rome
had already commenced the Propagand amongst
these people, whose unfortunate political position,
torn by Turk and Persian, particularly seconded it.
Some of their kings were constrained to ask succours from Rome, whose first condition was, as we
may say, the conversion of their people to the faith
of the Holy See.   Notwithstanding these advan-

tages, Rome did not succeed in her views; the people determined never to sacrifice the faith of their fathers. It was known that at the Council of Florence the union with the Catholic Church was signed by some Armenian bishops, who are represented on the frescoes of the library of the Vatican at Rome as prostrated at the feet of Pope Eugene IV. The Armenians upon this transferred the patriarchal see from Sis to Eczmiadzine, so as to remove as far as possible from the Roman Propagand; and like the Russians, they solemnly rejected the decrees of the Council of Florence.

Dating from 1439—that is, from this epoch until the end of the sixteenth century—the Popes, despairing of the success of their enterprise, left the Armenian as well as the Russian people in peace. But at the end of this term, when religious persecution burst out in Western Russia, they renewed their proselytising activity amongst the Armenians with redoubled vigour, and upon a more plausible basis. In 1584 Gregory XIII. ordered a college to be founded at Rome, where young Armenians could be educated at his expense; but as he died the year following, it was not established, and it was the school of the Propagand that took charge of the few pupils that offered. It was not till seventy years later that the idea of Gregory

was acted on by Alexander VII., when the celebrated missionary Clement Gelanus was placed at
the head of the school then founded.   From 1650
to 1659 Gelanus was occupied with his great work,
in quarto, written in the Latin and Armenian
languages, directed against the dogmas and the
ceremonies of the Armenian Church.   This work
failed in its aim, for instead of attracting, it only
repulsed the people, and soured them against
Popery.   This book was so full of false ideas
concerning the Armenian Church, that afterwards the Romanists themselves were ashamed of
the errors of Gelanus, as well as of the incoher-
ence of his reasoning and deductions.   Among
these the Marquis of Serpos was particularly
distinguished, in his work on the Armenians in
Turkey, published in Italian at the close of the
last century.   The students (Armenian) of the
Propagand, enchanted with the spirit of this work
of Gelanus, on which their theological education
was based, looked upon him as their oracle, and
returned to their country, young, inexperienced,
and completely ignorant of their countrymen, from
whom their Roman Catholic education completely
separated them.   Therefore, so far from attracting
the Armenians by Propagand, they destroyed all
desire for a union with Rome.   " Nihilo tamen
minus," said Gelanus, "extra Romanum Eccle-

siam errare hoc tempore, quam antea videbatur
Armenios." This remark may be applied to an
epoch which preceded the appearance of the work
of Gelanus.

Mekhitar, himself an Armenian, who consequently knew his countrymen more thoroughly than
the Roman Propagandists, placed the rational foundations, so to speak, of Romanism on the Propagand. Mekhitar was born at Sebastian, in 1676,
and in this Armenian city was converted to Catholicism at the age of eighteen, by the French missionary Antoine Beauvilliers. At Constantinople
his co-religionists were so indignant at his apostasy,
that to save his life he was obliged to hide amongst
the Capucins, and in the house of the French
Ambassador, and afterwards to fly to the Morea.
When this latter country was occupied by the
Turks, he took refuge in Venice, where, after some
years, he was authorised to found a convent on one
of the small islands situated in the lagunes, which
convent he called Saint Lazare. Clement XI. gave
this community the rules of St. Benedict for their
government. It was definitely established in 1740,
and contained a printing press. Mékhitar died in
1749.

At the close of the last century the Mekhitarists
founded convents at Trieste and Vienna; and at the
commencement of the nineteenth century the com-

munity at Venice was transformed, without any change in the rules, into an academy, with a branch at Paris.

If the conversion of the Armenian people, the aim of Mekhitar, only attained very restrained limits, the means he employed for conversions afterwards proved very useful, though pursued with a totally different object to that intended. The Mekhitarists established Armenian printing presses, which have published and translated a considerable number of works of general utility. They cultivated Armenian literature and history, and in short afforded the people the means of attaining civilization, while rejecting, as up till the present they have done, all tendency to Roman Catholicism. Thus we see that the measures originally calculated on as the surest means for proselytism led to a totally different result, which may in time produce a true and popular civilization, based on the fundamental doctrines of the Armenian Church.

As to the position of the United Armenians in the Roman Church, and their transition to Latinism, we find that their ancient ceremonies and idiom were left them; that their priests married, but that they were obliged to recognise the supremacy of the Pope and the dogmas of Catholicism. There can be no doubt, however, that little by little the ceremonies were changed, as was done in the service of the United Greeks in Western Russia; and we actually see in the churches of the United Armenians in Russia, that the sacerdotal vestments and the greater number of the rites are purely Catholic. It is true that the service is still celebrated in the Armenian language, but the organ is used in the second half the liturgy. The closed sanctuary of the Eastern Church remains, but the screen which veils it exists no longer, and in its place there is a small altar as in the churches of Rome, so that the first half of the Mass is celebrated by a priest in the sanctuary, and the second at the small altar. Armenian Romanism is in the Armenian Church, in short, what the Union was in the Russian—it had the same aim, used the same means and the same modes of conversion. It was thus that the primitive Armenian Church gradually comprehended, and comprehends still, this new doctrine, and it was thus that it comprehended also the government of Catherine II.

As regards the settlement of the Armenians in Russia, we find them as early as the fourteenth century in Volhynia and Podolia, where they carried on commercial speculations, built the Armenian churches of Balta, Luck, and Mohilew upon the Dniester, and of Lwow, and freely professed their religion according to the Gregorian rite. But about the middle of the seventeenth century, the Roman Catholic clergy, elated with their success among the United Greeks, commenced to try their system upon the Armenians. Matthew Bembus, a celebrated Jesuit propagandist, addressed himself in 1629 to the Ruthenians, in hopes of converting them to Popery; the year following he applied himself to the Armenians. In chronological order, this was the first essay of the sort in the Polish provinces. Bembus in his writing tried to sow dissension between the Armenian clergy and laity, both of whom were naturally not disposed to abandon the faith of their fathers; and he cleverly invited the priests to Lwow to public controversies upon matters of faith. He spared neither protestations nor promises as to the inviolability of the Armenian rites, and promised permission for the priesthood to contract matrimony; in fact his plans were based on the same system as that used among the Russians : his promises and protestations never intended to be kept when the time should arrive to forget them. But the baits of the Propagand and of Bembus were unavailing among the Armenians of Gallicia, Podolia and the Volhynia.

Despairing of their conversion by the Propagand, the Romanists resolved to convert them by violence.

In 1626 Nicolas Torossowicz, a young man of twenty-three years and a concealed Catholic, residing in the city of Lwow, was elevated to the dignity of Armenio-Gregorian bishop of Lwow, when he swore to preserve the faith in all its purity, and to submit to the Patriarch of Eczmiadzine. It was well known that Torossowicz only took this oath for appearance' sake, and the people were upon the point of chasing him from the church at the time of his consecration. He was compelled to fly from Lwow, but protected by the Jesuits and their humble pupil Sigismond III. of Poland, he was reinstated in his diocese by main force and through the municipality of the town; first, however, openly passing over to Romanism. At his installation the police were obliged to burst the doors of the cathedral, and in this way he was consecrated pastor of an Armenian Catholic congregation, which in reality did not yet exist. As a *protegé* of the Papacy, Torossowicz did not fail to make a pilgrimage to Rome, to prostrate himself at the feet of Urban VIII. who confirmed him in the episcopal See, and elevated him to the dignity of Archbishop. We have evidence as to the effect this ecclesiastical violence produced upon the Armenian population, by a complaint addressed to their Patriarch, July 25th, 1631, still extant:

"The Catholic clergy and the police," says this document, "after breaking open the locks of the church door, forcibly introduced this cursed one. Why did not the earth open and swallow us, rather than that we should have assisted at such a sacrilege? This pretended bishop will not leave us our faithful flock, or any churches in which to celebrate our ceremonies, but even interdicts the burial of our dead. He seizes the priests who remain steady in the faith—who refuse to recognise his authority—beats them, chains them, and throws them into prison, from which they are not released till they are converted to Romanism. All this is done with impunity, as the authorities, both civil and ecclesiastic, uphold him, and he is backed by the Jesuits, who are for his cause. We have petitioned the king, but have obtained no redress, and God only knows when we shall. If we are even permitted a hearing of our case, it is doubtful if it lead to a discovery of the truth, as the Nuncio at Warsaw and other Romanists, particularly the Jesuits, defend this cursed priest with all their power. We have complained of such violence to the Nuncio, and he replied that all that signified nothing, as original sin being washed out by baptism, the actions of Bishop Torossowicz are absolved, since his recognition of the union with the Holy Roman Church. When we would pray as Christians should, he has left us no church in which to assemble, and the king, the Nuncio, and the Catholic priests cite the Roman canons, according to which the church follow their bishop as their chief. They use us as they did the Greek Church, which for more than twenty years could not obtain justice; and these persecutions exhaust our energy and drive us, against our grain, to the Union." We are constrained to add that we owe the publication of this interesting and historical document to a Roman Catholic priest attached to his own Church; its authenticity is therefore unquestionable.* The tears and sufferings of the Armenian people, touched neither the bigoted king nor the fanatical people, and Torossowicz remained in his see for fifty-five years until the time of his death in 1681. He was the first of the series of United Armenian bishops of Lwow whose spiritual authority extended over all the Armenian Roman Catholics domiciled in Poland.

To assist Torossowicz the Theatins were despatched by Rome to this quarter, amongst whom was the celebrated Gelanus, of whom we have already spoken, who died at Lwow in 1666. These priests would not submit to the Diocesan bishop, relying altogether on the Propagand. They founded the Collegium Pontificum at Lwow, in

---

* Wiadomose o Ormianach Polszeze. Lwow, 1842.

which establishment they supported twenty students
—of whom ten were Armenians and ten Ruthenians. On the termination of their studies, these
pupils were sent as missionaries to the East, and
especially to the Crimea, where they set up as Armenians. In 1784 the Emperor Joseph II. sent back
the Theatins to Rome, and closed their schools.

It was from Lwow that the Theatins extended
their proselytism over the adjacent countries belonging to Poland at this period—and especially by
reason of its vicinity to Kamienec-Podolsk. It is
necessary to say that in 1666 the union commenced
in this city with the arrival of the Monk Pidou, a
Parisian, when Archbishop Torossowicz followed
him in public procession through the streets of
Kamienec. Mohilew on the Dniester and Kamienec-Podolsk became the centres of the new religion in the south-west of Russia; at the latter
place there is still the ruin of an old temple of
this confession called St. Mary, with an image of
the Holy Virgin, which considered as miraculous,
was greatly venerated by the inhabitants. The
Armenian Catholic Church of Mohilew was erected
about the year 1742, the services being conducted
by the Latin clergy.

At the close of the eighteenth century the Polish
Armenians Romanised and Polonised themselves,

as we may say, entirely. They retained few of
their ancient customs and prayers, and the greater
their contact with the Poles, the oftener they fre-
quented the Latin Churches, appropriating the
Latin and Polish languages, and forgetting little
by little their own. But the number of convents
was inconsiderable; and at this epoch the total
population of Catholic Armenians in the Polish
provinces, did not even amount to ten thousand
souls. Monsieur E. Dulaurier, who studied the
Armenian Church, says with justice:

" The Catholic Armenians dispersed in Italy,
in Gallicia, and in France, having but few churches
have at least preserved their nationality, a fact
which is itself sometimes contested. If they rarely
succeed in making proselytes it is for this reason:
That two churches may unite and operate together,
a simple difference in some words and in the ceremonies may be easily arranged; but change the
doctrine upon the Procession of the Holy Spirit
and the Holy Eucharist, giving the latter in bread
alone, instead of administering it in two kinds;
reverse the order of the liturgy; put an uncovered
altar in the place of that one which is veiled with
mystery during some part of the service in the
Eastern Church; impose celibacy on the clergy,
and you have the points which constitute the great

and capital difference in the dogmas of the two Churches."

The conquest of the southern provinces increased the number of Armenian Catholics, and later still their amount was more augmented by the arrival of their compatriots of this faith for commercial enterprises, so that at the close of the last century they were dispersed, though in a limited number, throughout the different countries of Southern Russia, Georgia, Astracan, and Kamienec-Podolsk.

Heraclius II. recognising, as we know, the protectorate and supremacy of Russia, engaged himself not to enter into any direct relations with foreign powers, without obtaining the previous consent of the Russian minister at Tiflis; and from this date, Russia commenced to employ her legitimate influence over the country with regard to ecclesiastical and political affairs. To have a clear idea of these facts it is indispensable to throw a rapid glance over the progressive introduction of Romanism into Georgia.

At the beginning of the seventeenth century Roman Missionaries first visited this country, and later in 1615 some Capucins arrived at Gori as doctors. They took a house, as they pretended, for purposes of practice, and insinuated themselves amongst the population, converting them afterwards

to Romanism. Pope Urban VIII. being apprised
of the success of these priests, in 1626 sent a missionary named Avita-Boli to the King of Georgia, desiring him to try and gain the favour of this monarch,
so as to be able to establish a permanent mission
at Gori. This adroit diplomatist passed himself
off as a doctor, and affected particular veneration for
the ancient Iberia, so that he succeeded in winning
the good graces of the king, and entering into relations with Catholicos Zacharie, the chief of the
Armenian Church, through whose intervention permission was given in 1630 to the Capucins to
establish a chapel in this city. Avita-Boli also
influenced the sovereign to enter into amicable
relations with the Pope, and in 1631 both the king
and Catholicos wrote amongst other things to
the Pope, that the Christian religion was preserved
in Georgia since the time of Constantine the
Great, and that permission was accorded to the
missionaries of Gori to have a chapel. To this
the Pope on his part replied by very amiable
epistles. Four years afterwards other Capucin
Missionaries arrived in Georgia, intending to
establish a second permanent station at Tiflis;
but hearing from Avita-Boli that the people dis-
played hostile intentions, and that the clergy were
in strong opposition, they decided to temporise and

meantime the Propagand directed their activity towards the Armenians; converting them, not *en masse,*
but individually, and as opportunities occurred.
These priests were ordered to practise medicine;
they celebrated the liturgy in any sacerdotal vest-
ment; could absolve penitents from all sins without
exception; might assume different costumes; have
horses, servants, and even slaves. They could engage in commerce, borrow and lend money at
interest—in one word, the Propagand sanctioned
whatever these missionaries adopted. Nor was
this all; they might also adopt the luxury and
vices of the country in which they lived; they
might act and bend to the customs of the people
among whom they were, in order to discover and
profit by their weaknesses. The rules of their
Order were temporarily suspended to enable them
better to deceive society; they were interdicted
going barefoot or asking alms. During nearly
eighty years they inhabited only the house they at
first rented at Tiflis, and here they clandestinely
celebrated their services, but were only known publicly as doctors of the king and the nobility. They
succeeded in gaining the favour of those nobles
whose interests could serve them, by their servility
and flattery, at the same time showing themselves
useful to the lower classes, by their treatment of

the sick, and by the distribution of medicines. Never losing sight of their principal and primary aim they drew the Armenians to their faith, explained the dogmas of their own religion by a light suitable to their hearers, developing more and more in the minds of these simple people the idea that the Roman Church was the only infallible and orthodox one, out of which there was no salvation, and persuading their dupes that the man who embraced their faith, on becoming an orthodox, was no longer amenable to local authority. By these tricks they founded two permanent missions, one at Koutais and the other at Akhalcich at the end of the seventeenth century. Under King Teimouraze they had intimate relations with the Orbelian princes, and especially with prince Soulkhane, whom they helped in the publication of his Georgian dictionary. By such services they secured the protection of the Lords; and Heraclius II. permitted them to have a chapel at Tiflis. Having in this way won public confidence, they entered into relations with the Catholicos Antoine, who became their powerful protector, and who is even suspected of a penchant for their Church. Heraclius sent this prelate to Russia, and prevented several families passing over to Catholicism; but if the secular efforts of the Roman missionaries were not crowned with success, they had nevertheless a satisfactory result for the Propagand; the Latin Church without being considerably spread, solidly established itself in Georgia.

The Empress Catherine, not tolerating in her own empire the arbitrary measures of the Court of Rome, could still less permit an open Roman Propagand, and a clergy who relied exclusively on a foreign power to proselytise among other Christian confessions under her direct protectorate. Her first act, therefore, was to deliver them from foreign priests, to give them enlightened and educated pastors chosen from their own countrymen, who at the same time were the subjects of Russia. In 1784 she accordingly placed the Catholic Armenians under the superintendence of the Archbishop of Mohilew, charging him to establish proper schools for the education of the people, according to the dogmas of their religion, and from time to time to send some of the pupils to the Armenian College at Lwow. Rome approved of this last regulation, not dreading much at first, as only two pupils were despatched at this period, and if the number were not augmented the missionaries could not so soon be replaced either at Astracan or in Georgia by real Armenians. The subjection of the Catholic churches to the Bishop of Mohilew put an end to the reign of the Propagand, although this subordination was also incomplete, as the canons of the church required that only an Armenian Catholic Bishop had a right to consecrate the priests of this sect. But as there was no Armenian Catholic bishop in Russia, they were obliged to have recourse to the bishop of Lwow, a foreign prelate, who was often disobliging and actually malevolent. This measure, however, effectually freed them from the Propagand; and Siestrencewitz commanded the Catholic priesthood in Georgia not to have any communication with foreign authority. This necessarily put an end to conversions, which was the only aim of the missionaries in the country. The Propagand was in a tumult; Rome defended the cause, and the 19th of July, 1785, the Pope sent for Prince Youssoupoff, and told him that Siestrencewitz should not extend his power to the Armenian Catholic clergy who had their own bishops, but said nothing as to the Propagand or the missionaries. Cardinal Archetti, whom Youssoupoff consulted upon this affair, proposed the appointment of an Armenian Catholic bishopric in Russia, and in this manner to free the clergy from all dependence on strangers. But neither this advice or the assistance of the Pope was accepted by the Empress Catherine. Siestrencewitz preserved his

authority over the Armenian Catholics, and, notwithstanding the constant opposition on the part
of the Armenian Catholic Bishop of Lwow in all
that related to the consecration of the priesthood,
the people were never afterwards interfered with
in the performance of their religious duties. For,
though with difficulty and notwithstanding preme-
ditated malevolence, the Government could always
have Armenian Catholic priests. Thus two great
inconveniences were quashed :—proselytism on the
one hand, by Roman priests in an empire professing the Greek faith ; on the other, the erection of a useless new Latin diocese, which through
its exterior attraction was eminently qualified to
take the place of the Propagand and fulfil its
mission. The news of the measures of Siestrencewitz arrived at Rome at the same moment in
which Youssoupoff took steps to secure the elevation of the Archbishop to a Cardinalship, and failed
not to influence its refusal. Thus Siestrencewitz
sacrificed the highest dignity Rome could confer
to his convictions as a statesman.

The majority of the population in the Western
Provinces annexed to Russia did not belong to the
Roman Catholic religion, but to the United Greek
Confession. Catholicism had been violently im-
posed on them, notwithstanding which a large pro-

portion of the population retained their faith,
though persecuted and pursued by the Latin clergy
and by the Polish government, and for centuries
had neither received nor expected succour from any
quarter but Russia, whose people were of the same
religion and the same race.   But political circumstances had often hindered the Russian government
effectually helping the Russian martyrs of Lithuania.
Nevertheless, when occasions presented, exertions
were made in their favour.   John III. Grand
Duke of Russia, reproached Alexander of Lithuania for forcing the Russians to embrace the Roman
Creed, building churches in several cities exclusively
inhabited by members of the Greek Church, and
complained that the Latin clergy obliged them to
apostatise.   The Czarine Sophia, comprehending
all the advantages Poland would receive through a
Russian alliance at a period when the Turks
menaced that country, insisted that a clause should
be specially inserted in the treaty she concluded
with that power, 6th May, 1686, at Moscow, by
which the Russian Lithuanians should be secured
the full and free right of worship according to conscience.

But treaties, intercessions, and promises were
vain.   Only force could withstand Roman fanaticism, and the state of Russia at this time did not

permit this. In vain the Russian ministers at
Warsaw interfered for their co-religionists—in vain
they supported their petitions on the fact of special
clauses, in treaties, confirming religious liberty to
the people—they were informed that Russia was
not permitted to interfere in the affairs of Poland,
as if the Lithuanians were slaves. They were
told, that according to the laws, the king himself had
no right to order the lowest noble to do anything
contrary to the constitution—that every noble was
the master of his own estates, and might do as he
chose, but that as for the United Greeks their
ecclesiastical affairs depended entirely on Rome.
By the treaty concluded between Sophia and Poland,
four dioceses were preserved in Lithuania: Luck,
Peremyse, Lwow, and White Russia. Originally
there were nine Greek sees in the country, but
contrary to this treaty only one remained up to the
time of the Emperor Peter—that of White Russia,
—the other three were given to United Greeks, as
well as the greater portion of their convents and
their churches, and the parishioners were violently
converted to *the Union.* Peter interfered in favour
of the Greeks in Lithuania, but unfortunately not
with that power which carries conviction. When
Augustus II. received the crown of Poland, the
Russian troops had hardly time to quit the country

when they were sent against the Swedes. One would suppose from his position *vis-à-vis* the affairs of Poland, that the voice of the Czar would have been attended to ; but we find in the year 1718 that he complains in an epistle written to this king, that his intercession in favour of the Russians had not preserved the Greek bishoprics, which contrary to treaties had been changed into United Greek Sees, and that the Russians were violently converted contrary to all the principles of international right. "The human conscience," he says, "rests with God only, and no sovereign has a right to proselytise by violence." He demanded that the Russians should enjoy their faith, and not be forced to embrace the Union against their will. Again in 1720 the Emperor reiterated his demands, and the same year Augustus II. granted the free exercise of the Greek faith in Lithuania. But the edicts of the Kings of Poland were rarely executed, and the people remained as in past times, subject to their ancient yoke. Peter, who after the taking of Nisztadt was declared Protector of the Russians in Lithuania, believed it his duty to address himself directly to the Pope, and deputed the Jesuit Priamo, who was returning from China through Russia to Italy, to carry a letter from Count Golowkin, written by order of the

Emperor to Cardinal Spinola in 1723 ; in which
having forcibly manifested the persecutions endured by the Russians, he begged him to put a
curb on the provocations of the Polish clergy : to
consider that existing treaties secured the Russians
from Polish persecution ; but that notwithstanding, it was repeated and continued ; although
in his own dominions, the Emperor bound by no
concordat in favour of Roman Catholics, permitted
them to build churches and enjoy the Catholic
faith freely. Count Golowkin added, that if this
just demand produced no result, the Emperor
would be obliged, to his own great regret,
to withdraw those privileges from the Roman
Catholic communities in his empire. Priamo, at
the same time received a memorandum of the
latest despatch from the Russian ambassador at
Warsaw, detailing the sufferings of the people of
Lithuania. "They imprison the Russian priests,"
it is said therein, "which has before been represented to the Pope, simply because they refuse to
join the Union. They tie their hands and whip
them ; they bind them quite naked to stakes ; they
cut off their limbs and execute other horrors ; the
Jesuits invade the convents and carry away the
images venerated by the Greek people ; disperse
their funeral processions, and celebrate this ser-

vice as they themselves choose, breaking the crosses." Such violence, at which the heart turns sick at the recital, moved not Rome *the Christian*. The Pope replied* by pretending that this information was incorrect and incomplete, and prolonged the affair so long by requesting enlightenment on various points, that at last it ended in nothing. But the facts were too glaring to admit of denial. The successors of Peter the Great interfered in the same cause. Catherine I., Anne, Elizabeth, and Peter III. all entreated the Kings and Diets of Poland to stop these shameful persecutions, but in vain. The Russian martyrs were abandoned to themselves, but they defended their faith by patience and long suffering; by the development of their ecclesiastical instruction—upon the basis of which has since been founded the Academy of Kiew—and by their fraternities which conferred inestimable benefits during this bloody religious struggle. Only those countries united to Russia, such as Little Russia, enjoyed entire repose—countries in which there was no trace of the Union or of Romanism, since their annexation to Russia in the seventeenth century. A writer at the close of this epoch says: "Long ago one met with Catholics in those

---

* Through the medium of the Nuncio at Warsaw, as well as directly through the Polish Government.

countries bordering on Poland, at present there are actually none." In the time of Peter the Great there were some Catholics in Smolensk, but the number was extremely limited. They had neither church nor clergy, and a priest from Moscow visited them from time to time to celebrate the necessary services of the Church and the requirements of religion. It was from places in the vicinity of Poland,—places already annexed,—that Russia received her information as to the state of her co-religionists in Lithuania.

Under the reign of Catherine Russia commenced to take an active part in the affairs of the Greek communities of Lithuania ; and from her accession to the throne, the Empress devoted particular attention to the sufferings of her co-religionists there. Assisted and sustained by Protestant governments, she eventually delivered the Faith and the conscience of these people from the frightful persecutions of the Roman Catholic clergy.

Persecution had begun, as we have seen, with the entry of Romanism into Lithuania, and had continued until, and been strengthened by, the *Union;* but at the date 1717 it commenced to reach such proportions, that towards the second half of the eighteenth century, its crimes could be neither justified or palliated, and brought down upon their authors a just and retributive vengeance.

At a time when Europe made gigantic strides towards the disfranchisement of religious tyranny, the Lithuanian Greeks were a prey to fanaticism and bigotry. They were forbidden not only to build, but even to repair their churches; they were deprived of the right of representation in the Diet, and held ineligible for government situations. Roman Catholics exercised the censorship of eccle- clesiastical Greek books, and professors of the orthodox faith were constrained to pay tithe and imposts to the Latin priesthood. They were obliged to take part in religious Catholic proces- sions, and were judged before Roman ecclesiastical tribunals. Their monasteries, schools, seminaries, and bishoprics were done away with by force. The celebrated Bishop of White Russia, George Konisky, advocated the cause of the Lithuanian Greeks with the Empress, but his representations were not seconded by the Foreign Office, which first sent them to be examined by the United Greek bishops, thus retarding the march of affairs, and post- poning the solution of several important questions indefinitely. The Empress comprehended at a glance the true state of the case; secular ex- perience had demonstrated that the exchange of

diplomatic notes was not sufficient in transac-
tions with the Court of Poland, more especially as
the royal power in that country failed in authority,
and also that persuasions and prayers produced
no effect in places where the Roman clergy predominated. .

The news having reached Rome that the Russians
had presented memorials to demand the amelioration of their co-religionists, Pope Clement XIII. in-
stantly requested King Stanislas Augustus to make
no change in their favour;* and when it became
evident that something must be done for them, as a
Diet had been called for the regulation of the affairs
of Dissenters, this Pope addressed a very violent
epistle to the king, in which, amongst other things,
he said that if he accorded any privileges to the
Catholics he would let the wolves enter the Lord's
flock, that he would sully his name, and that his
reign would be marked in history as the epoch of
the decadence of Catholicism, during which all the
restrictions of the rights of Dissenters—restrictions
made for the benefit of the Holy Church, and which
had been acquired by the arduous labour of several
centuries, had been abrogated. At the close of
his letter he said, "Will you be with or against the

* Letter written on parchment, dated 18th April, 1767. See
Archives pr. of Moscow.

Christ who has said, 'Those who are not with Me are against Me?'"

Expecting neither equity nor justice, and seeing that no Christian pity was to be hoped for on the part of the Chief of Roman Christianity, Catherine resorted to the only means in her power to succour the Russians of Lithuania. Prince Repnin occupied Warsaw with his corps d'armée, and at the commencement of 1768 the restrictions published since the year 1717 against Dissenters were abrogated, and they were permitted to construct and repair their churches, to establish seminaries and schools; the clergy were liberated from tithes and imposts, and from the jurisdiction of the bishops of the United Greeks; they were eligible for public offices, guaranteed liberty of conscience according to their faith, and all violent conversion to the Union was interdicted. The Empress of Russia, at the same time, assumed the Protectorate of the Russians of Lithuania, and, dating from this epoch, she interfered more actively in the affairs of Poland, took part in the partition of that kingdom, and greatly co-operated in its dissolution. The hatred which the Poles bear to the memory of this Sovereign is only too natural. Besides many treaties and stipulations not respected by Poland, the defence of the Russians in Lithuania served as

a pretext, it is true, for Catherine to arrive at her
political aim. But who furnished the pretext?
Who provoked the presence of Russian troops on
Polish soil to guarantee, at the close of the
eighteenth century, rights of conscience inherent
in human nature—the right to worship God according to the ordinances of one's own church? It
would have been a strange thing if Catherine had
been deaf to the complaints of her co-religionists in
a country bordering on her own powerful empire,
especially as experience had demonstrated that
fanaticism could only be combated by armed force.
Thus, amongst other causes leading to the destruction of Poland, it was religious fanaticism that
contributed most powerfully to her partition, and
the Empress Catherine was only the instrument of
this destruction, forced to it, as she was, by political reasons, to save the tranquillity of her own
empire. The rights of the Russians, recognised
by the Constitution of 1768, were confirmed in 1772,
but nevertheless they were constantly violated,
limited *de facto*. Thus, interment of the dead was
not permitted during the services which took place
in the Catholic Church, bells were not allowed to
be rung, &c. These persecutions only ceased with
the annexation of the Western Provinces to Russia.
It was then only that Lithuanians of the Greek

rite, and those United Greeks who had been violently converted, found their aspirations and their hopes realized by the intervention of Russian power.

While according the Roman Catholic population of her empire entire liberty of worship; founding for them dioceses;—organizing and reforming their clergy;—Catherine did not forget her duties to her subjects of the Greek faith in Western Russia, and effectually she fulfilled them. At the period of the annexation of these provinces, the Greek Sees, previously abolished by Rome, commenced to re-appear; seminaries and schools were founded, the clergy received proper treatment, and the Russians having preserved their faith in the midst of persecution and distress, were rewarded for their long suffering and great patience by liberty to live and die in the faith of their forefathers, without fearing persecution for their religious convictions.

The Government also directed its attention towards the position of the United Greeks, a people occupying a false position, as belonging by their dogmas to one Church and by their ceremonies to another. The clergy of this confession not only did not contribute to a complete fusion of their flocks with the Roman Church, but far from it, they prolonged the transitory and abnormal state of the

Church, the causes of which were to be found in the composition of the clergy—in the separation existing between the regular and secular priesthood—the first leaning to the side of Romanism, the other sustaining jealously traditions of the Greek rite, and hindering the population from being Romanised.

In the United Greek, as in the Greek Church, there existed only one single monastic order, founded on the Statutes of St. Basil the Great, and denominated Basilians. But in its organization this fraternity only preserved the name, its tendencies and its institutions being quite Roman. This last result was the work 'of the Jesuits. Soon after the construction of the Union, the general of the Jesuits, Aquaviva, obtained in 1613 authority from Pope Paul V. for members of his Order to enter this congregation, without demanding a special permission. Once in the United Greek Convents, the Jesuits began their reforms after their own ideas. At the commencement of the seventeenth century, Joseph William Routky having become United Greek Metropolitan in 1617, convoked the Archimandrites and the Priors of the Convents, and proposed to establish a novitiate in one of the monasteries, after the fashion of the Latin Convents, and in another a school for the Latin sciences ; in

short, to introduce the rules and monastic statutes
of the Roman Catholic Orders. He proposed the
election of a Superior who for the term of his office,
four years, should regulate all their affairs, and
establish uniformity of rules and costume as well as
a similar ritual. Thus the United Greek Basilians
should don the costume of Latin Order. The
Superior was subordinate to the authority of the
Metropolitan, but the right of the diocesan bishops ~
to meddle with the convents was forbidden. Thus
the election of a Provincial, the institution of a
Novitiate, and the non-subordination of the convents to the episcopal jurisdiction, were all Papist ·
innovations, the only difference being that the Provincial of the Basilians was reputed to be subject
to the Metropolitan. One may easily suppose that
this plan of Routky, decided on 4th October, 1624,
met with approbation, and on the 10th August, 1631,
Pope Urban VIII. gave it his sanction. As in the
course of time the Order of the Basilians became
more numerous, Pope Benedict XIV. separated them
in 1744 into two departments, Russian and Lithuanian, and commanded the Basilians to elect every
eight years, besides the Provincials, a general of the
Order with the title of Proto-Archimandrite, a dignity unknown in the Eastern Church. This dignitary was subject to the Nuncio at Warsaw.

Organised in this way, the Basilians founded schools, their plan of instruction differing little from that of the Jesuits. Their pupils were despatched to Roman Catholic colleges to finish their studies,—to Rome, Olmutz, Bronusberg, and Wilna. They acquired considerable estates and founded new convents, and in prosecuting their aim they endeavoured to extirpate the Union of which they formed no part, except in name and costume. In reality this fraternity became a Roman Catholic Order, disdaining their *confrères*, the United Greeks, and pluming themselves consequently on the esteem and sympathy of the Roman clergy, who gathered them, as one may express it, into their lap, permitted them to participate in their rights and privileges, and treated them as equals. Therefore the Basilians soon caught the spirit of the dominant clergy. At the close of the last century, when public opinion in Poland pronounced against the cupidity, tyranny, and vices of the Roman priesthood, the Basilians were included in the general condemnation, and forced to fight for existence—for the prolongation of their privileges. Forced as it were to fight for their future, they addressed petitions to the King, to the Diet, and to the Pope. The Diet in 1775 confirmed some of their requirements, and they relied on Rome, whose faithful and docile servants they had been, to protect them, and with whom, through the General of their Order, they had already direct relations. In 1785 Pope Pius VI. addressed a petition to the King of Poland, pressing him to defend the Order at the approaching Diet, as the brethren were protected by Rome for their zeal in the cause of the Union, and not to permit them to succumb under the animosity of which they were the object. He reiterated this petition in 1786. But if the Basilians merited the animosity of the Poles, they yet more deserved that of the people and the secular clergy of the United Greek Confession. The monks treated the secular priests of the Union with disdain, looking upon them as beggars, as ignoramuses, as something altogether inferior, though they were themselves the authors of this poverty and ignorance. From the bishops, who were in their hands, and who knew the strength of the Order at Rome, they took all the most important ecclesiastical functions, both in the consistories and in the parishes, and profiting by their power, deprived the secular clergy of their endowments ; both of those destined to the support of schools and seminaries, as well as of the churches. They thus deprived them of all means of education, so that the secular priesthood was composed of poor people, drawn from the lower

classes of the population. Their children were
made citizens, and later they even became peasants.*

The Basilians treated the secular priests like
slaves; they tied them, beat them, and maltreated them in every way. Their arbitrary
violence against the parochial clergy attained such
a height, that at last Rome herself interfered in
defence of the United Greek priests. This interposition certainly did not arise from sympathy with
their sufferings, but from the politic desire not to
alienate them entirely, as the people would certainly
follow their pastors, if, disgusted with their treatment, they seceded from Romanism; their number too, surpassed the Basilians; the churches
which they had were numerous, and their influence
over the people was incontestable. These considerations induced Benedict XIV. to write, in
1753, to the Metropolitan and bishops of the
United Greeks, in which he traced all these evils
to the ignorance of the secular clergy; to the disdain which they showéd them, that they never
rose to ecclesiastical preferments—situations reserved for the monks—from which they were

* The Constitution of 1764 authorised the Polish proprietors
to convert into serfs the children of the United Greek priests,
who at the age of fifteen years had not yet accepted a profession.

debarred. The Pope therefore, to put an end to such disorders, desired them to give places to the secular priests, and by thus presenting an aim for their ambition to render them more zealous. Nevertheless, this prescription was not executed, the Basilians remained the chiefs of the clergy as before, and became towards the end of the eighteenth century a thoroughly Latin Order, so that Roman Catholics and Poles entered the fraternity, and in time surpassed the number of United Greeks.

These Basilian monks, that is to say, those by birth Latins, were generally elevated to the dignity of bishops, and in this way all the administration of the United Greek Church centred in the hands of Romanists. It is therefore easy to understand the hatred of the low United Greek clergy to the Order. To them they attributed their abasement and their beggary; they regarded them as apostates of the United Greek Church, hastening its overthrow; and if they kept silence, it was because they were impotent against so affluent an Order, supported by riches, by political privileges, as well as by the Roman Catholic and the Polish Government. The people sided with the secular clergy, but it was just at this epoch that they also were oppressed by the priests. It was in this state of antagonism and disorganisation in which the ecclesiastical hierarchy seemed tending towards dissolution, that the Russian Government found the United Greek population at the period of the progressive annexation of the Western Provinces to Russia. It was only natural that this union was ardently desired by the people, who were more attached to the Greek rites than to the Latin dogmas, which were to them incomprehensible; while the Greek rites, celebrated in a language incomparably more Russian in its idiom than Polish, ensured their sympathy; so that, according to all probability, the major part of the lower clergy waited with greater impatience than the people, the advent of Russia,—that is to say, the greater part of the secular priesthood looked to Russia for deliverance from Roman Catholic persecution. The Basilians only would gain nothing by a change of power, as the loss of their privileges would be sensibly felt, and as they were for the greater part composed of Poles they were evidently hostile to Russia.

The population of White Russia was principally United Greek, under the authority of the Archbishopric of Polnek, whose Metropolitan Jason Smogorjewski remained in Poland. The Empress Catherine provided for the administration of the

United Greek clergy of this district a particular diocese, the regulations of which were based on those applied to the Roman Church. The secular clergy as well as the monastic orders were subordinate to the bishops, and the same rules as those laid down for the Church of St. Petersburg were extended to them. This regulation abolished the dignity of General of the Order, and the reunions of the chapter were rendered unnecessary. But the Empress was in no hurry to name a bishop to this diocese, for as we have seen, and as she well knew, the United Greek bishoprics were nothing less than dioceses violently snatched from the Russians to give greater *éclat* to the Union; to serve in fact as another instrument in the hands of the Propagand among the people of the Greek Confession. For several years this diocese was regulated by the Consistory, to the great displeasure of the Pope and of the Metropolitan Smogorjewski, who, although remaining, would administer it. The Empress, in 1782, replied to the complaints and the pretensions of Rome thus :—" The Consistory instituted by us administers the diocese confided by us with success and to our entire satisfaction ; we therefore see no reason to change this administration, especially as we hear no complaints from our subjects of this Confession; so that

reports to the contrary are inexact." Count Czer-
nischeff, in the name of the Empress, announced
also to the Metropolitan Smogorjewski, through the
medium of the Governor-General of White Russia,
that the nomination of an archbishop to a diocese
situated in the empire of Russia, was solely an
affair of the imperial authority; and that therefore
the intervention of any foreign ecclesiastic on the
subject of a vacant diocese, the consecration of the
priests and the general regulation of the Church,
was altogether out of place; moreover, how could
he, after being made a citizen and prelate of
another State, serve at the same time two sovereigns? At length, the Empress, in 1784, selected
an archbishop for the United Greek See of Polock,
elevating Heraclius Lissowsky to this position, and
completely subordinating all the convents and the
clergy to his administration.*

By this subordination the Basilians lost, so to
speak, their Roman nationality. They both complained to Rome and revolted against the episcopal
authority. To end this disobedience some of them
were exiled, that is to say, in Poland, and at length
Prince Youssoupoff obtained, in 1785, a confirmation of their subjection to the archbishop appointed
by the Russian Government; this decree according

* Receuil des Lois, t. xxii., No. 16122.

him the power to make any changes he judged
necessary for a term of three years, conditionally
that such changes were not incompatible with the
doctrines of the Roman Church. It is worthy of
remark that the prelate to whom they refused
obedience was a monk of their own order, who was
quite as much imbued with the exclusive and independent spirit that characterised the ecclesiastical
Latin communities as could be.

But the Basilians formed only a small part of
the United Greek population. The people themselves, who had been torn from the orthodox faith
by cruel persecution, had nevertheless religiously
preserved the rites bequeathed to them by their
fathers, and gladly hailed the authority of the
Russian Government, from which for centuries
they had expected succour, and from whom they
had nothing to fear for their conscience. Nearly
all the lower clergy, closely allied as they were
by their manner of living and their language to the
people, detesting Romanism and the clergy that
oppressed them, were always favourably disposed
to the Eastern Church. A religious movement,
antagonistic to the Union, had manifested itself in
the western districts, and had even spread into
provinces not then annexed to Russia, the people
being disposed to abjure a faith distasteful to them.

This proceeded to such a height that the United Greek Polish priests were obliged to exhort their flocks to remain attached to the Union, and published at the same time epistles containing reproaches to those who made a difference between the Liach religion and the Russian religion, and explained that the Union and Romanism were the same thing.*

But the Greek people, notwithstanding these efforts to preserve them in a foreign fold, never confounded their rites with the Latin; and as to their sentiments, they remained much more Russian than Roman. Their return to the Oriental Church began with the annexation of the western provinces—that is of White Russia—when they felt that they might and could call themselves as belonging to her without fear. If conversions to the faith of their ancestors were not more rapid throughout the country, it must be attributed to the influence of the Jesuits, without whom, undoubtedly, the people would have thrown off the Union; and thus this Order, after having been recognised and their authority established by the Government, for a long time hindered the interior reunion of Russia with her co-religionists of the

* Epistle of Etienne Lewinsky, administrator of the diocese of Luck, 27th May, 1789.

same race. But in the southern and eastern
countries, where the mass of the people had succeeded in preserving their ceremonies even under
the domination of Poland, the Jesuits could never
firmly establish themselves, and the united Greeks
living in the middle of a Russian population only
counted through compulsion as belonging to the
Union. The Government and the Russian priesthood not only did not oppose this tendency to
return to the orthodox faith, but even encouraged
it. Victor, Archbishop of Isiaslaw and of Bresclaw,
in 1794, addressed the following epistle to the
united Greek people, furnished with the benediction
of the Holy Synod :—

"It is notorious that at an epoch unfortunate for
Russia, a large portion of her subjects professing
the Orthodox faith, having been torn from their
native country and subjected to the yoke of Poland,
soon experienced bitter persecutions for their faith.
All that the most refined cruelty could invent was
devised to turn the children of Christ from the true
faith, and when these means failed of success,
violence constrained them to a union with Rome.
But the impenetrable decrees of Providence put an
end to the sufferings of a people belonging to
orthodoxy, who were for that cruelly persecuted
by the Poles. The hand of the Most High has

delivered them from foreign domination and reinstated them under the beneficent sceptre of
their true sovereign.   The Empress Catherine II.
having their material and eternal happiness in
view, has reunited these people of the same
race under one sceptre, and instituted for them
a legal hierarchy, nominating us to this holy
ministry.   In the quality of pastor, on whom
has devolved the mission of caring for the souls
of our flocks, we invoke you, in the name of
the Holy Evangelists, of whatever age or station
you may be—all belonging to our diocese, whose
fathers, grandfathers, or yourselves may have
turned from orthodoxy to the Union—to return
within the pale of the Eastern Church.   That no
fear or apprehension on the subject of such conversions be entertained by the timid or the waver-
ing, we declare that all menaces or false insinuations
of the forcible separation of these provinces from
the Empire of Russia are vain, and that no human
power can destroy their political union with their
brothers and co-religionists.   No Roman Catholic
authority need be feared, neither the power of
Poland ; for we know that our august sovereign,
though protecting foreign religions, and according
to every one liberty of conscience with the profession of the dogmas inherited from his fathers,

never tolerates that any one passing to the Orthodox Church, whose grandfathers, fathers, or they themselves shall have been constrained by fraud or violence to abandon their primitive creed, and would now return to it, shall suffer, and has therefore provided a legal support to which they can apply. We ourselves, depending on the doctrine of the Saviour and the apostles, and convinced of the excellence of the Greek Church, glorified since the time of Christ by the holiness of its dogmas and the miracles of the Fathers, exhort you, as your pastor, to enjoy the full liberty of the orthodox confession which has from time immemorial animated and exalted your ancestors, as well as many among yourselves. Persecution is past: all constraint on matters of religion has become impossible. Turn to the bosom of the Church your Mother, enjoy a quiet conscience in faith and truth, which will lead you to a state of divine grace, that each of you, in professing the doctrines of the Orthodox Church, may fulfil his obligations of loyalty towards the sovereign of the State, according to his social position."

It is evident that the people, though attached to their rites, preserved a mixed religion, influenced no doubt by the fear which the Polish nobility and the Roman Catholic priests had imbued in them, both of whom continually menaced them that their country would again return to Poland, and that then they should be punished as apostates. But from the moment that the Government and the Church together enlightened them on the impossibility of such a return, and dissipated all false apprehensions, nearly all the united Greeks of Podolia, the greater part of Volhynia, and a large proportion of the population of the Government of Minsk and in White Russia, consisting in all of about a million of souls, re-entered the Russian Church, headed by their priests, who always had a penchant for orthodoxy. No violence obliged this movement ; on the contrary, a ukase expressly forbade everything of the kind, and the priests who wished to remain in the Union were given the liberty of choice either to emigrate abroad or reside in the empire ; in the latter case, they and their families should receive pensions from the Government.

Those parishes of the United Greeks that returned to the Russian Church, were incorporated with the Greek dioceses. After the second partition of Poland the following United Greek bishoprics entered the empire : the metropolitan bishopric, the archbishopric of Polock, part of which had been already annexed conjointly with White

Russia, and the bishoprics of Pinsk, Luck, and Brest.

In 1795 these bishoprics were abolished as un-necessary, and the few United Greek churches that remained, as well as the convents, were subjected to the jurisdiction of Lissowsky, Archbishop of White Russia, who should regulate them on the same conditions as those of his own diocese; that is to say, all the clergy without exception were subordinate to him, and the independent Monastic authority of the Basilians was annulled. The Metropolitan Rostocky, the bishops of Luck, Levinsky, Gorbazky of Pinsk, Mlozky of Brest, as well as the suffragans of the Metropolitan, were all pensioned by the Government. The latter re-ceived six thousand roubles per annum, the bishops three thousand each annually; but with regard to Rostocky, who had been educated at Rome, it was stipulated that he should reside either there, or in St. Petersburg, but not in any of the newly annexed provinces. The other bishops were left liberty of choice to reside abroad, or in Russia; and the ecclesiastical funds and properties were placed under the administration of the Government.

The Basilians, the most zealous fanatics of the Union, were not at heart United Greeks, but Roman Catholics. They themselves would never join the Greek Confession, and their numerous convents were altogether superfluous in a country where they had no congregations.   They were also nuisances to the Orthodox clergy, as the only aim of the Order was the propagation of Popery, and the conversion of the lower classes.   The Empress Catherine having herself examined the catalogue of their convents, ordered those to be closed that were useless either for religious or educational purposes : the monks to be transferred to the other convents of the same Order in Russia.

The Empress had indeed a right to say of the United Greeks, " Having broken the chains that weighed so heavily on the conscience of the population professing the orthodox religion, we do not doubt that the other people of the same race will follow this salutary example."   A few years longer of the rule of this sovereign, and the Union had ceased to exist, not that the Government suppressed it by violence, but neither justice nor obligation required the support of this half church, which deprived of artificial foundations would consequently fall of itself.

In truth, it could hardly be expected that a people who had endured so many sufferings for the faith of their forefathers, should hold to a Church and a priesthood that had been imposed on

them by violence and persecution, especially as
they now formed part of an empire where the
orthodox faith was dominant. The majority of the
United Greek priests, condemned and scorned by
the omnipotent Latins, would they not also desire
to re-enter the pale of the Oriental Church? Constantly in the midst of their people who were
devoted to them, would they not encourage and
imitate them? It was not a new religion which
they embraced, they only returned to that for
which their forefathers had shed their blood and
sacrificed their lives. The Basilians only formed,
so to speak, a sect among the United Greeks—
they alone remained faithful to the Union in the
Southern part of Western Russia; but two years
sufficed to dissolve this sect in these districts,
so that it soon became impossible to distinguish
either those who remained faithful to the Greek
faith, or those who returned to it. This religious movement was so natural and so logical
that Europe, rarely charitable towards Russia,
found little to say against it. Even in our own
days there are bigoted Roman Catholics who sometimes avow that it was the sympathy and attachment of the people to the Eastern Church and
not violence, which diminished the number of the
adherents of the Union. The secular clergy, as

we have said, always retained a *penchant* for the
Russian faith, and exercising a great influence on
the masses, were the principal instruments in
assisting the Greek bishops to draw them into the
bosom of the Church. But the most striking point
is, not that a million and a half of United Greeks
entered the Orthodox confession in the space of two
years, but that half a century later we still find
under the sceptre of Russia a very numerous
population professing an abnormal faith, which
holds that there is very little between a Church
from which they are separated, and that to which
they belong by name. One can only be astonished
that civilised Europe knew so exceedingly little
about this half Church—about the state and spirit
of its clergy—the relations between it and the
people of the orthodox creed—its composition, its
regulations and its aim—that its definite abolition
under the reign of the Emperor Nicholas should
have been interpreted as an arbitrary and iniquitous
act of an autocratic government. If Catherine had
not preserved the Jesuits in White Russia—if her
useful reign could have been prolonged, and the
number of the Basilians diminished—if the Russian
government had only thrown aside the pernicious
and arbitrary influence of the Latin clergy, the
Union, as we have sufficiently demonstrated, would

have been an impossibility. The aim of this
system was Romanism ; but from the moment that
it was dissevered from its leader, and that the mass
of the people with their clergy separated from it,
the Union had nothing to do but return to the
Greek fold. Having attained no positive result,
though forcibly driven towards such, it was only
natural that it returned to the point from which it
had departed. Even by its very spirit it showed
a state of transition that would, sooner or later,
ensure its disappearance. Rome had for two centuries laboured to produce and support it, and in
two years its traces had vanished in Podolia and
the Volhynia.

Western Russia numbered among its population
many different sects (not counting the Jews),
Catholics, Greeks, and United Greeks, ordinarily
inhabiting the villages and the towns. But
Samogitia and the western district of Lithuania
which bordered on Poland, presented an exception,
as nearly all the people belonged to the Catholic
faith ; even in Podolia, where after the conversion
of the United Greeks mostly all the population
adhered to the Russian creed, some Calvinists who
had resisted and survived the persecutions by the
Jesuits and the Polish government, were found
scattered over Samogitia, and even possessed some

churches at Wilna and Sluck. The people of these
countries, living in common, notwithstanding religious differences, were of the same nationality—
generally spoke the same language and inter-
married.   This act of social life offered the Roman
priesthood a new instrument for conversion : an instrument much more efficacious than offered by
the mere requirements of common interests and
mutual wants, which in most cases take precedence
over religious attachments.   The Roman clergy
therefore forbade mixed marriages, except in cases
where the non-Catholic consented to join the
Roman Church.   The Empress Catherine put an
end to this manifest oppression, which was heavily
felt in a country whose geographical position often
rendered these marriages necessary.   In 1768 a
treaty was concluded between Russia and Poland,
in which it was stipulated that mixed marriages
between Greeks, Catholics, United Greeks, and
Calvinists should not be hindered, and that the
nuptial benediction should be pronounced by the
priest of the confession to which the bridegroom
belonged.   Should a Catholic priest refuse to
sanction such a marriage, the religious ceremony
could be accomplished by a Dissenter, and the
union would be legal.   As for the children of such
marriages, the sons should be baptized and educated

in the faith of their fathers, the daughters in that
of the mother. But the nobles were permitted the
right of making this point the subject of a marriage
contract. These regulations were established also
for the inhabitants of these countries after their
annexation to Russia.

Thus the most important questions relating to
the administration of the Roman Catholic clergy,
were solved and resolved by the Empress Catherine
II. The Russian government finding itself for
the first time *vis-à-vis* a priesthood whose hierarchy,
though demoralized and disorganized, was strongly
supported by a numerous population professing the
same faith, proved itself firm, independent, and
just, and exhibited a discrimination that would do
honour to a government habituated for a long
series of years to such questions. There can be
little doubt that Catherine based her enactments for
the Catholic Church upon those of neighbouring
States professing Catholicism, particularly Austria,
but she never followed her model in that which deserved to be set aside. The interior constitution
and the interests of Russia would, however, have
prevented her modelling her reforms solely after
the patterns of a State, whose dominant religion
was directly antagonistic to that of her own
empire. Adopting a rational system, Catherine

designed with precision the principal basis of this
administration ; marked the points where the State
might possibly come in contact with the Church,
and strongly determined their respective limits.
Time interfered to prevent the accomplishment of
all her designs, as it was only a little before her
death that Russia recovered the provinces so
violently wrenched away from her ; but upon nearly
every single head the Empress had indicated her
opinions, and marked those points which most
merited attention. The relations of the government with the Court of Rome were put upon a
stable and positive footing, and her ordinances on
this question became for Russia what the maxims
of the Liberty of the Gallican Church became for
France. The organization of the hierarchy, traced
by her, gave force and influence to the ecclesiastical
power, abolished the arbitrary will of the Latin
clergy, and consequently purified the Church from
the vices of its priesthood ; vices that in the last
days of Poland, had contributed to debase this
Church in the eyes of the people and weaken their
religious sentiments. It was with this aim that
the Empress intended the secularisation of the
ecclesiastical estates, in the possession of which
the monks lived in luxury and idleness, thus
obliging them to become instead, the useful mem-

bers of the Church. The clergy which until then, forgetting their vocation and their vows, thought only of politics and worldly affairs, were placed by her in their proper position and civilized. By confirming liberty of conscience to her Catholic subjects, instituting dioceses, and favouring and promoting ecclesiastical educational institutions, Catherine put a stop to Roman proselytism among other sects, particularly in that of the established religion. Fanaticism and violence, under the name of religion, were interdicted, and every one was furnished with the opportunity of worshipping and living according to the precepts of his faith. To the Greek Church she restored the faithful, torn from her by brute force; in a word, Catherine not only changed the administration of the Roman Catholic Church in her empire, but completely re-organised the priesthood, without trespassing on the dogmas of their faith. She turned them from a political institution—a position they had arrogated to themselves, and in which they had brought much evil upon Poland—to their true vocation—the fulfilment of duties they had sworn to undertake and never accomplished; and she afforded them instead the means of being useful to religion and their flocks, to the populations who required to find in their pastors, spiritual fathers and not politicians. If in this she discontented the priesthood, she at least satisfied the people.   Among such reforms, faults are inevitable, and we cannot pass over in silence the principal mistake of this great sovereign, which was the protection she afforded the Jesuits ; but her profound wisdom, and the political measures she planned and carried out compensate for this unfortunate error.   Let us not forget at the same time that the regeneration of the Catholic Church in Russia, whose decadence manifested itself at the close of the last century, was inaugurated by a sovereign who did not belong to it, but who professed a creed which even in her own time had been persecuted by Catholicism in Poland.   It was this very Church that had cruelly trampled on her own, which some years later she forced to be purified, and raised from the degradation into which its servants had plunged it.

END OF VOL. I.